away ...
ab window. I did my last ...
leaving the poor ... the
I wore a open the ... throu
rather late for ... ble.
precepts of his ... a
told one, that is ... a
n others faults, in common conversa
charity of the heart, & the spirit
loved. Mr Edwards here later & a
the green wreath for our St Anthon
words to bind on wreath. "In memo
Cooper. Earl of Shaftesbury -- Just a
Mr Edwards is a really generous
man, & it is a great pleasure to
he had set out in life meaning to
that he gave back all money that
the people who gave it - he says
he should give every day a little more tha
What a splendid principle if
n that!! I have dropped seeds
the Home Arts - society in need of
of the Building News & been interested
the arts & handicrafts through its ma
he may help us from the proceeds of
I should be glad if I can turn
in the direction of this great ...
The queen came down Kensington
with flags - our household had a ...
more lucky, as the moment after ...
Mulberry R., a down pour of rain
to ride - for it was too uncertain

ra copper – & I put hopeless &
ps to such strides, so I turn on
like he comes back at him &
beside me making coffee for me –
so thoughtful – bless him, bless h
away from him keeping my
Eden, I went to 35 Dover St
her Loan & Gen Col Ex = Chaos
hard from morning to night –
splendid church embroideries sanct.
of things – but before I left at 6.3
& the rooms looked well –
Lawrence there morning hard
a Mrs Boord & her daughters hand p
heon in Berkeley Square
Mrs Robby Benson – bring my mar-
gment whom had had his knee
Lord Rosebery had been f
signor got something in-
us & thoughtful – gentle
lovely man
this morning out today & she
to work but the squabb
unite yet work together
thing & she says it is
– then she can do with
character training of public
suppose! What genuine

The Diary of

MARY WATTS

1887–1904

The Diary of
MARY WATTS
1887–1904

Victorian Progressive
and Artistic Visionary

Edited by

DESNA GREENHOW

LUND HUMPHRIES
in association with
WATTS GALLERY

First published in 2016 by Lund Humphries
in association with Watts Gallery

Lund Humphries
Office 3, Book House
261A City Road
London
EC1V 1JX

www.lundhumphries.com

ISBN: 978-1-84822-201-4

A Cataloguing-in-Publication record for this book is available
from the British Library

Designer: Oliver Keen

Set in Sabon LT and Chanticleer

Printed in China

Contents

Foreword

Mary Watts was a collaborator of genius. A designer in many varied media, she left few if any masterpieces made entirely by her own hands. But working with and inspiring others, there seems to have been nothing she could not achieve. Most famously she led the villagers of her adopted Compton in Surrey in the creation of the astonishing mortuary chapel over which they laboured for several years. She was the founder of the Compton Potters' Arts Guild, and the co-worker of a long list of distinguished, and more modest, craftsmen and women. But the collaboration that meant the most to her was with her husband, the celebrated artist George Frederic Watts.

Mary's diary opens in Cairo, with the Wattses on their honeymoon, and its culmination is marked in July 1904 by the death of *Signor*, as she refers to Watts (sometimes he is instead her 'little lamb'). She is telling a story: this book has a narrative, centred on its author's challenge to herself to make the very most of the wonderful luck she felt Fate had brought her. Marriage to Watts meant life in a beautiful studio-house in Kensington, where the great names of the day seem to have passed in and out almost daily. It meant also the opportunity to build her own home at Compton in the Surrey hills, Mary's beloved Limnerslease, the true centre of her life from 1891 to her death in 1938.

At Compton Mary's powers as a designer were revealed. Surely she must have amazed herself, as she surprises us, with the ambition, originality and quality of her work during these years in gesso relief, in sculpture, in ceramic and fabric design, and in architecture. Mary's diary describes her resolution to press on with this work, alongside her domestic cares. Her annually replaced 'Fatima' (Mary's nickname for the volumes of her diary) became her confidante and indeed support in her struggle to not fritter away the precious time granted to her.

Mary's marriage to Watts brought the opportunities to liberate her artistic talents, once she realised that her calling lay in three-dimensional decorative work. But it brought also many other responsibilities, not least caring for her much older and often delicate husband whose complete inability to manage anything like a professional career (despite his fame and success) tested her patience. Both often starting work before dawn, she could not bear to see him waste precious days returning to fuss over pictures long put aside.

Mary's diary ultimately tells a story of success. At Compton she realised her dream of creating a community founded on art and craft: few enterprises based on the principles of Ruskin and Morris turned out so happily. In collaboration with her friends and neighours, Mary created a very special place, one which always charmed and moved visitors, who saw that the entire project was based on Mary's love for Signor, who lived just long enough to see the completion of the Watts Chapel and the Watts Gallery at Compton in 1904, the year of his death.

During the twentieth century, the estate Mary had created was broken up, leaving only the Watts Gallery building as the exquisitely crumbling home to a collection of pictures and sculptures by G. F. Watts. But soon after the centenary of his death a revival began, and since then the Watts Gallery Trust has entirely restored the Gallery, bought back Limnerslease and taken on the management of the Watts Cemetery and Chapel. Visitors are now once again invited to explore an Artists' Village comprising a sequence of buildings sharing a common aesthetic. There is nothing quite like it anywhere else in Britain. It has been particularly satisfying to create, as part of the restoration of Limnerslease, the Mary Watts Gallery in which are displayed many works created by Mary, almost always of course in collaboration with others, but all showing her distinctive universalising approach to pattern.

As this restoration work has been taken forward, Mary Watts has been our guide and she has spoken to us through her diary. When we have needed to orient ourselves in terms of architectural decisions, the language we use or the essential priorities among our objectives, we have looked to the woman whose story is told in this book and have sought to carry on that story. The transcription, annotating and editing of Mary's diary has been an enormous labour for Desna Greenhow requiring great scholarship and the kind of optimistic but steely perseverence that we associate with Mary herself. Watts Gallery Trust is hugely grateful to Dr Greenhow for what she has achieved in bringing the diary of Mary Watts to publication, and we are so glad that this book will bring new generations of readers and visitors into the world that she created.

Dr Nicholas Tromans, Brice Curator, Watts Gallery – Artists' Village

Introduction

George Frederic Watts and Mary Fraser-Tytler married on November 20, 1886. Watts suggested, in the first few weeks of their marriage, that she should write a diary, chronicling their daily life together. It turned out to be a cementing element in their relationship, and a fascinating document in its own right. Most importantly, Mary wrote it for herself, not anticipating sharing it with the world or with anyone else. This is clear by the tiny, difficult handwriting, and its voluminous nature. It has not been completely transcribed until now, more than a hundred years after it was written. 'Signor', as Watts was nicknamed, never tried to read it, and so it remained a narrative by Mary with herself, about their relationship and on the joint lives they led.

Watts was 69 and Mary 36 when they married, and the diary covers the 17 years they were together. Some of the volumes have disappeared, but we are left with an overview of a delightful and interesting joining of two lives, conducted at the centre of the artistic and social world of London and, in contrast, in rural Surrey, in the last decade of the 19th century. The diary amounts in its full unedited text to 300,000 words (which it took two years to transcribe and edit), and is now available for researchers at Watts Gallery Library & Archive. This book, above all, is intent on keeping the flow of Mary Watts's lively writing, and to show the detail she gives us of those years and that relationship. Watts died at 87 in 1904, after what had been a very happy and productive time for them both. Their relationship was close, and Mary brings out its strength and quality, while revealing Watts's high profile, the awe and respect he commanded as an artist, and the affection in which his friends held him. These elements could have made for a difficult start for Mary in a world of which she knew little, but the strength of her personality helped her to cope magnificently, and to develop her own unique artistic persona.

Watts was a central figure in the artistic scene in London, and for their first few years together they lived in his house in Kensington, close to many of his friends. Some of them were the best regarded artists of the day, and most of them were top-ranking in the eyes of the critics and the public. Mary had enjoyed a free childhood in the Scottish Highlands, in a literary family, part of the Scottish intelligentsia. She studied at the Slade, and then worked on portraiture in Edinburgh and London, where she met Watts. They had a teacher/student relationship for some years before they came together as a couple. As her diaries clearly show, she had the great advantage of a liberal upbringing within a successful and educated stratum of Scottish society, and her own personality gave her the added advantage of a sense of humour, and strength and determination.

An interest Signor and Mary had in common was in social reform, and the benefits of philanthropy by the haves towards the have-nots. One of the great enjoyments in their marriage was their evening reading, often on these topics. Watts got up in the morning at four o'clock, Mary often joining him, their bath-time conversation giving Mary the chance in her diary to give us an entertaining side-light on Watts's waking mind, fully active, speaking on a striking thought about the universe, or a political problem of the moment, or a new painting by a friend, or an obscure element in the religious beliefs of an ancient culture. They were both extremely serious about the wrongs in their world. Watts's philosophy as it appears in his paintings moved from social realist depictions in his early work, which show homelessness in London, the Irish Famine and the evictions, and poverty and suicide by oppressed women, to his later symbolist paintings of universal themes, oppression of the vulnerable through greed and vanity, and the blindness of most of society towards progress in human understanding, and spirituality, in the post-Darwinian era. Mary voices their similar views in some of her writing, and they both became involved in several important movements. They supported Samuel and Henrietta Barnett in Whitechapel, and later in Toynbee Hall and Hampstead Garden City. They both held the view that women's rights to equality should be fostered, and they were active in the Home Arts and Industries Association, which built creative classes in dying crafts in small rural communities. Here, Mary gave an active lead when she came to build and decorate her extraordinary Cemetery Chapel in Compton in Surrey, with the help of almost an entire community.

In London, they lived among the circle of Watts's close friends, particularly Edward Burne-Jones and Frederic Leighton, and, through Mary's diary, we get to know these two quite intimately. The entries report conversations with friends and sitters, and, of course, many between herself and her husband. This makes for entertaining and vivid reading. Watts was a lively conversationalist with his sitters. His approach to painting portraits was that he would never undertake a likeness until he knew a person thoroughly. He was considered one of the finest portraitists of the 19th century, and the aristocracy, as well as people in all fields of public life, asked him to paint themselves and their families. He offered to the nation through the new National Portrait Gallery the likenesses of many of the most important figures of the day in what he described as a 'Hall of Fame'. These filled several rooms at the new gallery. Watts completed some of his best portraits in his late years, and we are given a strong idea of several of them in the diary as they emerge on Watts's canvases. The portrait of Walter Crane, the painter and illustrator, is considered one of his best, most insightful likenesses, painted when Watts was 74.

London winters were becoming very unhealthy in the late 1880s, with frequent impenetrable fogs. Once, Mary writes, a journey home from Notting Hill to Kensington proved so difficult that she needed to accept a lift from a milkman on his horse-drawn float, along the pavement! When she congratulated the milkman on driving through the fog, and asked him how he managed it, he said he always followed a certain drain that he could just pick out below him. She became more and more determined that she and Watts would spend their winters in the country. For two years they stayed with friends, Andrew and May Hichens, in their house, Monkshatch, near Compton in the Surrey hills, from October to March. Watts had known May since she was a child, when he was living with her parents in their house in Holland Park in London. Gradually the idea took root that the Wattses might build themselves their own country retreat close to Monkshatch. Andrew was a stockbroker and a great enthusiast for Watts's work, and he offered to pay for the building work and the land, with a view to Watts buying it from him at a later date. The decision was made late in 1890, and they commissioned the Arts and Crafts architect, Ernest George, to design the house. It was christened

'Limnerslease', the word 'limner' being an archaic name for an artist, and 'lease' having several inferences: the fact that they would, to start with, lease it from Andrew; that it would give them a new lease of life; and, reflecting an older meaning, that they would garner a golden harvest from it. The diary for 1891 gives us a sense of the excitement they both, and she particularly, felt as the dream she had of a house that was a real home for her and her beloved became reality. She threw herself into furnishing and decorating it, and designing and planting the garden.

In the country, Mary was able to develop her own artistic talent. She had been taught by the French sculptor, Aimé-Jules Dalou, exiled to London from his native Paris for ten years in the 1870s. He taught her how to work with terracotta, from which he was producing, at that time, superb figurative portraits of French peasants. In London, she was helped by a contact of Edward Burne-Jones to extend her knowledge to working in gesso relief. Before the building of Limnerslease was completed, Mary was already designing and making panels to decorate the ceiling in their new drawing room, to be known as the Red Room. In white gesso, the relief depicts, in the centre, the Egyptian winged sun, and radiating from it four rectangular panels show positive human attributes: a sense of renewal, with a butterfly coming out of a chrysalis; industry, with bees in the cells of a hive; produce, with corn sheaves and grapes; and love, with Egyptian love symbols. As with each of her artistic works, Mary writes of its progress as it emerges.

In July 1891, the house was ready to move into. Watts had a new studio and, very soon, his largest and most ambitious painting *The Court of Death*, as yet unfinished, was brought down to Surrey. It was installed with the clever device of a 'picture slot' in the floor so that it could be lowered or raised on pulleys, allowing him to work on it at any level. He had been working on a series of drawings in red chalk, shown at Agnew's Gallery in the spring, and sold to the Whitworth Gallery as a group. They were much admired, even by those who had not warmed before to Watts's work, and precipitated a visit from the novelist and poet Thomas Hardy, who displeased Mary by saying he must 're-do' (that is, reassess) Watts. She could never see any reason why anyone should not admire, unconditionally, all his work, as soon as they first saw it. Another unexpected visit was from Oscar Wilde, who had just published *The Picture of Dorian Gray*. Mary found him unexpectedly easy and pleasant company.

Their years from 1891 onwards followed the pattern of summers in London and winters at Limnerslease. Watts suffered greatly from the deaths of his friends Frederic Leighton, Alfred, Lord Tennyson and Edward Burne-Jones, but he worked on stolidly, through much of the decade, on his large equestrian sculpture, *Physical Energy*, at Little Holland House. He painted portraits of George Meredith, the novelist, at Limnerslease, and of Cecil Rhodes in Kensington. In his late 70s and into his 80s he produced some of his most heartfelt, symbolic work. *Can these Bones Live?* is a comment on the shrouding of England in a pall of greed and neglect, *The Minotaur*, a condemnation of the exploitation of the young, especially women. Finally, nearly at the end of his life, he was exploring one of his interests, creation, in *The Sower of the Systems*, a near-abstract work.

Meanwhile, Mary gained confidence in her own abilities in the happiness of her country life. When, in 1895, the village of Compton bought land for a new cemetery, she persuaded Watts to back her idea of building a chapel there. He agreed to pay for it with fees from his portraits. She took advice from a recently retired architect, George Tunstal Redmayne, on the design for the building itself. She wanted its plan to be circular with a cross running through it, basing it on some of the Crusader churches and on the original Church of the Holy Sepulchre in Jerusalem. Redmayne worked in Surrey on a series of commissions for his relative by marriage, Edwin Waterhouse, founder of the accountancy firm Price Waterhouse. The house he designed for Waterhouse, Feldemore, uses the small bricks we see in the Watts Cemetery Chapel, which give it a tall, narrow, Byzantine appearance.

In her ceiling decorations for Limnerslease Mary had drawn on symbols from many cultures but, for the Watts Cemetery Chapel, she went to the symbols she had known so well in her childhood in the north of Scotland, from early Celtic Christianity. She recorded in her diary her adventures in the British Museum, studying the Lindisfarne Gospels, and she obtained a facsimile of the Book of Kells, another superb Celtic illuminated manuscript.

Combining her interests, Mary began to run classes for people in the local community in terracotta work, as part of the Home Arts and Industries Association scheme, and invited help from four experienced craftsmen to work with her on the chapel project. Whereas the design was Mary's, as her sketchbooks show, the extraordinary result, a unique blend of Celtic symbolism and Arts and Crafts vision, was a communal effort, some of it by people who had done nothing creative before they came to the classes at Limnerslease. There were sometimes as many as 40 people there on a Thursday evening and, on Saturday mornings, the children's class had similar numbers.

The difference in the ages of the Watts couple had to mean an unhappy ending for Mary. In 1904, Mary's diary is filled with the path of Watts's last illness, her reactions, the hopes and fears for his recovery, his death in July and her immense grief and sense of loss that followed. Yet the autumn and winter of the same year is full of her commitment to what he would have wanted: for her to live for the future, and to create it in the most positive way she could. She organised the casting of *Physical Energy*, to be sent to South Africa as a memorial to Cecil Rhodes. She finished the interior decoration of the chapel, painting the angels' faces as early as August, only a month after Watts was dead. She worked with Sir Edward Poynter, President of the Royal Academy, on the retrospective exhibition of Watts's work planned for the end of the year. She worked on pottery designs, and found a pleasant married couple to look after her apprentice potters. She celebrated with her ward Lily when she became engaged to a man with whom she was delighted.

In her last entry for 1904, Mary wrote, 'I have followed, worked, loved as you did, beloved. Now for me it must be all looking forward, forward.' She had many years of looking forward ahead of her. She ran the Compton Pottery, and designed for it well into her 80s; she helped their ward Lily to bring up her children at Limnerslease after her husband, Michael Chapman, was killed in the First World War; she was President of the Godalming Suffrage Society; she designed the decorative scheme for the Military Chapel at Aldershot; she managed the Watts Gallery, and organised numerous exhibitions of Watts's work. She wrote an almost complete catalogue of his paintings, a three-volume memoir of Watts, *Annals of an Artist's Life* (1912), and her own understanding of her magnum opus, the Watts Cemetery Chapel, *The Word in the Pattern* (1905).

Mary more or less abandoned diary-writing after 1904, adding only one or two entries in a journal about incidents that struck her in the years 1906–8. She was trying hard, and succeeding, from then onwards to look forward.

Dr Desna Greenhow, Editor

The Diary

1887–1904

The text published here has been edited down from about 300,000 words to roughly one third of its original length. Adjustments have been made to Mary's punctuation for the sake of clarity but the text is otherwise unaltered.

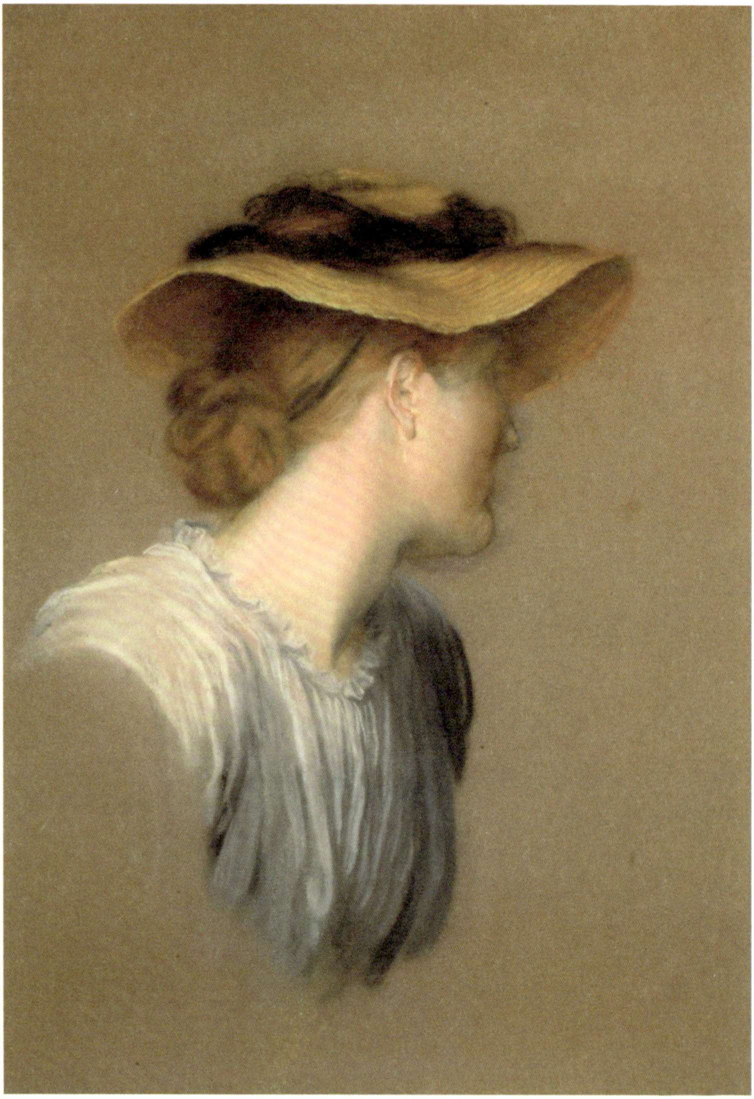

G.F. Watts, *The honeymoon portrait. Mary Watts in a Straw Hat*, 1887, pastel on paper, Watts Gallery

1887

The newly married couple took a long honeymoon for the first half of 1887, first to Egypt, travelling on and near the Nile for three months, then on to Constantinople and Athens, and finally coming home slowly by ship to England at the end of May. In her first diary entry, Mary wrote simply, 'I begin my life with Signor by beginning the oldest history of the world.' The nickname 'Signor' dated from his return, in the 1840s, from three years in Florence. It was the name all his friends used.

They enjoyed and sketched the physique and the 'beauty of line and colour in the drapery of the people' they saw around them, and the 'lovely lines of cliffs, great sandstone ridges' on the river banks. At the great temple of Karnak Watts exclaimed, 'Such pillars should only support the sky.' Mary was determined to use the Egyptian symbol of the winged sun for a design in their house in London.

Writing in tiny script in the early mornings, she did not hold back in the diary from describing the tenderness between the two of them. She had ordered a small, squat book with a full page for every day of the year in it. She christened it 'Fatima', thinking that it resembled a small, fat, voluble woman who might well bear that name. A new volume for the following year arrived each autumn.

Once back in the house in Kensington Watts had built himself in 1871, this was a time of adjustment for Mary. They were surrounded by Watts's friends and fellow artists, several of them doubtful if the new marriage would succeed, particularly given the 30-year age gap between them. She was warmly welcomed, however, by his closest friends, Edward Burne-Jones and Frederic Leighton. They were delighted to find how she admired Watts as a painter, and how warm she was to the new people in her life.

Watts opened his studio, and later his gallery, on Sunday afternoons to all comers. This tradition on the part of artists provided a popular weekly outing for Londoners; in Watts's case it often included the opportunity to see him working and talk to him. It was also a chance for friends to visit each other. Soon after they returned from the honeymoon, Mary wrote of an afternoon in June when Sir Edward Poynter, soon to be President of the National Gallery, and Sir Richard Burton, the explorer, were among the visitors. 'I enjoyed my afternoon seeing people like that & finding a response to all one's dearest interests' was her comment; it was a prelude to her very full life in the London social, political and intellectual scene.

In August the Wattses visited May and Andrew Hichens, in their house in the Surrey hills. Watts had known May since she was a child when he had lived for over 20 years in her parents' house in Holland Park. This was the start of a close friendship between the four of them, which would lead to the Wattses building their own Arts and Crafts house close by in 1891.

SATURDAY, JANUARY 1 *New Hotel, Cairo* Signor[1] put out his hand to me before daylight & told me it was a New Year & blessed me.

Pyramids & the Sphinx[2] by sunset & by moonlight. I begin my life with Signor by beginning the oldest history of the world.

SUNDAY, JANUARY 2 Sitting under the Sphinx, with its great mysterious face burning with sunlight. I sat up above & heard the young Sheik talking to Signor about Allah. He preached him a little sermon. The Sheik was delighted & translated it for the others.

---

1. Watts's nickname, dating from 1847, when he returned to London after four years in Italy. **2.** Watts made studies on the spot for his painting of the Sphinx. Mary quotes him as saying, 'An epitome of all Egyptian art, its solemnity, mystery, infinity'. M.S. Watts, 'Manuscript catalogue of G.F. Watts' portraits and subject paintings', 3 volumes, Subject catalogue, p.135. Further citations to the manuscript catalogue will be to M.S. Watts, 'Portrait cat.' or M.S. Watts, 'Subject cat.' as appropriate.

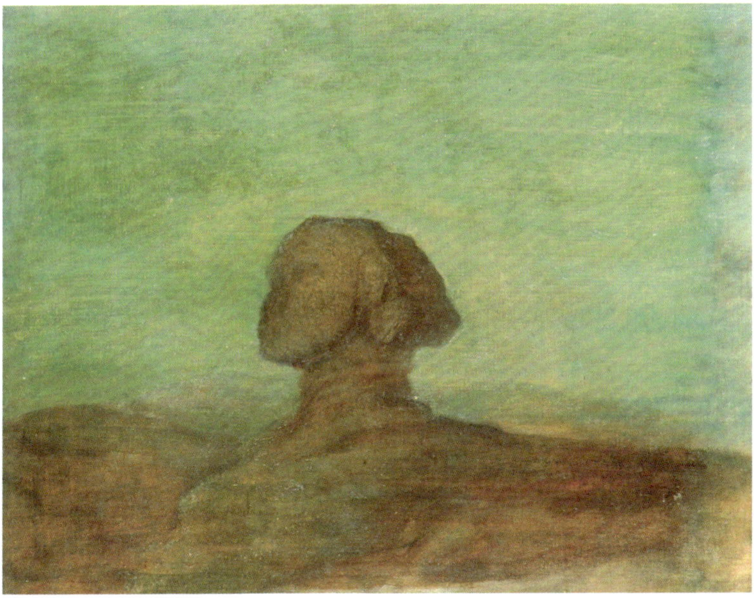

G.F. Watts, *The Sphinx with its great mysterious face*, 1887, oil on paper, Watts Gallery

'We want to grow feathers to make wings, to get up to Allah. If man does a good thing it makes one feather. If man does a bad thing it makes heavy. If he want too much backsheesh it make gold in his shoes. Nothing so heavy as gold. If he have gold shoes he can't fly up to Allah.'

'That's right' they all said, & were very pleased, & showed their beautiful teeth.

MONDAY, JANUARY 3 One last look at the Sphinx at four o'clock. The sun was just behind its head. It looked grander than ever. Signor feels it to be a symbol of time, something strong, calm & inexorable with a smile that is cruel.

TUESDAY, JANUARY 4 Left Pyramids & went on board our 'Dahabeah'[1] at five o'clock.

---

1. A sailing boat for travellers, used on the River Nile; it was the usual means of travel before 1900, when it was overtaken by the steam boat and the train.

WEDNESDAY, JANUARY 5 Anchored on the Island of Roda. Drawing from the deck.

Signor much delighted with the fine chests & square shoulders. He has often argued that the scapula should be large, & has made it so in his athletes, but cannot find it in the models in England. The calf of the leg, too, he thinks should be long.

The throat starts, in the finest examples of the human form, from a flat basis which gives it the grandeur of a fine column, & the chest should be square and ample.

SUNDAY, JANUARY 23 Every hour seemed to make clearer to me the priceless treasure of this nature & mind now my own, & he tells me he is grateful too! I think my happiness reflects something of him. Made a list of his portraits for the Nation,[1] adding some still to be done.

MONDAY, JANUARY 24 Curtains & shutters opened at seven & a glorious sun streamed in. 'Light & warmth' Signor said, delighting in it. He said he hoped he had not given me the impression he valued intellect as the highest emanation from God, for he holds that the spiritual has a far higher place.

WEDNESDAY, JANUARY 26 When I looked for my dear one's hands this morning, I found them both crossed upon his breast. I said 'Don't do that, Signor' & he, 'I often lie so'. 'Oh, don't' I said 'it is too much like "Well done, thou good & faithful servant."' When I next touched his cheek it was wet with quiet tears.

My dear one has painted & sketched some figures, such nice, great lines he sees in all these people. I feel as if I was blind in comparison to him. I am trying to read in the new book he has opened to me.

THURSDAY, JANUARY 27 A lovely day, the most perfect we have had on the Nile, warm & yet a steady little breeze & my dear one able to sit on deck & see the things we passed. We passed under some grand cliffs & felt how distinctly they had suggested to the builders of the great temples, pyramids & Sphinx, the idea of line & size.

---

1. Watts, over many years, painted the 'portraits of the makers of the Nation', to be called 'The Hall of Fame', which were donated to the National Portrait Gallery.

My dear one was so grieved this morning in his quiet way because a little bird Zidan had brought us, who had got hurt upon the deck, after living some hours, fell back & fluttered out its little spirit before our eyes. 'Goodbye' he said. He is very tender & would like, like St Francis, to speak to the birds. Their tameness here delights him.

S. kissed me tonight saying 'We are very fond of each other.'

FRIDAY, JANUARY 28 Signor & I looked out upon some lovely lines of cliffs, great sandstone ridges that are on either side of the river. They were beautiful. 'Do you feel you have seen more than you ever did before?' he asked me. I feel it dimly & cannot find words for it but it is powerful all the same. I feel that things, the smallest details of daily life, and the majestic sweep of line, the glory of the rising sun, is in keeping, parts of a great design, & I perceive that it makes things lie before me like a great work of art.

MONDAY, JANUARY 31 The mountains this morning were wonderful, the light almost pink, & the shadows almost magenta. Colour, Signor thinks, is life. A black & white drawing is a most beautiful thing, but put a touch of colour & then it must be all colour, filled as the Venetians are with glow & light.

TUESDAY, FEBRUARY 1 Met an American artist. He is much interested in Signor, thinks his exhibition in New York has had a great influence on American Art,[1] & is producing a reaction against the French school of impressionists.[2] Intensely interesting to me, to see my beloved through the eyes of the world.

WEDNESDAY, FEBRUARY 2 *Visit to Karnak* What is to be said? 'Such pillars should only support the sky,' Signor says. 'I feel much in sympathy with the old Egyptians, though not so much perhaps as with the Greeks.' The quiet & the size is what he loves to aim at in his lines.

THURSDAY, FEBRUARY 3 Saw Rameses. Signor & I woke to talk of the great Temple at Karnak. Marvellous though he feels it to be he says

---

1. This was Watts's one-man exhibition at the Metropolitan Museum, New York, in 1884. **2.** Impressionists had been given that title for over 20 years; Mary's use of a small 'i' in her mention of the school mirrors that of Watts, as do her critical feelings on the movement, about which numerous negative comments are recorded in the diary.

there is something in the line of the cheek of the Sphinx which touches him more. There Ruskin & he differ, for Ruskin finds more beauty in almost everything else. To the lines of the human form he is blind.

FRIDAY, FEBRUARY 4 We have been two months & a half married & never been away from each other for half an hour. I used to think I could not be happy unless I was much alone every day. Here I am never happy unless with Signor.

'Are you really not longing to be alone?' he asked me, 'not finding drawbacks? Ah, just as you expected, & yet you expected a very great deal. You make your own happiness out of what I have to give you, which is nothing.'

MONDAY, FEBRUARY 7 Drew some hasty lines of drapery.[1] Signor begs me to do it as often as possible.

'The eye gets as it were in tune with the law of form & line, & by constant study, even hasty notes, the mind acquires that knowledge of the natural law, which is necessary for the ideal.'

THURSDAY, FEBRUARY 10 *Philae* Our day at Philae. Signor delighted with it & is sorry we are going to have to leave so soon, our boat dismasted for the journey down.

FRIDAY FEBRUARY 11 *Aswan* S. said 'For great Art there are three things that should never be lost sight of, largeness of style, beauty & infinity. In feeling, Egyptian Art is what I have for 30 years definitely, & always indefinitely, thought the only possible direction that art could now take. In their Sphinx & in the Rameses, delicate detail in the form is wanting, though the majesty and mystery is superb.'

SATURDAY, FEBRUARY 12 *Aswan* He asked me today what had struck me most in Egypt. I answered that the thing I was least prepared for was the beauty of line and colour in the drapery of the people. That no one had spoken of.

MONDAY, FEBRUARY 14 We are drifting slowly down the Nile, & are sorry to turn our face from the sun. Signor says it is contrary to all he endeavours after, & he does not like it at all.

---

1. See illustration on page 24.

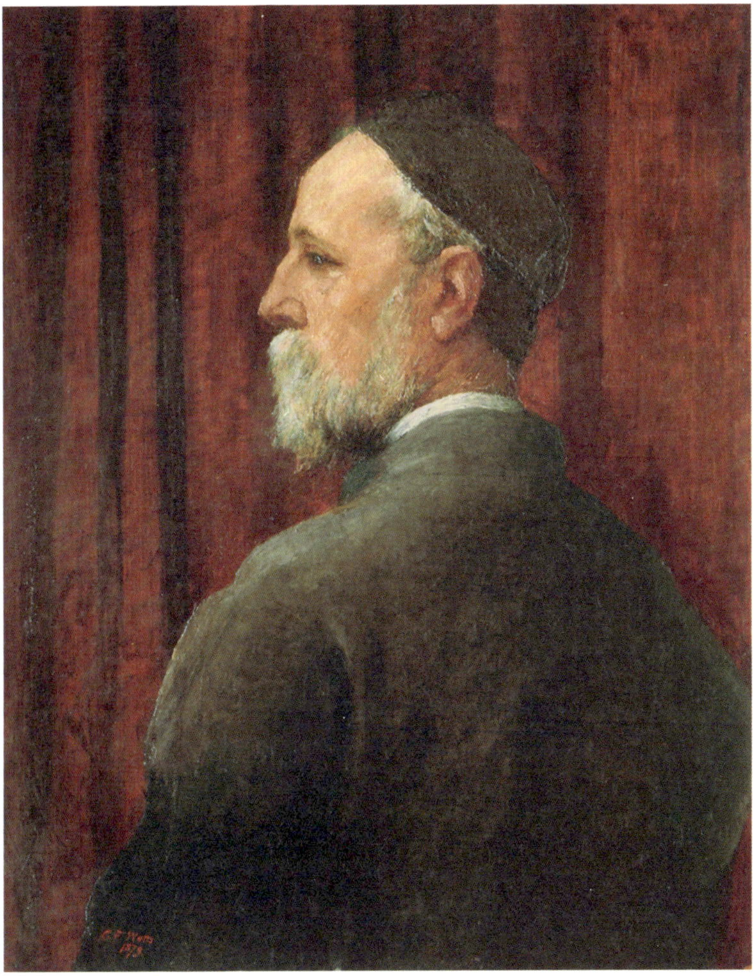

G.F. Watts, *Self-Portrait*, 1879, oil on canvas, Watts Gallery

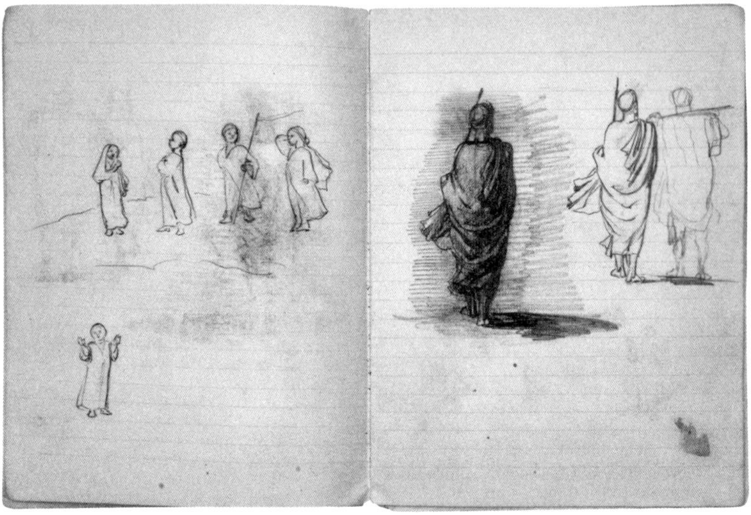

Two pages of Mary Watts's notebook drawings from Egypt, 1886, Watts Gallery

TUESDAY, FEBRUARY 15 A very hot day, but on deck till luncheon. Talking a good deal of the possibility of making the best decorative art highly ideal. We mean to have the winged sun at Little Holland House,[1] an example of which we saw yesterday in great loveliness of proportion. We will work something out of this.

WEDNESDAY, FEBRUARY 16 Woke this morning to talk about the possible development of my ideas for design. My loved one says 'How happy we are to have interests that are more than interests in common. It is very rare' – He throws himself into the idea of it warmly, & when I say there is one very important thing needed, to find out if I am able to design, he says to prepare myself for it now as far as I am able in this quiet time, & that I shall probably find myself able, when the time comes to try.

1. The house in Melbury Road, Kensington, that Watts had built in 1876 and where he and Mary would begin their life together.

SATURDAY, FEBRUARY 19 Joined by Mr Hamilton Aidé,[1] & went to Karnak, after mooring in the dahabeah close by. Signor charmed with some of the sculptures & one small one particularly which expresses the form as well as Greek art, he says.

MONDAY, FEBRUARY 21 Sketching the sunset & had a shawl wrapped round me suddenly. Sent for, with loving thought, by my dear one.

WEDNESDAY, FEBRUARY 23 *Watts's birthday* GFW 1817

He said to me this morning 'The many happy returns depend on you.' I had not wished him that trite wish. There was no need to put the desire of my whole life into words at all. I kissed him silently at two this morning & thought of the night, years ago, that had seen the beginning of the life which has affected many so greatly & so nobly & which is all my world now.

WEDNESDAY, MARCH 2 Signor says the greyness of the moment after sunset is accounted for by the contrast of the sunless earth against the sunlit sky. The afterglow is the reflection of that flame colour in the sky, produced by the sun being at the angle that its rays strike through the densest part of the atmosphere, nearest the earth.

TUESDAY, MARCH 8 We are gliding down the stream fast. It is, we say, unpleasant, & besides we are sorry to leave the Nile. The great serene beauty, the clear far horizons & the sense of size which Signor feels here affects him more with a sense of divinity, than a thunderstorm on mountains, or the wildest sea. He feels calm nature, all light, more beautiful when she is in extremities, as it were.

SUNDAY, MARCH 13 *Last day on the Nile* A lovely last day on the Nile. No wind & not too hot a sun.

MONDAY, MARCH 14 Left our *Vittoria* at half past one having spent 70 days on it. A very wonderful world we have seen in our wooden house. 'Inside a wooden house oftimes a golden room you find.'[2]

---

1. Charles Hamilton Aidé (1826–1906) was a novelist, playwright, songwriter, society personality and a constant visitor to the Wattses. Several of his rhymes were in common parlance, for instance: 'I sit beside my lonely fire, And pray for wisdom yet; For calmness to remember, Or courage to forget.' **2.** Henry Wadsworth Longfellow.

TUESDAY, MARCH 15 A delicious desert air blew in at our windows this morning, & we went out to walk in the desert & see the eight or nine pyramids to be seen from here.

FRIDAY, MARCH 25 Signor has been asked some time ago to paint a little child, the daughter of a Greek here. Of course he refused, but a few days ago, he told me he thought he would make a sketch of the head, & if the father liked it enough to give £100 for it, it would be a good thing. 'You see' he said 'it would be useful to buy things here.'

'How wonderful' I said to myself, seeing visions of Syrian embroideries & Persian rugs, etc. 'Yes' he said deprecatingly, 'You see I do really want a pair of those trousers.'

TUESDAY, MARCH 29 *Halouan* In the evening glow we walked to the clear space over-looking the Pyramid plain, & sat down to watch the sun sink. We were very happy, this feast of light, & glow before our eyes, & an air like a moorland blowing in our faces. We grieved to think our time in Egypt is to be counted in days.

FRIDAY, APRIL 15 *Athens* We woke early & went up to see the coast of Greece. Piraeus at nine today & Athens soon after.

A blue sky with great loose clouds moving along the hills. There had been rain & it had left just enough to make a blue atmosphere, on blue hills above bluest seas. I had had some fears about seeing this wonder of the world. *The Apex of the World* after all one had seen in Egypt, but it does not compete. It is the child, but so different in such different surroundings.

We looked out through the pillars of the Parthenon & saw the same blue wonders that had been the power that stirred Homer, Phidias & all those wonderful men of that wonderful age. He spoke to me of those giants of the past.

WEDNESDAY, APRIL 20 *Constantinople* My dear one not well, the cold here affects him. I found *Pride & Prejudice* & began to read it to him. No novelist delights him more. It is so finished & so complete, so without effort, just the right words used with reticence & such graphic power.

We heard the cry to prayer this evening when I was lying by him. I said surely one ought to answer to it. 'Yes' he said 'prostrate ourselves before the principle of Goodness.' 'Can we have contact with a principle?' I said.

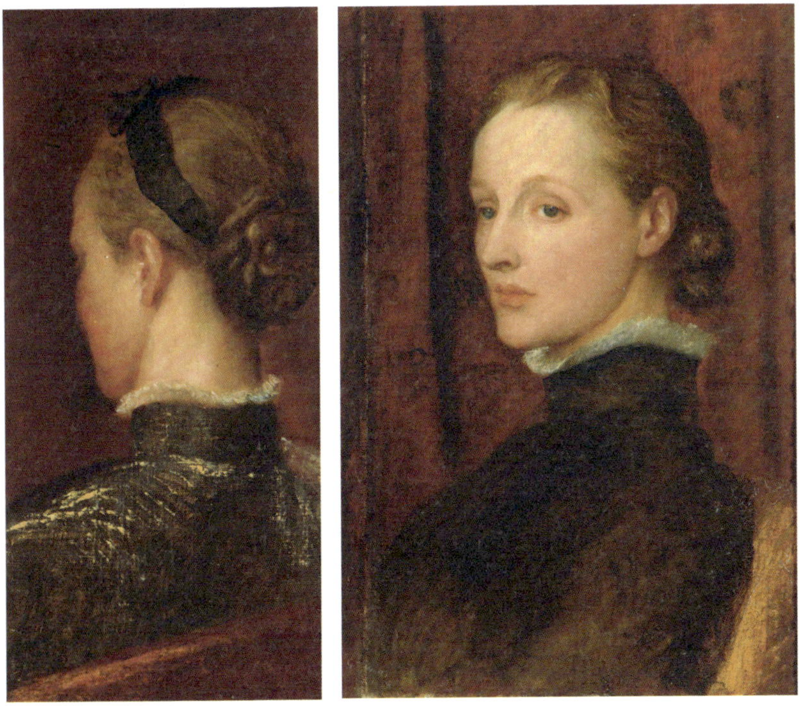

G.F. Watts, *Portraits of Mary Watts in Constantinople*, 1887, oil on canvas, Watts Gallery

'I need a spirit I can speak to, even if I can only say Holy Holy Holy.' 'Ah, that is better' he said.

I was sad to tears today because his love of life is so faint. He held me in his arms, & told me I was a reason for its being dear, & when he talks of leaving it he thought only that we should go together.

TUESDAY, APRIL 26 He began, because his hand was wearied by idleness, a sketch in oil, of me.[1] Painted straight off, in four colours, on single prime canvas with white, light red, burnt & raw umber, a lovely flesh colour. It was all drawn in burnt umber, which is a very good useful colour but must be used carefully, transparently, over light ground or else it darkens & becomes very heavy. Talking of painting with varnish, Signor says that it must be used with the white ground & again with the colour.

MONDAY, MAY 16 *Athens* Went up early to the Acropolis, a heavenly air blowing in our faces, & all more lovely than could be described. Went into the Museum. Signor is pleased with fragments there, *The Winged Victory*, & many splendid things. 'No one' he says 'understood how to give a kind of tremulous palpitating beauty in every line of drapery as the Greeks at their best periods. It is the music of form, light, & colour!'

THURSDAY, MAY 26 Our last day at Athens. Signor held me in his dear arms & said the curtain of six months' delight was not going to fall. 'It cannot be so delightful at home' he said, but I know I only need one thing to have delight.

'We have been six months together & you do not love me less.'

My picture has become most lovely. 'The wife of his idea', I call it. We drove to the cemetery & to the Pyx. & there saw the most perfect view of the Acropolis that we have yet found.

FRIDAY, MAY 27 Turned our faces homewards. Sorry to see Athens growing smaller & smaller till it disappeared & is only a dream of beauty now – a joy for ever in our minds. The sea blue & calm, with nice fresh air, pleasant, for it had been hot in Athens.

1. See page 27.

TUESDAY, MAY 31 A fog.[1] In the afternoon Signor & I had been struggling against sleep, went down & had tea to help us, & came up to see a lovely sight the mist began to lift before our eyes. Out of a veil of cloud, out of a silvery pearl sea, rose clear blue peaks with sunny snow upon them every line pure & clean against the sky, but tender like a dream, lost at the foot in a thin grey stretch of mist.

'What a vision' we said, & were so thankful we had seen it, & so sorry no one else felt the pleasure of it. It went like a thing breathed upon in a mirror. Mist came up again and it was all blotted out.

SATURDAY, JUNE 4 England on a June evening, rich, peaceful & picturesque. The Kent trees looked very fine. Just saw the gothic towers of Canterbury. Delighted in the harmony.

SUNDAY, JUNE 5 *Little Holland House* Awoke in my own room. The sun shines on us. My dear one went to see his beloved Sir Frederic.[2] He loves him I think better than any other man alive. I say he has a different tone of voice for speaking of him! I went from church to my gallery. I sat in front of the great *Chaos*. The child's thought saying in the dark, was with me: 'Dear God, are you here?' & very near the great spirit seemed. My dear one's mind, so spiritual & so creative, glowed out upon me from the canvas. Sunlight & all the impressions of nature are there.

Signor came back happy from a visit to Sir Frederic finding, of course, great delight in talking over Athens & Egypt & finding agreement.

MONDAY, JUNE 6 Began our life. Signor awoke at a quarter to four & said that I must not get up unless I liked it 'but it will be very nice if you can'.

---

1. 'A summer sea fog drifted about us one day, through which Corsica was suddenly revealed like opal and pearl, and then lost again. A disabled ship loomed strangely through the fog, and the two pictures *Off Corsica* and *The Sea Ghost* were painted later from the impression of that day.' M.S. Watts, *George Frederic Watts: The Annals of an Artist's Life*, Macmillan, London, 1912, vol.2, p.83. 2. Sir Frederic Leighton (1830–96), painter of historical and classical subjects, President of the Royal Academy (1878–96). They met in 1855, and were close friends for the rest of their lives, and neighbours in Kensington. 'Forty years of unbroken friendship' were the words written by Watts on the laurels laid on Leighton's coffin. See portrait of Leighton by Watts on page 33.

G.F. Watts, *A Sea Ghost*, 1887, oil on canvas, Watts Gallery

We got down to the studio about four & found Emma[1] had lighted the fire. Coffee, & then work till half past seven, baths & breakfast. I ran down to Stratford for the day. My darling Choons[2] looks worn & sad. He very much altered. They would not tell me that I was changed which I said was disappointing! I ought to be. I am in many ways.

TUESDAY, JUNE 7 Again awoke, and down at four. I busy arranging things & Signor at work.

Mrs Burne Jones[3] came to see us. Met me very warmly. She said she felt a pity sometimes for all the lives that were not cast as hers is amongst the daily creation of beautiful things. Surely it is the most quiet & the most lovely of lots. I feel it every time I go inside my door!

---

1. Emma was Watts's housekeeper at Little Holland House for many years, and married his sculptural assistant, George Thompson, in 1891. **2.** 'Choons' was Mary's elder sister, Christina. Her husband, the Rev. Edward Liddell, was suffering from an undiagnosed mental condition. They were moving to St Albans where he had a new appointment at the cathedral. **3.** Georgiana, wife of Edward Burne-Jones (1833–98), painter and designer of the later Pre-Raphaelite Movement. He was a friend of Watts from the 1850s onwards; they corresponded and saw each other regularly throughout their lives. Edward started life as Edward Coley Burne Jones, and his surname was not hyphenated as Burne-Jones until after his death. See photograph page 112.

SATURDAY, JUNE 11 Busy day! but still I began to paint at four this morning in my own beloved's studio.

He proposed to go to see Buffalo Bill this afternoon & was pleased.[1]

We have had all our pictures hung. I am rich in my walls! *The Sisters* that I care for so much is opposite to me in the dining room always & I like it better every day.[2]

Mrs Prinsep, who, alas, has faded & darkened through being painted with turpentine, was done in two days, having just made a careful sketch.

SUNDAY, JUNE 12 Sir F. Leighton came to see Signor this morning. I saw him for a moment when I came in from church. We sat in the garden. All still. No roar of London to be heard & thrushes & blackbirds singing, the red & white may blossoming. Emma & I had a long talk. Lord Wemyss called.[3] Emma said to him 'When are you going to make my master a lord?', an idea that she often propounds. It makes me feel as if it might be possible that such a thing should be offered, & I shiver. O! I should dislike it nearly as much as the Crown of England. They are, I hope, equally impossible.

MONDAY, JUNE 13 Went to the National Gallery to wait for Signor & looked about, finding my old friends among the pictures in new places, but looking better than ever. Signor came in but only to fetch me & we went on to the Grosvenor, & were very much pleased, liking the *Pan* by Burne Jones more than any other.[4]

FRIDAY, JUNE 17 Aunt Mela[5] came at five & had a kind, loving greeting from my dear one.

She is won by him at once. 'He has kept his soul like a little child's. Who can fail to love him as one does a darling child, & reverence him as a great intellectual being with a life's experience behind him.'

---

1. Buffalo Bill Cody brought his Wild West Show to Britain in 1887 to celebrate Queen Victoria's Golden Jubilee. The Queen attended a performance, as did most of London society. **2.** Portrait by Watts of the two Pattle sisters, Sophia and Sara. Sara was married to Thoby Prinsep, and Watts lived for many years with them in 'old Little Holland House' in the grounds of Holland House, as their resident artist. Their household was a magnet for artistic and literary London from the 1840s to the early 1970s. **3.** Francis Richard Charteris, 10th Earl of Wemyss (1818–1914), friend, liberal politician and amateur painter. **4.** *The Garden of Pan* by Edward Burne-Jones, based on his travels in Italy in 1872, shown for the first time at the Grosvenor Gallery. **5.** The sister of Mary's father.

SATURDAY, JUNE 18 Talking of Turner, Signor said he would be inclined to place him after Titian. 'He cannot do trees like Titian, but he can do better in some respects.' He has grown to understand & value Turner more & more. 'When I did not see Turner, I learnt to value him, in Italy where I was reminded every day of him.'

MONDAY, JUNE 20 After our early work, I working, Signor painting, we must off to see the Academy & got there about nine. Found a good many things that he liked. Came back through the decorated streets.[1] The colour pleased him & he wished that London oftener looked so bright. Such cheerfulness is too unusual. Millais's pictures are too bad this year. A bad omen, their all falling off their easels the last day. His good genius must have pushed them.

TUESDAY, JUNE 21 Kept Jubilee today, by beginning to paint in my own studio. Signor talking today about Holman Hunt[2] said that he distinctly mistakes the true principles of dignity, fancying that he can get it by crowding his canvas with a mass of unnecessary detail, which simply confuses instead of impressing & elevating.

The earnestness of his work places it, not withstanding, upon a very high level.

A perfect day. Signor looked in very often to my studio & kissed me, very pleased to find me working.

SUNDAY, JUNE 26 I had a morning's rest, and got up for an early breakfast & church with Emma. Mr Poynter came,[3] who I liked, though he came in saying he had come to see Mr Watts. However I was not snubbed & liked him very much.

Sir R.F. Burton came.[4] He was charming. 'I am very glad to see you here.' What could I want more? I showed him the picture of Signor as a

---

1. The streets were decorated for Queen Victoria's Golden Jubilee. **2.** William Holman Hunt (1827–1910) was a founder of the Pre-Raphaelite Brotherhood in 1848. He remained true to its ideals throughout his career. **3.** Sir Edward Poynter (1836–1919), painter of historical and neo-classical themes. Director of the National Gallery in 1894–1904. Knighted in 1896. He married Agnes Macdonald, sister of Georgiana Burne-Jones. **4.** Sir Richard Francis Burton (1821–90), linguist, scholar, explorer, adventurer. Watts painted his portrait (unfinished) in 1879–80. Remonstrating with him for not completing it, a friend said 'Burton might very likely murder you for this.'

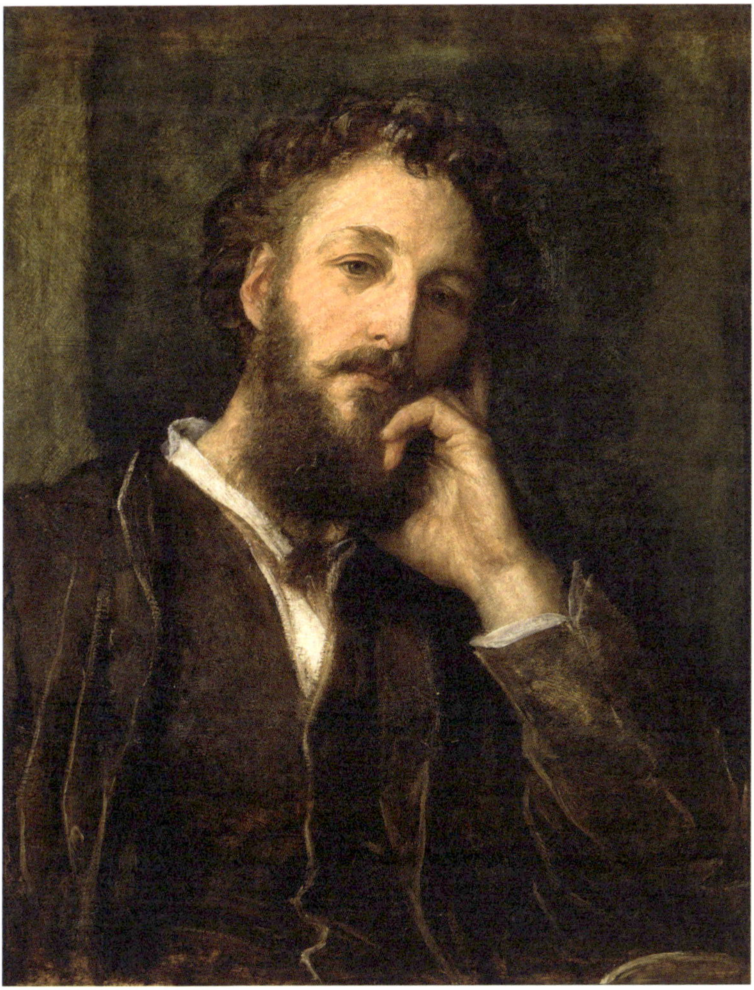

G.F. Watts, *Portrait of Frederic Leighton*, 1871, oil on canvas, reproduced by kind permission of Leighton House Museum

boy.[1] He said it was one of the most interesting things he had ever seen. I enjoyed my afternoon seeing people like that[2] & finding a response to all one's dearest interests. It is very different from any entertaining I have been accustomed to. We went to the Prinseps.

SATURDAY, JULY 2 We looked over a delicious book of early sketches arranged in a scrap book for him by Mrs Nassau Senior.[3] He goes so far as to say they are good because done with such extreme care.

Went to the R.A. again. Signor woefully disappointed with the Leighton Medallion,[4] thinks it detracts from the true principle of relief, the edges blurred into the ground instead of sharp & the form so weak.

SUNDAY, JULY 3 Sat for a few minutes to Signor, & had a quiet morning not doing much, but enjoying it all the same. Sir Charles Newton[5] here in the afternoon. He thinks that Ruskin's want of perception for the beautiful in the human or lower animal form is an unconscious result of his religious training, a feeling that such beauty is carnal & wicked.

My darling asked me tonight if I would take care of him when he became an old cripple! He said nice things, wished we had married 10 years ago. I seem to have an undue amount of happiness now.

TUESDAY, JULY 5 Began my first lesson with Moore.[6] Signor pleased that I like it.

Found a beautiful portrait of Mrs Leslie Stephen.[7] He thinks he has lost something of colour in his later picture & he pointed out to me that

---

1. Self-portrait of Watts at 17, often taken to be of Shelley or Keats (Watts Gallery). **2.** Watts held an open studio on Sundays. **3.** Mrs Nassau Senior was a life-long friend of Watts. He painted one of his finest full-length portraits of her. She compiled two scrapbooks of his sketches from the 1840s and 1850s. One is owned by Watts Gallery. **4.** Sir Frederic Leighton was commissioned by the Royal Mint to design the reverse side of a medal struck in 1887 for the Queen's Golden Jubilee. The Queen's portrait on the front was designed by J.E. Boehm. **5.** Sir Charles Newton (1816-94), archaeologist and Keeper of Greek and Roman Antiquities at the British Museum. Watts joined him on his expedition in 1856–7 when he discovered the mausoleum of Halicarnassus, and Sir Charles stayed with Watts and Mary in Constantinople on their honeymoon. M.S. Watts, *George Frederic Watts: The Annals*, vol.1, pp 163–6, and vol.2, pp 75, 78. **6.** Watts arranged for Mary to have lessons in drawing and painting with a painter, 'Moore', possibly Albert Moore (1841–93), an artist of classical themes. **7.** Julia Jackson, married first to George Duckworth, then to Leslie Stephen. She was the mother of Virginia Woolf and Vanessa Bell.

when he wished to keep the grand monumental characteristic of a sitter, he found himself obliged to sacrifice something to it.

FRIDAY, JULY 8 My dear one very anxious I should do my best under Mr Moore. He came behind me this morning while I was writing down some notes from my lesson, & kissed me saying 'We may yet do some good work in the world.'

SATURDAY, JULY 9 The Barnetts[1] came yesterday & we had a pleasant time of it, both full of enthusiasm for Signor's works. In one hour and a half he made the most wonderful likeness of Mr Barnett. Mr Richmond came in afterwards & was very nice about all he saw.[2] I showed him my picture of Signor at 17. He was delighted.

FRIDAY, JULY 15 I painted on the lawn this morning. My dear one across his big horse[3] looked down upon me.

MONDAY, JULY 18 Mr Burne Jones came to see us. I said to him that he ought to go to Egypt, next year. Later all the costume drapery will be gone.

'No', he said. 'I have Egypt in my mind. It would be too sad to go there now. Like seeing a friend on a death bed.'

Signor painted Mr Barnett from two till six, & finished in that one sitting a very fine head, which he had prepared with colour from the one he began towards the end of the sitting last Friday. It is on yellow canvas, which gives it in this simple painting a beautiful luminous effect. He was very tired after it.

---

1. Canon Samuel Barnett (1844–1913) and his wife, Henrietta, were social reformers and philanthropists. They worked tirelessly for the poor in St Jude's parish, Whitechapel, and were involved with the University Settlement, Toynbee Hall, where Barnett was Warden. They were also instrumental in the development of Hampstead Garden Suburb in London. Watts presented the portrait to Mrs Barnett. It is now in the National Portrait Gallery. **2.** Sir William Blake Richmond (1842–1921), painter and sculptor. He designed some of the mosaics below the dome and in the apse of St Paul's Cathedral. In the 1860s Watts had designed two of the mosaics (St John and St Matthew) for the spandrels below the dome. Because of various delays, they were not installed until 1890. **3.** Watts's twice life-size sculpture *Physical Energy* (see page 37), on which he worked for over 20 years from 1883 until his death in 1904.

WEDNESDAY, JULY 20 Mrs Richmond Ritchie[1] here & telling Signor that she was in difficulties at having to write on Ruskin. Signor gave her two points, one that he had a vein of cruelty, which he himself was almost inclined to be proud of, & the other that he is blind to the beauty of animal form.

THURSDAY, JULY 21 Went over to Sir Frederic Leighton's to see the great picture of Andromache.[2] Saw his beautiful house & court.

FRIDAY, JULY 29 My dear one working away to have the arm taken off the rider that it may be finished, made moveable.[3] I, making some designs, Signor walking in & out.

I tried to put the Egyptian wings upon the arch above the door but found it would not compose. It should be on a straight bit of wall, as it always is in Egypt.

Went to see Mr Burne Jones, found him painting his *Sleeping Beauty*, a wonder of colour & detail. He has promised to send me a man who can make the gesso (for the wings).

SATURDAY, JULY 30 Life seems like a dream of fine weather, green pastures, & still waters. My loved one working at the rider, & I with my easel below him in the garden designing for the Porch.[4] Mr Burne Jones sent his man, to arrange about teaching me to work in hardened plaster, & I hope it will lead to much.

---

1. Mrs Richmond Ritchie née Anne Thackeray (1837–1919), the eldest daughter of William Makepeace Thackeray. She wrote several novels. The character Mrs Hilbery in Virginia Woolf's *Night and Day* is believed to have been inspired by her. Watts painted her, and met her first on the Isle of Wight and then at old Little Holland House. **2.** *Captive Andromache* (1886–8), the wife of Hector, captured by the Greeks in the Trojan War. The painting shows her as a humiliated captive, paraded among a crowd of Greeks. **3.** Burne-Jones commented on *Physical Energy*, 'that horse of his is getting bigger than the world, it is, and too heavy for Europe to hold; if he keeps putting more clay and stuff on it, it will go smash through into S. Africa' (Thomas Rooke, *Burne-Jones Talking*, John Murray, London, 1982, p.31). Ironically, the first cast did end up in South Africa. **4.** This was to be a design of the Egyptian winged sun, in plaster, to decorate the porch at Little Holland House.

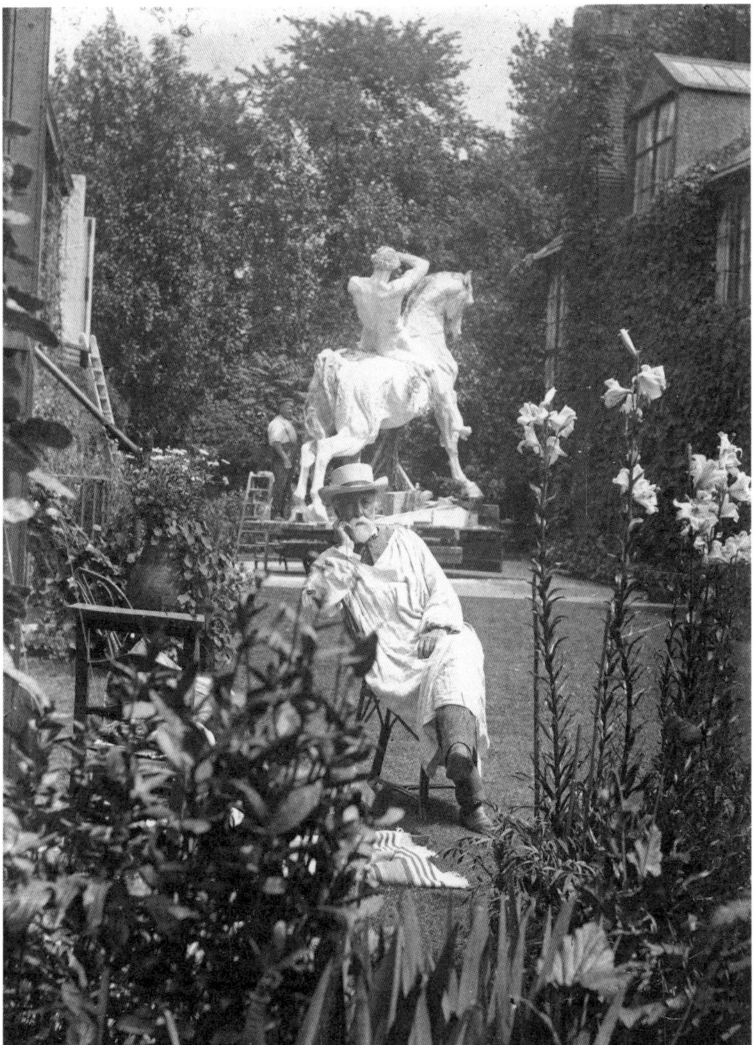

Watts in Little Holland House garden with his sculpture
Physical Energy in the background, 1890s

Gerry[1] came at half past one, & we went to Buffalo Bill. We all liked it, not too old or too tired to be amused, & came back to our serene home for a nice little bit of rest.

SUNDAY, JULY 31 Aubrey de Vere[2] came to see us & was very charming. Some American strangers asking leave to see the horse came to Signor, & Mr de Vere & I went into the studio. He spoke to me of my great happiness & said '& you must feel you have set his life to music'. We went into the Gallery for it was late before he left, & as he passed through the dining room he looked at Millais' *Poor Seamstress*[3] & said 'Remember to pray for all such, out of yr. happiness.'

TUESDAY, AUGUST 2 At seven this evening Lady Somers[4] & Miss Vaughan came in unexpectedly. Signor was a good deal moved. It is pain to him to separate the woman he reverenced so in the old days, from the woman he thinks she has become now. Her firm nature has missed its full flowering time, he says. The soil of life was not what it should have been. I was greatly moved by seeing his beautiful angel, since though she is not that any more to him, I could have thrown my arms around her for the sake of the past, but instead had to be quite stiff & off-hand.

FRIDAY, AUGUST 5 My dear love has just been up to have tea by me. Says he has been working at the back of the rider hard all day & thinks he has improved it. 'How wonderful' I said 'that you still feel there is something to improve.' 'Ah' he said 'if I felt that it was merely to be improved!'

1. Geraldine Mary Liddell, sister of Edward Liddell, Mary's brother-in-law. She was a frequent visitor to Limnerslease and Little Holland House. A fine pianist, she played at their concerts and was instrumental, with other friends, in buying a grand piano for Watts in 1893. Watts painted her portrait in 1898 (M.S. Watts, 'Portrait cat.', p.94). **2.** Aubrey de Vere (1814–1902), Irish poet and critic, prominent in the London literary scene. **3.** Also known as *Stitch Stitch*. Given by J.E. Millais to Watts as a present in 1876 in return for painting his portrait for his 'Hall of Fame' in the National Portrait Gallery (1871). **4.** Lady Somers (1826–1910), born Virginia Pattle, one of the seven sisters Watts knew well in his youth. He had been in love with her, drew her many times, and painted several portraits of her. Virginia Pattle married Charles, Earl Somers, and lived the life of an aristocrat without, Watts felt, the opportunity of developing her own talents.

TUESDAY, AUGUST 9 My loved one said to me today that I did not quite help him as I might, to be better & more kind in spirit. 'How could I' I said 'unless I were to become quite an angel?' & – 'then wouldn't you want a little devil sometimes to play with?' He tells me he thinks he could play with angels, & not find them monotonous.

He says to me 'Charity thinketh no evil.' I say 'Yes, but Charity's wife does.'

FRIDAY, AUGUST 12 Lady Somers sent me a necklace which Signor asked me to send back.

SATURDAY, AUGUST 13 A very busy morning finishing off many things before going to Monkshatch.

Met May & Andrew[1] at Clapham, & found a very pretty place at the end of the journey. The house put down in such a lovely spot like some old garden & so complete, & done with so much taste & thought. We sat in the 'studio' & in the evening May played the organ so deliciously – a very beautiful nature.

SUNDAY, AUGUST 14 *Monkshatch* A very lovely day. We looked over Surrey with its beautiful English character & Signor said it was as lovely as anything he had seen in his life. Nature so various.

I went to church with May, & Signor had his in his own Cathedral, at home in the garden. After luncheon we walked together on the 'Hog's Back' & rejoiced. The air was full of insects. I never saw such numbers of butterflies. May played all the evening, she has a lovely organ, a surprise of Andrew's for her when they came back from Italy one year. It is very delightful to see two such perfectly completed lives. Signor is never tired of dwelling upon the beautiful unspoilableness of her nature, & I am as much fascinated by it. No one ever so kept her eyes from beholding vanity, without effort, just because the nature is great in its simplicity!

---

1. May was the daughter of Sara and Thoby Prinsep, with whom Watts had lived in their home, 'old' Little Holland House, and so he had known her as a child. She married Andrew Hichens, a stockbroker, and they built themselves Monkshatch in the village of Compton in Surrey. Watts and Mary spent the winters of 1889 and 1890 with them, fell in love with the Surrey hills, and the plan for building their own house, Limnerslease, in the same village, was hatched.

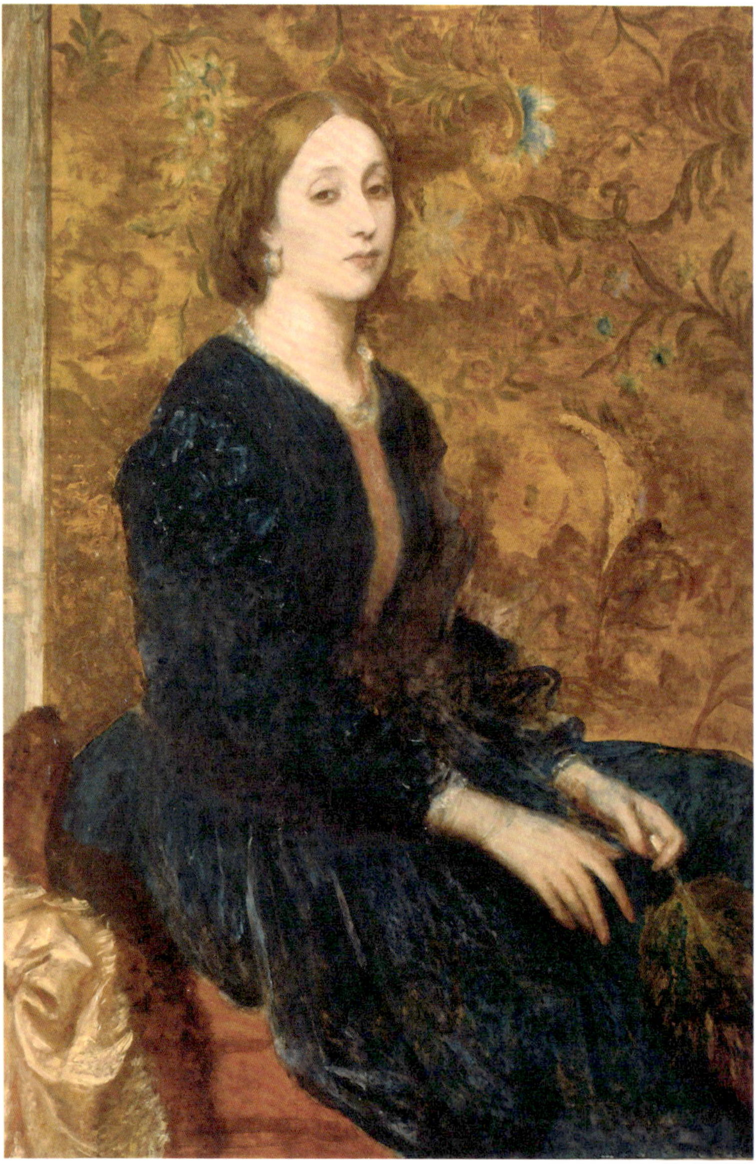

G.F. Watts, *Countess Somers*, undated, oil on panel, Watts Gallery

FRIDAY, AUGUST 19 *Little Holland House* Hanging the Gallery. The great dray horses have been stretched again.[1] We have hung them low, as almost everything Signor paints looks best on a line with the eye. I think it is then that the beauty of the work lies in the pure faithful rendering, making no effort after effect. So many pictures look better for being at some little distance because of the clear pictorial excellence to which everything else has been sacrificed.

SATURDAY, AUGUST 20 Our own dear home. How cosy it was, a fire in the drawing room for it is colder, & a lamp, & I sat by my darling while he lay down in my little golden niche, which he has got very fond of.

MONDAY, AUGUST 22 Mrs Stillman[2] here for a long time, I think her so dear & so beautiful, a lovely soul shining out of her beautiful eyes.

WEDNESDAY, AUGUST 24 'What hard working people we are', a light all over his face when he said it. A little quiet time in the gold niche. I read some Bret Hart & Austin Dobson to him. He likes both, the dainty finish of Austin Dobson especially.

MONDAY, AUGUST 29 I was busy writing out Signor's letter for *The Times*.[3] At last he is giving out his ideas about the National Monument.[4] I sent Alfred to *Times* office & he bought *The Times* of April 25th '85, with an account of Alice Ayres, who Signor wishes to take as a typical case. I have composed the letter from sentences Signor has used in speaking of the scheme from time to time.

TUESDAY, AUGUST 30 *Monkshatch* A lovely morning. Signor & I walked for some time among the lovely growth all round, great branches of red brown dogberry, a bright green bryony climbing up. Nature so beautiful

1. Watts's painting *The Mid-day Rest* (Tate). 2. Marie Spartali Stillman (1844–1927), Greek Pre-Raphaelite painter, as renowned for her beauty as for her painting. 3. Letter to *The Times*, September 5, 1887. The letter was headed 'Another Jubilee Suggestion', putting forward a plan to commemorate 'heroism in everyday life'. 4. This was Watts's idea to celebrate the heroic acts of ordinary people who had saved others from death, often sacrificing their own lives to do so. This idea bore fruit 13 years later with the *Memorial to Heroic Self-Sacrifice*, in Postman's Park near St Botolph's church, Aldgate. There are 53 memorial tablets, the first being: 'Alice Ayres, who by intrepid conduct saved 3 children from a burning house in Union Street, Borough, at the cost of her own young life. April 24, 1885.'

& so different, the country so lovely under the passing effect of cloud shadows which Signor says makes English landscape, which depends on beauty of detail & variety in light & shade, more than landscape which has a wider range & greater nobility of line.

THURSDAY, SEPTEMBER 1 *Little Holland House* Wind & rain, Signor down early, & came back again to lie down, partly I think because the studio is a little dreary to him in those early hours now when he is alone.

Signor resting & laughing much over Miss Austen's *Emma* which I was reading to him.

WEDNESDAY, SEPTEMBER 7 I told Signor today that the only sad part in my life now was that in all my life before I married, my one object was my work. To do something well at last! All this past year I have been conscious that the strenuous effort after that is past. Instead of my work, I focus on him. He is grieved because he says it is a wrong view. If in mastering the anatomy & getting a thorough knowledge of form, I would remember that I am acquiring a possession that will make me not only of more use & value to him, but a more useful member of the human family, I should regain some of my earnestness.

It will take me a little while yet to get over being under the shadow of his great work. I know until I do I shall do nothing, for whenever there is a difficulty to be got over, I feel so much the loss of being able strenuously to overcome. I am overcome at once by it. I say I can't & it is no use trying.

FRIDAY, SEPTEMBER 9 'How well we suit each other' he said tonight. 'Do you really feel that?' I said, for I can never have too much reassurance tho' I have no fears now. 'Absolutely' he answered.

This day last year (the 9th) our darling little Sonnie[1] fell from his pony. A life full of promise, a name so precious, a lovely promising disposition, in an instant of carelessness ceasing for ever, & oh the sorrow & anguish of heart to see the life ebb away.

---

1. Mary's nephew Charles Fraser-Tytler, who died at three years old after a fall from his pony. He was the son of Mary's half-brother, Edward Fraser-Tytler and his wife, Edith. They lived at Aldourie Castle, near Loch Ness, where Mary had spent some of her childhood. The Wattses later designed a bronze triptych in memory of Sonnie and Mary's father and brother, all three named Charles Fraser-Tytler.

TUESDAY, SEPTEMBER 13 Mr & Mrs Barnett came for the final sitting. Mrs Barnett is quite delighted with the picture. She & Mr Barnett have been long playing the game of her saying 'Now, Samuel, look as you do in Mr Watts's picture.' It is a wonderful painting & she came back after saying goodbye, to tell Signor again how much she liked it. She said she knows now what is their dearest possession.

SUNDAY, SEPTEMBER 18 This has been a somewhat unusually golden day, beginning with sunshine pouring in upon us at 7 this morning, a lovely air & the pleasant sound of church bells. We went out for a walk going down by Addison Road & wishing we had Bedford Park to walk in to please our eyes. Instead we looked out for what we could find, & a branch of a great chestnut tree pleased Signor with its majesty of line, so much lost by modern landscape painters, so little understood by the public. We turned up Holland Park Road & down the Holland Walk, & peeping into the beautiful old place made Signor think he would ask for Lady H.[1] She had left some days before, but we saw Lane, the dear deaf old master of the household, who was so proud to take us into the interesting rooms. I saw the hand of my darling in almost every room, on little brackets, friezes, ceilings, pictures, & it all culminated in a grand picture of himself. I hope to be allowed to copy it or have it done. I am so glad & thankful to have seen it & know that it exists – the true link between the boy of 17 & the man of 40.[2] I was fascinated with all I saw. Signor promised to take me back in the afternoon to see the garden. We found Dixon, & went round to see what does well & came away with a lovely bunch of flowers, having had a real pleasure walking through all the lovely old garden, & rejoicing at being among such beauty, the distant roar of London just loud enough to remind one of what was outside. Ugliness & toil making us all the more sensible of the joy of lovely things that toil not.

---

1. Holland House, the London home of Lord and Lady Holland, was in Holland Park, which they also then owned. When Watts was living in old Little Holland House, in the Park, he was a constant visitor to the house, and created some of its most decorative features, having been the Hollands' friend and guest in Florence for several years in the 1840s, before they returned to England. 2. G.F. Watts, self-portait, 1845, private collection.

WEDNESDAY, SEPTEMBER 21 Again working at the cement work, with gloves on, for Thompson[1] frightened me by saying that if I would excuse him he would say my fingers won't look like fingers again for a century. Glad to say they do still resemble them, but have got into gloves as they smarted a good deal.

Photographs came from Hollyer.[2] I am so pleased with a picture he did of me. I put it by Signor's & like the little illustration of our lives.

SUNDAY, SEPTEMBER 25 *Manchester* A grey miserable day, the hideousness of the town not to be described. We drove to the Exhibition[3] & were met. Too dark to see much, but saw much that delighted us. Sir F. Leighton astonishes him. He looks so wonderful – *The Summer Moon* & *Death of Hercules*, so beautiful. Signor deeply disappointed with his own work, it was dark, though, so we could not see it, but as I came in & saw *Una & the Red Cross Knight* without knowing whose it was, I said 'That is great work.' The portrait of Burne Jones is the only bit of his work there wh. he allows is good.

MONDAY, OCTOBER 3 Mr Jowett[4] came to sit to Signor. He tried to paint him earlier but he is a very difficult subject & the picture was not satisfactory. Signor made me come & sit near that he might talk to me. I enjoyed it very much, rather an exaltation to be perched between these two. Both simple & kindly & no one now frightens me as Signor used when I came to him with my tongue cleaving to my mouth with awe.

Jowett told us a nice story of two pessimists drinking coffee. One says to the other 'Life would be a hell but for coffee' & his friend answers 'It is a hell with it.'

---

1. George Thompson (d.1904), whom Watts took on as his sculptural assistant in 1880. He worked with both Wattses in many practical ways, and had a great admiration for them. Mary was particularly fond of him, and enjoyed his sense of humour. She talked about him as their 'pillar'. **2.** Frederic Hollyer (1838–1933), photographer and engraver, famed for photographing the works of artists in the second half of the nineteenth century and making photographic portraits of them. He produced albums of nearly all of Watts's paintings. **3.** The Royal Jubilee Exhibition at Old Trafford, Manchester (1887). This was an elaborate undertaking, with new buildings constructed specially to contain the exhibits, in what was then the Botanical Gardens. It was open for five-and-a-half months, and attracted between four and five million visitors. **4.** Benjamin Jowett (1817–93), Master of Balliol College, Oxford. The portrait had been started in 1872, but was not finished until 1887.

WEDNESDAY, OCTOBER 5 Mr Jowett telegraphed to put off his sitting. I was glad for I was very tired by yesterday. I sent Alfred off with a variety of notes over to Mr Jowett & returned some sketches of Miss Nightingale.[1] Signor has had them for 20 years, having once tried to paint her, but giving it up because he did not think he could do her justice, she had been so altered by illness.

THURSDAY, OCTOBER 6 I had a nice letter from Miss Nightingale. Signor so pleased. 'The greatest woman in England' he says. 'My dear child' he sometimes says to me, 'that is the part of your life in which I can feel I give you something really good. Many delightful & great people have been very kind to me & I have made them my friends, & now we can make them yours.'

TUESDAY, OCTOBER 11 Mr Jowett did come. We found him here after taking a walk through Holland House Garden. He sat & talked, Ethel[2] & I on each side of him.

I hear he whispers to himself now & then, repeating the same word over & over again.

THURSDAY, OCTOBER 13 Went to the National Gallery. It was dark, but still we were delighted, Signor feeling the exquisite delight those Old Masters can give, lost now in these modern times. Such clear true line & colour serenely glowing. We felt very proud of our gallery. Went in to see the Turners. Perhaps the dark day was bad for them but we felt a sort of disappointment

FRIDAY, OCTOBER 14 Ethel very much amused by Emma, who told us the new housemaid had asked if she might throw away an old pair of Signor's boots. 'She didn't know what she was talking about,' I told her. 'Why, they'll be worth, when the master's dead, quite a £100.'

SUNDAY, OCTOBER 16 A lovely day. Signor & I walked to the Round pond & enjoyed the clouds, the breaking sun & the shadow, the autumnal trees, the yacht races & the children.

Came back to find Julia & her children.[3]

---

1. Watts started a portrait of Florence Nightingale in 1864. It remained unfinished and is at Watts Gallery. **2.** Ethel Fraser-Tytler, Mary's eldest sister. **3.** Julia Stephen and her children Vanessa (later Bell), Virginia (later Woolf) and Adrian. Julia was a good friend, and she and her children visited often, both to Little Holland House and, later, Limnerslease.

FRIDAY, OCTOBER 21 Mary Anderson[1] came to sit. She brought a beautiful bunch of roses. Better than them, her beautiful self, with a fresh mountain air about her, that left a feeling of health with us after she left.

'She has the nature of a child' Signor says.

MONDAY, OCTOBER 24 We walked right down the park till we came to John St, when he remembered his old studio – 30 Charles Street,[2] & we went up to the old room which, though changed, has still the same walls. The door & small bedroom where he slept are gone.

TUESDAY, OCTOBER 25 Early shopping & then back to find Mary Anderson standing for her picture. We drove to Hampstead together, feeling quite friends in the few moments we have been together. She told me that Gladstone[3] had said to her that he envied her sitting to Signor. 'I sat to him once when I was exceedingly busy, yet I never found the two or three hours were over without having regret. I know no man who charms me in conversation as Watts does.'

Came back from Hampstead to find my darling in his golden niche. I had been with charming people but came back to be more increasingly thankful for what my golden niche holds!

WEDNESDAY, OCTOBER 26 We went to pay a visit to Burne Jones, he & she, & we sat together in their little drawing room & did not go to the studio. They have Michelangelo's *Night & Morning*, which Signor does not care for. Mr Burne Jones stood up for them. Signor thinks M.A. the greatest of all artists, but his sculpture by no means on a level with the painting. He thinks he was prevented by the obstinacy of his material from dashing in his thoughts (his wax sketches as fine as can be). From there we went to Holman Hunt & saw his very impressive picture of the *Flight into Egypt*, with all its strange ugliness of surface, flesh made of a

---

1. Mary Anderson (1859–1940), American actress of great beauty. She toured Britain in *The Winter's Tale* and *The Merchant of Venice* in 1883 and 1887, and was a great success. Watts painted her twice in 1885–7. **2.** Watts used this studio between 1848 and 1850, before he moved into old Little Holland House with Sara and Thoby Prinsep. **3.** William Ewart Gladstone (1809–98), Liberal politician and four times Prime Minister. He finally retired in 1894, aged 84. He was famous as an orator and a powerful politician. Watts painted him twice, in 1859 and 1876–80, and they enjoyed each other's conversations.

hard stable material reflecting every sort of colour, wh. makes a most unlovely impression. The dignity & moral influence of his work always surprises me.

SATURDAY, OCTOBER 29 Walked into the house with Mary Anderson who arrived at the same moment. She sat for some time to Signor, the picture growing more & more lovely.

Signor well & ready for his dissipation at night.[1] Julia came, a little before dinner. Signor remembered that he ought to wear evening clothes. They had not seen light of day for years, so there was considerable 'racing & chasing'. White tie & studs quite unattainable. Alfred came to the rescue & lent a tie. Then came difficulties of warm things underneath, ones which upper clothes would not meet.

'You really must go without me' – 'I fear you & Emma must go.' I kept out of this distressful scene. Emma almost in tears, all the wardrobes & drawers disembowelled in heaps on the floor. White shirt became an impossibility, there was no room for it, so the remembrance of a thing called a dickey[2] came to Signor. Alfred volunteered one, too large. Kensington produced one.

In the end, though rather late, we set off. Emma's parting cry 'I'll not forget this if I live a hundred years.'

Mary (Anderson) was on the stage in red & purple. The first impression was disappointment. The dress is ugly, designed by Tadema.[3] The trial is beautiful. She moves so grandly, is so divinely beautiful in her pure white. We could find nothing to criticise in her acting. The dance as Perdita surprisingly graceful, & the descent of the statue so grand & so pathetic.

MONDAY, OCTOBER 31 Signor heard from C. Hallé telling him about the trouble in the Grosvenor Gallery.[4]

---

1. They went to see Mary Anderson as Portia in *The Merchant of Venice* and Perdita in *The Winter's Tale*. **2.** A false shirt front. **3.** Sir Lawrence Alma-Tadema (1836–1912), the Dutch classical subject painter who settled in England in 1870. He designed many costumes for stage productions. **4.** The Grosvenor Gallery was set up in 1877 and showed the Pre-Raphaelite artists' work and the work of artists who had difficulties with the Royal Academy. In 1888, the directors, J. Comyns Carr and Charles Hallé resigned and set up the New Gallery, taking many leading artists, including Burne-Jones, with them.

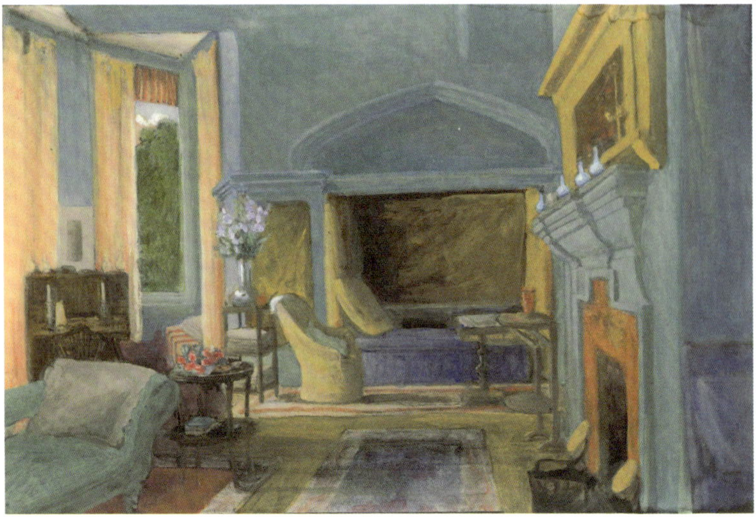

Madeline Wyndham (attrib.), *The drawing room at Little Holland House*, 1904, watercolour, Watts Gallery

Mr Burne Jones came also about the Grosvenor. Left me a lovely sketch. Pencil drawing & his blue *Fortune*[1] has come back too. Jowett sent us some books & a very nice letter.

THURSDAY, NOVEMBER 3 Packing & things sent off to *Britannia.*[2] Mary[3] came to sit, & saw her picture which she was delighted with. It is indeed a poem of beauty, strength of youth, & purity. She had luncheon with us.

Burne Jones came in & said 'You are much too happy.' He has been about the Gros. Gall. or rather the New Gallery that has been decided upon.

SATURDAY, NOVEMBER 5 *SS Britannia* Left home at ten o'clock. A tremendous crowd of people seeing friends off.

The ship is huge, new, & clean. Saloon has carved oak panels & wainscot, small tables, 7 at ours, 4 Scotch Australians.

---

1. E. Burne-Jones, *The Wheel of Fortune* showing Fortune in a blue gown looking down at three figures (also blue) of the slave, the king and the poet. 2. Signor and Mary were to sail to Malta for the winter on the SS *Britannia.* 3. Mary Anderson.

SUNDAY, NOVEMBER 6 All on deck, still in the Channel. Stopped near Plymouth & sent off letters with pilot. Passed Eddystone. Squally & darker. Told to expect rough weather.

MONDAY, NOVEMBER 7 We passed through a terrific night of noise, roll, & sounds of misery! The bows were nearly always under water & we rolled to an angle of 20 degrees, hearing afterwards that *The Captain* rolled over at 18, but our Captain was pleased with the way the ship behaved & said he did not have any anxiety for her. At times I felt anxious, the thought of Signor's unfinished work was the one that oppressed me most. It was impossible to sleep. I watched the skies from my post, or the phosphorous in the waves, when we went down into the depths. I was only up during the day, though feeling very miserable. Sat on deck with lashed chairs, deck often like the steep side of a roof.

TUESDAY, NOVEMBER 8 The morning looks radiant. Left the bay late last night, & since then the swell has been gradually subsiding. A lovely warm day. Signor up & sat on deck & felt thankful that the worst was over.

WEDNESDAY, NOVEMBER 9 Thermometer 69. Such a lovely day, as calm as a pond. The ship not rolling in the least, but making great way. We passed Gibraltar at one o'clock. Signalling 'All well' 'Rough weather in the Bay'.

SATURDAY, NOVEMBER 12 *Villa Micallef – Sliema* Arrived in the harbour at eight a.m.

Saw Gozo before I got up. Malta came in sight soon after. Our journey safely over, & yet both Signor & I had had strange presentiments about it, & on Sunday night we both felt that they were likely to be realised! A new ship, untried in bad weather, may have given us this feeling, but all is safely over now. The house delightful. We shall soon be quite at home and happy.

Lunched at the hotel at Sliema. All luggage came safely. Nothing lost, & my dear love safe from snow & cold & fog, able to be out every day & light & warmth to help him in his work.

SUNDAY, NOVEMBER 13 The delicious sun streamed in this morning, in time for us to have our baths. We had watched its first gleam upon the top of the window, & the gradual broadening till all was glowing –

Valletta lay looking pearly against the glowing sky, & our green olives & pines a beautiful rich foreground.

MONDAY, NOVEMBER 14 Signor at work & pleased with the light in the drawing room. He says the diffused light is probably a very instructive one, his things look darker than he thought.

WEDNESDAY, NOVEMBER 16 After luncheon Signor & I went to Valletta. Paints & a milk jug had to be got & came back in Signor's pocket.

We found letters here, one from Mr Burne Jones telling Signor more about the Grosvenor. They are not launching out upon a gallery as yet. He says he only means to go on 'as a quiet little painter painting pictures', & 'Exhibiting my pictures where you do'.

SATURDAY, NOVEMBER 19 We arose this morning & talked of this time last year. 'All that we can say is that we ought to have married long ago' he says.

SUNDAY, NOVEMBER 20 Wondering what other married people see of each other. 'Married a year, but having lived five together' my own love says. What a record of happiness this 'Fatima'[1] is. So seldom apart for an hour, a constant interchange of thought, no books read but together, what a sublime life it is for me. Every day teaches me its value more. The morning was too stormy for church. Signor wrote some letters & then we read together.

After luncheon we walked part by the sea, more calm today, & afterwards through field paths where to our great joy we found a great promise of wild flowers.

Our evening spent reading *Cranford*. It belongs to the same class as Miss Austen, but the pathetic is too much there for Signor.

MONDAY, NOVEMBER 21 The delicate sharpness of all we see here delights him at every turn. Yesterday as we left our door we happened to look up to the top of our house clear against a turquoise ground, the sun just delicately tracing out the cool stone carving, which was all in shadow – but such shadow! The warm greys that even the old Venetians would look cold against! Signor longs for Mr Burne Jones.

---

1. Mary's nickname for her diaries. They were all written in small, fat, identical volumes, and she saw them as a short, voluble woman, who might well have been called 'Fatima'.

SATURDAY, NOVEMBER 26 Signor telling me today about his *Alfred*.[1] I have never seen it & did not even know the story, King Alfred inviting the English to beat the Danes at sea, where they thought themselves invincible. Our first naval victory. A grand subject.

'How little you have changed in your ideas of the direction your art should take' I said.

'I don't think the direction has changed, it has developed.'

He has often told me that knowing that Ruskin & such earnest men as the P.R.B.[2] thought him mistaken had done him much harm.

He was in front of his day, & is so still.

THURSDAY, DECEMBER 1 Had our pleasant walk about nine, & found it rather too hot coming home!

I went to a reception at the Palace in the afternoon.[3]

SATURDAY, DECEMBER 3 Had my first Italian lesson. I went into the garden & was tempted by roses, narcissus, hibiscus & other lovely things to spend the morning picking & arranging flowers. I enjoyed it to its utmost. We lunched alone & walked to Valletta, did much shopping. A jolly looking curly headed youth was wanting to sell me roses, would put in a golden hearted bud into Signor's button & of course I had to buy a bunch of them – for two pence.

Signor has begun a new subject, the great figure holding the sphere on his knee.[4] I think it promises to be most suggestive.

---

1. Watts's painting *Alfred Inciting the Saxons to Prevent the Landing of the Danes* (1846, oil on canvas). It was Watts's entry in a competition to decorate the new Houses of Parliament in the category 'English History'. It hangs in the Palace of Westminster (The Parliamentary Art Collection). **2.** Pre-Raphaelite Brotherhood. **3.** The Governor's Palace, Valletta; Malta was a British crown colony. **4.** Watts's painting, *The All-Pervading*. The Creator is shown as a figure that may be either male or female. In his preface to the catalogue for the exhibition at the New Gallery in 1886, when the painting was first shown, Watts refers to 'a winged figure, holding in her lap, "The Globe of the Systems"', Barbara Bryant, '*The All-Pervading*: Before the Altarpiece and After', in M.S. Watts *et al.*, *The Word in the Pattern: A Facsimile with Seven Essays* (2012). A small version hangs above the altar in the Watts Cemetery Chapel, finished by Watts in April 1904, two months before he died (see page 225).

MONDAY, DECEMBER 12 A dear letter from Choons with a wonderful account of Edward.[1] She can see how in spite of herself there is a strong hope beginning to rise in her heart. Signor wrote again about the *Love & Death* he wants a friend to buy. He sends an account of the bequest by Sir Joseph Whitworth to Manchester of £47,000.

My dear love looked at me with a wistful look. I thought it meant that he would like to give them the *Love & Death*, but that it was a loss of £3000 immediately, & at least £5000 in the future.

'Darling,' I said. 'Could not you give them the picture?'

'I should like to' he said, & it was settled by his writing at once to Agnew. 'I say we' he said. 'You are associated with me in this'.

TUESDAY, DECEMBER 13 After luncheon to see some pony races at the Polo ground. Sliema, a golden city, a gold reflection, the harbour calm but for a gentle ripple that caught the part of the sky behind us which was bluest & made the sea bluer than the sky above it.

'You don't repent of being generous yesterday?' I said to him. 'Certainly not' he said, 'not more than I did about the baronetcy.'[2]

WEDNESDAY, DECEMBER 21 A black edged letter from Andrew was brought in to me. I opened it & sent for Signor to break it as gently as I could. The friend of 40 years, kind, warm hearted, original, impulsive, gone into the quiet land.[3] Death seems to be more cold & still, when the life it takes has been so full of movement, enthusiasms, affections, anxieties! My dear Love felt it much. He put his head down upon my shoulders & sobbed like a child. The first thing he said was 'I am glad she knew you were a darling.'

Afterwards he said 'Ah, how sad the dismemberment of that sisterhood seems to me, like the pages of some beautiful book torn out one by one.'

He says it is strange that to him to whom Death is an ever present thought, & that knowing for some weeks now that Mrs Prinsep has been dangerously ill, the news should come with such a shock. He looks pale today, but after writing letters to Val[4] & Andrew, he went back to his great solemn mood.

---

1. Mary's sister Christina and her husband, the Rev. Edward Liddell. **2.** Watts was twice offered a baronetcy but refused it both times. **3.** Sara Prinsep (1816–87), in whose house Watts lived from 1851 to 1875, had died after a short illness. **4.** Valentine Prinsep (1838–1904), painter, son of Sara and Thoby.

FRIDAY, DECEMBER 23 Signor lay rather quietly. I turned round & saw an unusually sad look on his face. At about ten minutes to nine Signor said – 'I should like to go out. I don't feel better for missing my morning walk.'

'I wish we were on our steps' I said, & not two minutes after I saw my dear one fall flat down upon the road, his profile turned towards me. He fell without an attempt to save himself. He was quite unconscious. I looked up & down the road. I saw no one. I felt what I had never known before. Alone, everything swept out of my life. Only a husk. Yet my love was not dead. I must get help. I rolled up my cloak & put it for a pillow under his head, I then ran at my utmost speed & soon saw some artillery, who ran to me, came back & found Signor had not moved. A moment or two afterwards, he raised himself up, his cheek was grazed, & blood was coming away. I tied a handkerchief round it, the men lifted him to the side of the road. One ran for water & one for a cab. I got him home in a half-conscious state. Joseph at the door helped him up. Alfred & Emma & I got him on to the bed, ashy white by this time, retching again terribly. We got some brandy down & laid him down quietly, I sitting beside him & holding his pulse, which mercifully I could feel was strong.

Perhaps I had grown too certain of my happiness. Perhaps I was counting too much on finishing this year with happy days, & my 'Fatima' for next year lying before me to be filled too. Now I must remember I am tenant only by the day, in my palace of peace & goodness & joy.

SATURDAY, DECEMBER 24 It was a windy & wet night. I heard the bells chiming & ringing loudly at Valletta, & told my darling.

'You must have happier Xmas's than this, my poor Mary' he said.

SUNDAY, DECEMBER 25 'I said you would be very dear to me' he said reminding me of what he had said when he first asked me to marry him.

He began to talk. Dear Emma brought the tea. She had been offering to get up an hour before if he needed it. He liked his cup of tea. Sat up for it. I saw his colour had returned. The voice was strong & natural, in fact in spite of his restless night, all bad symptoms had passed away. I put my hand into Emma's, the net curtain between us, & said 'A merry Xmas, Emma.' At the same time the tears coming rushing down my cheeks, hers doing the same. 'I wanted to say that, Madam, only I couldn't' she said, pressing my hand, crying quietly, that Signor might not know what fools we were.

A new joy & surely a happy Xmas. We had breakfast together again, the Doctor having been, & allowed him coffee & toast! When we were alone he asked me to put my head down upon his shoulder, & he held me in his arms. He knew I had been terribly frightened.

SATURDAY, DECEMBER 31 'My Best, my Best and dearest' he said to me this morning, 'I will tire you out soon. You will weary of me & then what shall I do? Such a rickety machine, I am, no sooner one part gets patched up, another falls to pieces. I am disgusted with myself, but I feel it most for you. There is no set off against all this for you.' How little he knows!

I asked him how I should end my 'Fatima' for 1887. He said 'Say that nothing could make us more to each other than we are.'

1891

Watts and Mary had spent two winters with Andrew and May Hichens in their house, Monkshatch, in the Surrey hills, above the village of Compton. Late in 1890 their friends persuaded them to build their own house, and Andrew found a piece of suitable land on a hill within walking distance. He offered to pay for the land and building, and to lease the house to them until they were in a position to repay him. They commissioned the Arts and Crafts architect, Ernest George, to design it, and named their winter retreat Limnerslease.

Mary was very excited that they would have a house truly theirs, and the first part of the year she spent designing and making a plaster ceiling for the drawing room, basing the idea for it on positive symbols of renewal, harvest and human endeavour, with birds of truth, love, rebirth and alertness, centred on the Egyptian winged sun. She also worked on landscaping and designing a garden, and on furniture and decorative ideas for a life that would contain studios for both of them, a dining room for entertaining, and a drawing room into which they could retreat to their own private space in the evenings.

Watts worked on a series of 12 red chalk drawings that were shown at Agnew's in the spring and bought by the Whitworth Gallery in Manchester for £2,000. They were delighted that the series was to be kept together, and also that the sale would provide building bricks towards the purchase of Limnerslease from Andrew. Many, including Thomas Hardy, who had not taken to Watts's work, came to see the drawings and they were at one time the talk of the Savile Club.

In the summer Watts's largest and most ambitious painting, *The Court of Death*, which was yet to be finished, was brought down from London to his new studio at Limnerslease. A 'picture slot' was inserted in the floor, through which the painting could be raised and lowered so that he could work on different parts of it with ease. In August he painted a portrait of Walter Crane, the artist and illustrator, often considered his finest. 'I have sat & looked at that picture with wonder & the man lives in it & holds one fascinated', wrote Mary in her diary.

Limnerslease and its surrounding land needed constant attention, and Watts asked George Andrews, an ex-policeman who had been working for him on the Isle of Wight, to come and live in Compton as estate steward. He remained a very valuable friend and ally for many years. By the end of the year their life at Compton was well established, and Mary looked ahead to 'the year undivined which begins tomorrow, & a feeling of thankfulness for the past one, which has given us our little home'.

THURSDAY, JANUARY 1 *Monkshatch* Good morning to 'Fatima' No.5. Good morning & a blessing from Signor very early. 'We must try to make a better use of this new year' says my angel husband.

'I don't believe we can' says his wicked wife.

For New Year's day we had the blessing of the sun, a bit of blue sky overhead, 'a good augury for the year' Signor said, and he has a good touch of superstition about him. It is natural to those with a childlike nature.

I ran down to the little house. They have got on well, our doorways are completed, just 6ft 3 high. A modern girl with a hat on must stoop to come in.[1]

FRIDAY, JANUARY 2 Signor interested this morning on his pillows by the thought of the dual nature. He believes we all have it, & can develop the good or not as we choose.

---

1. 'Modern girls', in 1891, would certainly turn up wearing hats. Building went on through the first half of 1891, and Mary played a great part in plans for the interior, and for the garden and woodland, as the diary shows. The name Limnerslease came from 'limner', a middle English name for a portrait painter, and 'lease', as they hoped the house would lead to gleaning many more fruitful years.

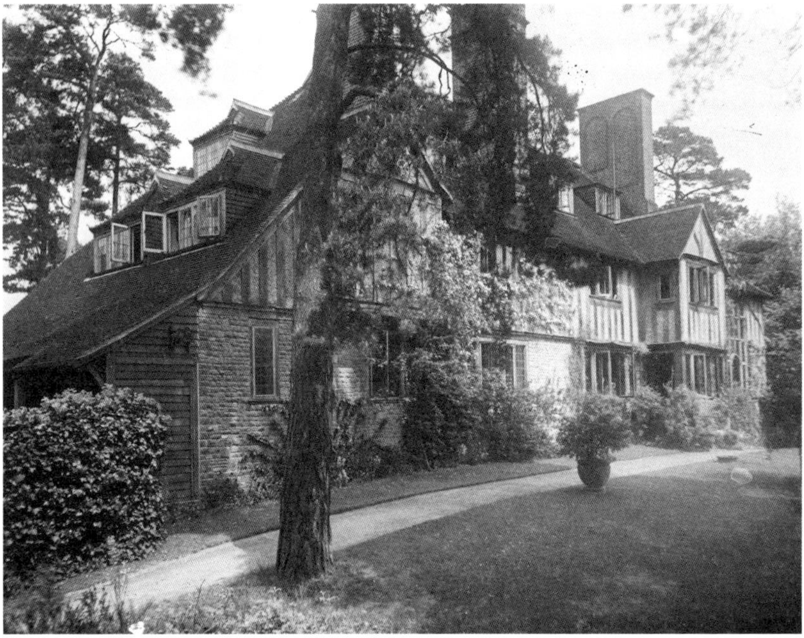

View of Limnerslease in the 1890s

He began to search out his 'Mr Hyde', but I told him I thought he was dead long ago.

SATURDAY, JANUARY 3 The outside world around us lies still & white & gives no hope of change. Signor works on in the library, with his red chalk.

There is a wonderful patience in his nature, he makes the best of things, very rarely saying that it grieves him to be doing no painting. He has not touched a brush since we came here.

He asked me to photograph the *Time, Death & Judgement*[1] wh. he has here & I am developing it & some others done out of doors. Took me my whole morning, with very little result.

1. G.F. Watts, *Time, Death and Judgement*, 1890s, oil on canvas, St Paul's Cathedral, on long loan to Watts Gallery.

SUNDAY, JANUARY 4 Our evening very cosy. We are getting on with the first vol. of *Modern Painters*.[1] We both delight in it.

MONDAY, JANUARY 5 I found I was quite wrong. The frost was soon 2 ft into the earth. The price for worms must be prohibitive.

Our birds are Signor's constant care.

TUESDAY, JANUARY 6 My ceiling[2] is begun in good earnest. Mr Peto[3] came down. He reminds me very much of what Gladstone was years ago, only his were fine, grey eyes.

He is very pleasant, though as an architect we could not quite find out that he had very definite ideas. He admired nothing here at the little house. When Signor pointed out the staircase with its curve which he admires, he only said 'what a curious thing the desire for curves was'. He did not even let his eyes rest on the red chalk drawings in the studio.

It was very nice going round the house with him, he especially pointed out what a pity it was that the pleasant rough plastering of the walls was lost in the finely polished mortar veneer.

SATURDAY, JANUARY 10 While I was very sleepy this morning at about six o'clock, in spite of a great many hints from dear one, his pillow put under my head, & other things all in vain, he took the candle & began writing. When he was done, & I was beginning to wake up, I turned to him & asked if he had been making a little philosophical theory upon sloth. 'Not exactly' he answered.

A visit to the little Limnerslease. Brilliant sun, Signor in delightful Arctic boots Mr Peto had chosen for him, & Andrew with us. I have long talks with darling little May, who I love more & more.

MONDAY, JANUARY 12 Marking small trees of scrub oak round the little house with Tyler.[4] Signor's tender heart won't allow more than three or four to go at a time. I feel we must have light & air to be well there, also

1. *Modern Painters* by John Ruskin (1843). In this, the first of Ruskin's four-volume study of what constitutes great art, he concentrates on landscape painting, analysing the importance of Turner, who painted from nature. **2.** Before the building of the house was finished, Mary had started work on white plaster panels to decorate the ceiling in the new drawing room, illustrating her interest in the symbolism of cultures from the past. **3.** Harold Ainsworth Peto FRIBA (1854–1933), partner to Ernest George. He worked with George from 1876 to 1892. **4.** A gardener. Two or three were always employed.

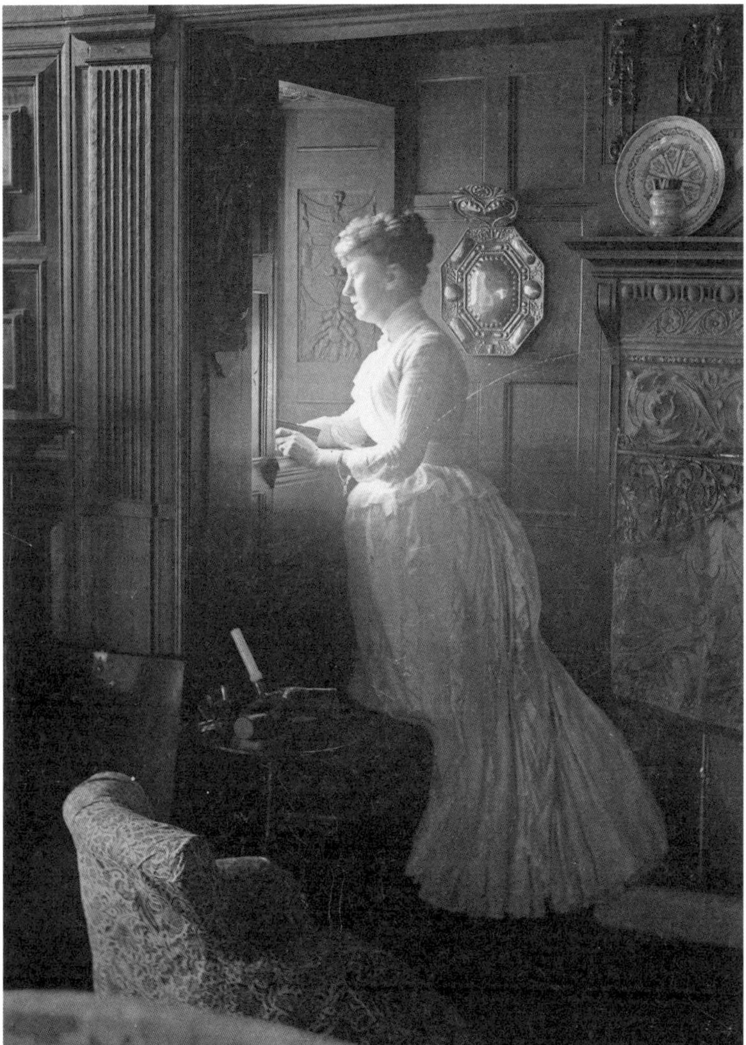

May Hichens in the music room at Monkshatch, 1890s

I should not want to have many deciduous trees round us in autumn, littering their decaying leaves about & making it damp.

TUESDAY, JANUARY 13 The peace of these home-driven days suits us well. I sometimes laugh at us, the little couple never separate, following the same moves day by day, till just before nine, each with our bedroom candle, each gone bedwards, to dream less happily perhaps than the dream of real life.

WEDNESDAY, JANUARY 14 I wrote to Mr George about the panelling for the drawing room.

Signor felt rather too deaf for reading, he said, so I began drawing a table I want made by the Home Arts people.[1]

THURSDAY, JANUARY 15 Hard work at 5 a.m., wings etc., the central panel.[2] Signor suggests me using felt steeped in plaster & glued on. It would make things go quicker & get the sharp edge so necessary.

SATURDAY, JANUARY 17 I have now to place my sliding door[3] of oak & my chimney pieces, then all will be going well.

SUNDAY, JANUARY 18 In the evening I was able to draw out the rolling door, which I think will be pretty.

TUESDAY, JANUARY 20 Too wet to go out, I slaved at my ceiling, Signor at his work. The chalk drawings take him as much time as many paintings would do.

THURSDAY, JANUARY 22 We walked down to our 'garden', the bare field now full of ruts & stubbles, but so sunny, & the garden in imagination so delicious. The peep up towards the house, the chimney stacks among the pines, the comfortable house in the heart of beautiful nature, was

---

1. The Home Arts and Industries Association, founded in 1884 by Eglantyne Louisa Jebb (1845–1925) to encourage and promote the survival of rural crafts and cottage industries. The Wattses were heavily involved in the movement, and Mary, when she came to decorating her Cemetery Chapel with terracotta tiles in 1896, taught successful classes for all comers from the neighbourhood. **2.** The central panel of the ceiling decoration shows the Egyptian sun with its winged rays. Mary had decided on their honeymoon in Egypt that she would use it in some of the reliefs she hoped to design. **3.** Mary had found this oak panelling in a furniture yard. The lower section is 19th-century, the upper part Jacobean.

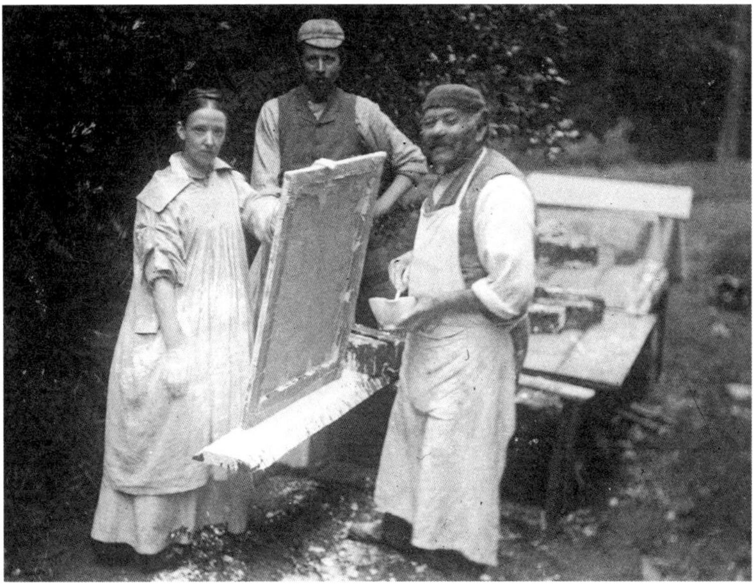

Mary Watts, George Thompson and another, moving panels for one of the Limnerslease ceilings, 1891, Watts Gallery

noticed by us for the first time. We walked back very thankfully, Signor quite brimming over with the pleasure of it.

The Academy elections[1] as commonplace, all three, as they well could be. More & more one regrets that Signor should even nominally be connected with such a dull stupid institution, where in future times all the greatest names of the day will be outside, Rossetti, Holman Hunt, Burne Jones & many more. Why does one go on hoping for any improvement? It becomes more & more impossible each year. Only love of Sir Frederic keeps Signor there.

SATURDAY, JANUARY 24 Andrew likes the ceiling, & I think he is pleased to find that it will be pretty inside as well as out. It has the promise of Golden years still to be gleaned & it looked sweeter to me than usual today.

1. The Royal Academy was going through one of its perennial upheavals. Sir Frederic Leighton was President but, with antagonism by existing members towards many of the artists of the day, it was becoming harder to take some of its rejections seriously.

SUNDAY, JANUARY 25 I gave my mind to the whole conception of my ceiling for some hours. It is to be the concrete expression of the spiritual atmosphere that Signor has round him, the aroma of his thought put into the silent language of symbols, graven as a memorial of him. I took the plan & showed it to him.

WEDNESDAY, JANUARY 28 How tender he is no one but me knows, & I can't write it for it is felt in silence. He seldom uses loving words, so much so that when I read to him a passage in *Blessed be Drudgery*[1] when a woman says 'If you love me, tell me so sometimes' he said 'Oh that must have been you.' If I was ever foolish enough to ask that, it is not because I really want it. The silent consciousness of being beloved, of being needed, almost constantly, what could any woman want beside?

THURSDAY, JANUARY 29 I work hard at the panels. I got Boulter the carpenter up for the day, & he stretched the canvases.[2] More than a day's work for him, it would have taken me a month.

Signor sketched out *The Girl at the Gate*,[3] in red chalk. It comes so quickly, & looks so light & beautiful when it is just laid in, almost like a thing breathed upon the paper.

FRIDAY, JANUARY 30 While I sit & write up 'Fatima' in bed, & wait for my bath, little lamb is up betimes & begins the intricacies of the scrubbing process, very long, & very complete, going from hottest bearable water to coldest possible, & ending in an air bath.

Sometimes, through the soap suds, come little monologues, political, ethical, or anything else under heaven's sun that may enter his wakeful brain.

We have Andrew & May here this evening & Signor is happy, interested by billiards.

---

1. *Blessed be Drudgery* (1890) by William C. Gannett (1840–1923). Gannett, born in Boston, Massachusetts, was a Unitarian clergyman and social reformer, interested in women's suffrage. 2. The panels for Mary's ceiling reliefs were worked in gesso on a canvas backing, stretched on a frame. 3. One of the series of red chalk drawings. *The Girl at the Gate* was an early title for *The Messenger* (February 1891), shown with the rest of the series at Agnew's in April that year.

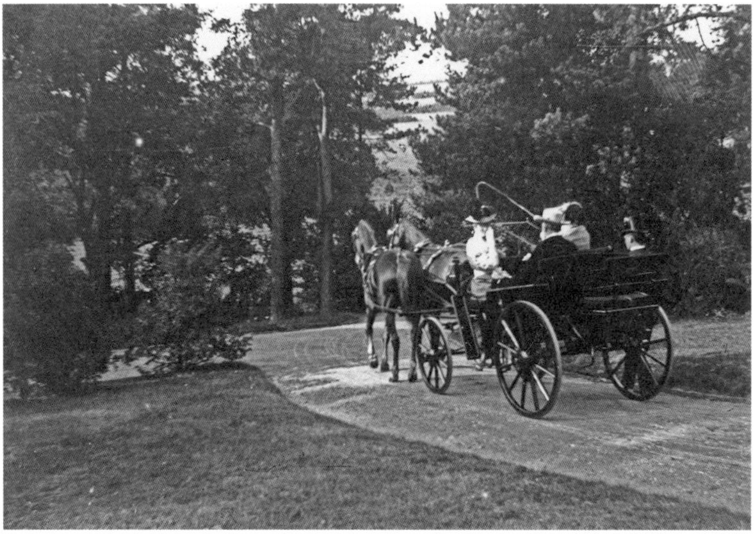

Watts and Mary setting off down the drive at Limnerslease, 1890s, Watts Gallery

SUNDAY, FEBRUARY 1 Picked the first primrose! Lovely! Sat out to have coffee, without hats or cloaks.

Signor again in travail this evening before tomorrow's journey. Difficult to console poor dear one because his 4 red drawings will be separated from us. I did not realise that the change at Woking would be so troublesome to him when I settled to go up by the 9.40 train. Must never to do it again.

MONDAY, FEBRUARY 2 *Little Holland House* We made our move, I am sorry to say both 'ragged to shatters' before we got into the train. We talked of it afterwards when he saw how tired out I was as we travelled up,[1] he being quite relieved, & he tells me he cannot control these fits of anxiety before travelling, any more than my nerves can be controlled where there is a constant rapping or loud noise.

1. The Wattses travelled often to and fro between Surrey and London by brougham to Godalming, then train and horse-drawn cab.

TUESDAY, FEBRUARY 3 *Little Holland House* Mr Burne Jones here in the evening, I having left a card at The Grange. Dear man, he has not been very well, a bad fall, a slight concussion afterwards. Georgie has been abroad, Phil[1] having warned them that the family were growing 'stagnant'. He told us a pretty little story of having seen, with Ruskin, in some gallery in Italy (Verona, I think) a letter of old Titian's, great scrawling letters to his name, & Ruskin went down quickly on his knees & kissed it.

THURSDAY, FEBRUARY 5 Signor painting for the first time since we came back.

FRIDAY, FEBRUARY 6 We go on bravely with the beef only, a small bit of dry toast, & black coffee at every meal.[2]

SATURDAY, FEBRUARY 7 *Monkshatch* It is wonderful to think that we are here from December to April, & so rarely see anyone & yet are never tired of being alone. Even Signor says he likes best the Saturdays we are alone. I had a lonely childhood, no friends, but sisters & cousins at Aldourie bred it in me. Later when as girls we ought to have made & had friends it was almost impossible to us, for peace sake, & because a friend of ours was generally denounced by Mamma.[3]

SUNDAY, FEBRUARY 8 This evening Signor began to talk to me as he had never done, about the future. We are so utterly agreed that it is useless piling up thousands for any one or two of the young generation. It so seldom carries a blessing, & is so often spent just as the donor would like least to see it spent. We have therefore arranged to leave the greater part, all but a few small legacies, to carry out Signor's monument to everyday heroes[4] & the rest to carry on the work of reviving the minor

---

1. Philip Burne-Jones, painter, son of Edward and Georgie Burne-Jones. **2.** The Salisbury diet, invented by Dr Salisbury, an American physician: ground beef boiled or fried, eaten daily, with very few vegetables or carbohydrates, taken with hot water. The diet was popular in the 1890s. **3.** Harriet Jane Pretyman, second wife to Charles Fraser-Tytler. Her relationship with her stepdaughters, Ethel, Christina (or 'Choons') and Mary, was always difficult. **4.** The idea was carried through some years later as Postman's Park, a cloister containing ceramic plaques commemorating everyday 'heroes and heroines' who had given their lives to help others in emergencies of life and death. See note for August 29, 1887 (page 41).

arts & handicrafts. We talked of the possibilities of spending much time down here, eventually, if he has a long life, many years still, of the 'Lease'. Also we might then ourselves carry out the 'Heroes'.

TUESDAY, FEBRUARY 10 Working like a tiger at my ceiling all morning, the glass door wide open, & the sun streaming in. I had all my panels out in the nice fresh breeze & it helped them much to dry. The wind is west. What a miracle of change it brings.

Our usual walk to little Limnerslease, where they are getting on so well these last two days. Signor oiled out the *Naples* which looks glowing.[1] Darling little one. How simple & childlike he is. He said to me today 'I think I should like to leave the chalk drawing of my *Hope* now, & finish it on my birthday.' He is still feeling tired & low, the effect of the beef diet only.

WEDNESDAY, FEBRUARY 11 Marie Stillman[2] has been promised the real shirt of the great Garibaldi, for Signor to paint from. His son Menotti possesses it. I think Signor will now make that portrait a fine one.

SATURDAY, FEBRUARY 14 Choons's birthday, a happier one than she has had since 1880.[3] I sent her the uncostly gift of photographs of Aldourie & the burn & bonny, bonny dell where our happy times were spent knowing nothing beyond our little world of half a dozen, & nature's great world. We worshipped the trees & flowers & moss & burn of that place, till it was akin to <u>illness</u> to be separated from them. Bless her & them, I still say, though forty years are passed since we first knew each other & that place.

WEDNESDAY, FEBRUARY 18 I have been foolish lately, feeling a sort of Aldourie love beginning in me for the little place. Signor has seen in my tell-tale face how much I care, tho' I have tried to keep my mind off it, have worked like a tiger, have tried to keep silence, hoping he would not know how much it concerned me.

---

1. *Naples* (1892), a first impression of Naples from the roof of the Hotel Nobile in 1888. Watts worked for some years on this painting, trying to recapture the effect this view of Naples had on him. **2.** Marie Stillman née Spartali. **3.** Choons's husband, Edward Liddell, had recently recovered from an undiagnosed mental illness, which lasted ten years.

THURSDAY, FEBRUARY 19 Began my day by running down to the little house by half past eight to see about the fixing of the drawing room mantelpiece.

Our evening with Ruskin. Signor has been so cute & has smelt out my birthday present for him, *The Queen of the Air*,[1] & is waiting with some impatience till Monday when he may have it. I am quite hard & unmoved when he says 'Let's have it at once.'

FRIDAY, FEBRUARY 20 The Festa will be kept by the men, as my darling has let me give them £3, & Mitchell[2] is to have an inscribed photograph with the date on it! He spoke charmingly, & said, looking down modestly & reddening, 'I am very proud of working for Mr Watts, I like his principles.'

The 'Limners - lease' is to be as a building one. Signor said he should like it to be a home for me, & Andrew's answer was 'We feel we are building it as much for Mary as for you.'

SATURDAY, FEBRUARY 21 Began keeping Signor's birthday. It goes over three days this year.

Our evening so happy, my darling allowed, as this was the beginning of the birthday, to have his *Queen of the Air*. He had really been longing for it since his eyes fell on it. What a different class of mind to most, & imagination is so rare, especially in that direction where we love to have the symbols & figures embodying some great truth, endlessly to be searched out & inexhaustible.

MONDAY, FEBRUARY 23 *St George's Day – Watts's birthday Little Holland House* My darling's real birthday. Another year if I am so blessed. Never let this feast be spread out over 3 days again, it dilutes its pleasures, & makes it no land mark.

The calm of the morning too disturbed by getting off by an early train, & by a weary wait at Clapham, or rather outside, while fog signals

---

1. *The Queen of the Air: Being a Study of the Greek Myths of Cloud and Storm* by John Ruskin, first published in 1869. Here Ruskin was renewing his idea of the concept of Divine powers in Nature for the age when the Christian faith no longer held sway.
2. The builder, working on Limnerslease.

went off all round, expresses flew past us in the darkness, & one felt far from easy. I saw dark lines growing round my dear one's eyes, from pure anxiety & nerve tension, a part always of an ordinary journey.

We groped home at last, to have a hearty welcome from Emma, Thompson & Phoebe,[1] who had prepared gifts! A pincushion & kettle holder for the new studio, & Thompson had cast Emma's hand & arm, & a very fine cast it is.

A dreary darkness outside – but thankfulness inside!

TUESDAY, FEBRUARY 24 Distinguished by a dense fog. Nothing was to be done, for Signor was inexorable about preventing my going anywhere in the dark. From the selfish point of view, he says, he must ask me to do nothing that gives him anxiety. Dear one! how much I feel that he draws life & help out of a sound & healthy life beside him, & if it were to collapse, his might.

Some light fell on us about two, & I was allowed to go out to see Mamma at Linden Gardens. Before I got back it was dense again. Only by the care of a kindly milkman from Holland Park farm could I manage to find my way up to Kensington, where my cabman, driving upon the pavement, had left me, & across to Melbury Rd. 'There is a drain I cross by, maam' he said patiently, used to darkness & danger, & wise & patient through it.

WEDNESDAY, FEBRUARY 25 A visit from Sir Frederic. The fog lifted as he came in. Delightful. No fog in his mind! When he talks he reminds me of exquisitely skilful piano playing. The management of words is so deft, so exactly right, no false note, & swift as thought is swift.

MONDAY, MARCH 2 Signor heard from Agnew in reply to his letter asking him to arrange for framing the chalk drawings. I went to George & Peto about the height of the staircase, which Andrew says Signor would now hit his head against. Then Mrs Coronio[2] came, who was very delightful

---

1. Phoebe was a much-loved maid. **2.** Aglaia Ionides Coronio (1834–1906), daughter of the Greek businessman Alexander Constantine Ionides, a major patron of Watts and his work. The portrait of the family (in the Watts Gallery), painted by Watts in 1841, shows Aglaia as a child. She, and others of the Ionides family, were painted at various phases of their lives by Watts.

as usual, full of bright thoughts. She was telling us about Morris[1] & his wonderful quick sight & length of memory. He drew her one day the whole & complete design & the pattern of the carpet in H. Hunt's picture *The Awakened Conscience*, & he had not seen it for 20 years. She had just seen it, & she said it was all correct, though not the woman's head. They had some discussion about it, so she took the drawing to H. Hunt, who said it was the most wonderful bit of memory as he had repainted the head ten years ago.

TUESDAY, MARCH 3 Went to May's & finding that darling thing on her pillows, she laughed consumedly at Rossetti's sonnet on Val,[2] which I learnt from Mrs Coronio yesterday.

'There is a creator called God,
Whose creations are sometimes most odd,
I maintain & I shall,
That a creature called Val,
Reflects little credit on God.'

THURSDAY, MARCH 5 Sixteen years since Charlie[3] said goodbye & went to exile & from there into the great unknown. What material there was in him, had the moulding hands better understood his worth & given something of deeper interest than the happy gamekeeper's life at Sanquhar,[4] & the training of Eton, to which he was sent so unprepared.

---

1. William Morris (1834–96), designer, poet and social activist. He was one of the major creative figures of the 19th century, producing a new kind of design for wallpapers, textiles and, with Burne-Jones, stained glass. Watts painted a fine portrait of him in 1870. In the 1880s Morris became an active socialist. In the last years of his life he founded the Kelmscott Press, which produced 66 books in seven years. **2.** The verse about Valentine Prinsep, son of Sara and Thoby Prinsep, May's brother, would now be called a limerick. The name was not invented for this verse form until later in the 1890s, but the form was well known from the 1840s onwards after Edward Lear wrote *Nonsense Songs*. The writer of the verse was Dante Gabriel Rossetti (1828–82). **3.** Mary's brother, Charles Fraser-Tytler, who died of typhoid in India in 1877. The triptych designed and decorated by Watts and Mary in memory of her young nephew (see the entry for September 9, 1887 and page 69) included two side panels in memory of her father and this brother. All three were named Charles Fraser-Tytler. **4.** 'Sanquhar' was a house in Forres, Moray, belonging to the Fraser-Tytler family.

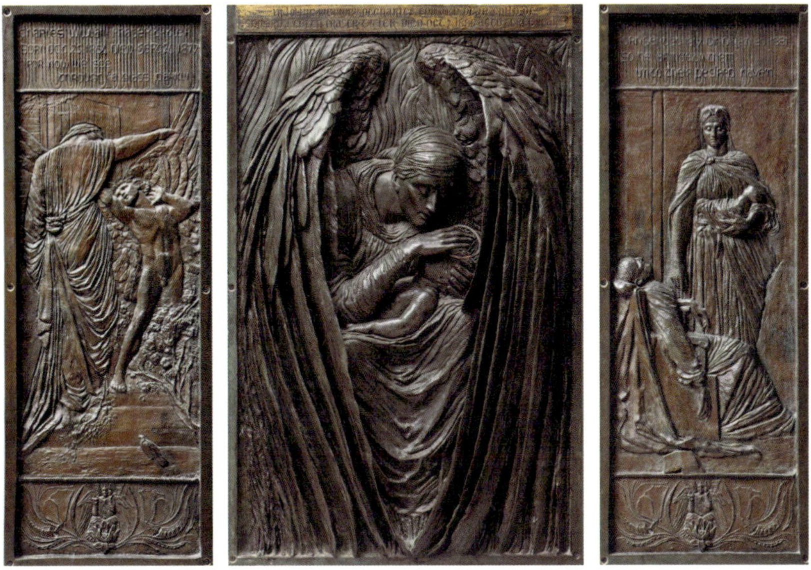

Mary Watts, Triptych in Memory of Mary Watts's nephew, father and brother, all named Charles Fraser-Tytler, 1891–3, private collection. Reproduced by permission of the photographer John Hammond

MONDAY, MARCH 9 *Monkshatch* Signor has been putting down some ideas on brown paper for a picture of *Joan of Arc*.[1] He says besides being a fine pictorial subject & of the sort he seldom makes use of, he wishes to do it as an Englishman, to show the French we are capable of doing justice to greatness wherever it is found.

Thompson here & working like a lion at my canvases. He & I have managed together to reduce the stack by four, of the unprepared ones. The working of them afterwards is nothing.

---

1. One of Watts's 12 red chalk drawings. The group of drawings sold at Agnew's, including *Joan of Arc*, was bought by the Whitworth Gallery after the exhibition.

TUESDAY, MARCH 10 Thompson & I again spent our morning & made the panels fly! & the plaster too. He is delightful as a companion. 'Stand them up perpendicularly straight, Madam' he says. His taste in furniture is good, he likes things simple & to the purpose. Cheap ornament he hates & he condemns always, as a thing 'all Vandyked about'. I am glad to say he says 'he is very fond' of my panels. The 'raison d'être' of them appeals to him.

Darling busy with his *Joan of Arc*, which I fixed for him in the evening, & we were together for a lovely hour with Ruskin's *Queen of the Air.*

WEDNESDAY, MARCH 11 *Monkshatch* The roads are blocked, & our butcher had to turn back his cart & ride here.

Thompson & I again busy, & were able to go down to the house.

Signor working at *Hope*,[1] dear love. The fact that it is to bring shekels, puts drags upon it. I long to see it finished. 'I find it difficult to respect myself' he says, '& I wish therefore to put something better into it than I have put before.' Pot boilers are impossible to him.

A cart took the first panel to the little home, the blessing Hand, the crowned heart, the palms of Peace. There it is, chosen accidentally because it was most convenient to send, & it looks well. Thompson says 'after all, madam I do believe it will be a success'.

THURSDAY, MARCH 12 Signor is very happy working at his *Joan of Arc* in water colour on a plaster ground. He seems to need the relief of something new while he works at things long in hand. He has never, I should think, except in the case of a portrait, begun a picture & finished it right out of hand, or worked at it steadily for any length of time. He does not work for effect at the present time. He prepares no fresh surprises for exhibitions or for visitors to his studio. He lets his beginnings be seen

1. *Hope*, oil on panel, 1891, Budgett version (Yale Center for British Art, see illustration on page 72). As well as the red chalk drawings, Watts was working on a new version in oils of his most iconic painting, of which there are seven versions. This version was painted for Richard Budgett, whose wife Ann had died young in 1887, and who had admired Watts. He paid 500 guineas for it. It is a symbolic rendering of Watts' pessimistic view of 'the world', although, he thought, in spite of its dire state, it still held just a tiny glimmering of 'hope'. He painted the picture in the 1880s and 1890s. (See Nicholas Tromans, *Hope: The Life and Times of a Victorian Icon*, Watts Gallery, Compton, 2011.)

from year to year, till the world says he does nothing new. This year he wanted to send in *Time, Death & Judgement* to the New Gallery, & I asked him not to. I knew I was taking the smaller view, but I am proud of his doing as good work as ever, & would like it to be known.

I worked hard all day, gluing on my felt designs. Signor went for a ponder up & down the terrace, but the sun had gone, & the fog was horrid, 'full of London smoke', he said.

TUESDAY, MARCH 17 'Fatima' becomes a burden to me at times. The moment I take her up, my brains lie down like a naughty boy's & kick. I am like the unfortunate nursery maid trying to deal with them.

WEDNESDAY, MARCH 18 S. is working out his *Joan of Arc* design on many sheets of paper, & still unsatisfied.

MONDAY, MARCH 23 Working out the thoughts for *Joan of Arc*. He has made five or six chalk designs, this last one, after time for quiet thought in bed, is far the most satisfactory to him.

TUESDAY, MARCH 24 Dear one downstairs painting *Hope*, which is still a difficulty to him. 'I lose all interest' he says 'in a design I've carried out so often.'

We enjoyed the chalk pits walk together. The glittering white walls with their rents & seams, the splendour of the dark bent yews, in their eternal green, grasping the cliff edge with such a grand strength, is endlessly delightful to us. So good for Signor's eyes to rest on these beautiful things, instead of being starved by a walk down Addison Road.

I worked hard & got 3 new panels well under my hand.

THURSDAY, MARCH 26 Signor went out for a moment before breakfast & came back saying it was like a morning in Malta. We were shining, & feeling giants in the pleasure of the sun. By nine o'clock I had all my wet panels out drying in the garden. On the landing they have remained wet since Thompson put them there. Then I packed the finished ones, more than a quarter of the ceiling, to be ready for Emma's cab. She came early & we went down together to the house, the ceiling going on in front in solemn procession. Signor ought to have joined the pageant, but chose the short cut to the glories of the procession. We spread them out over the floor & found them none the worse.

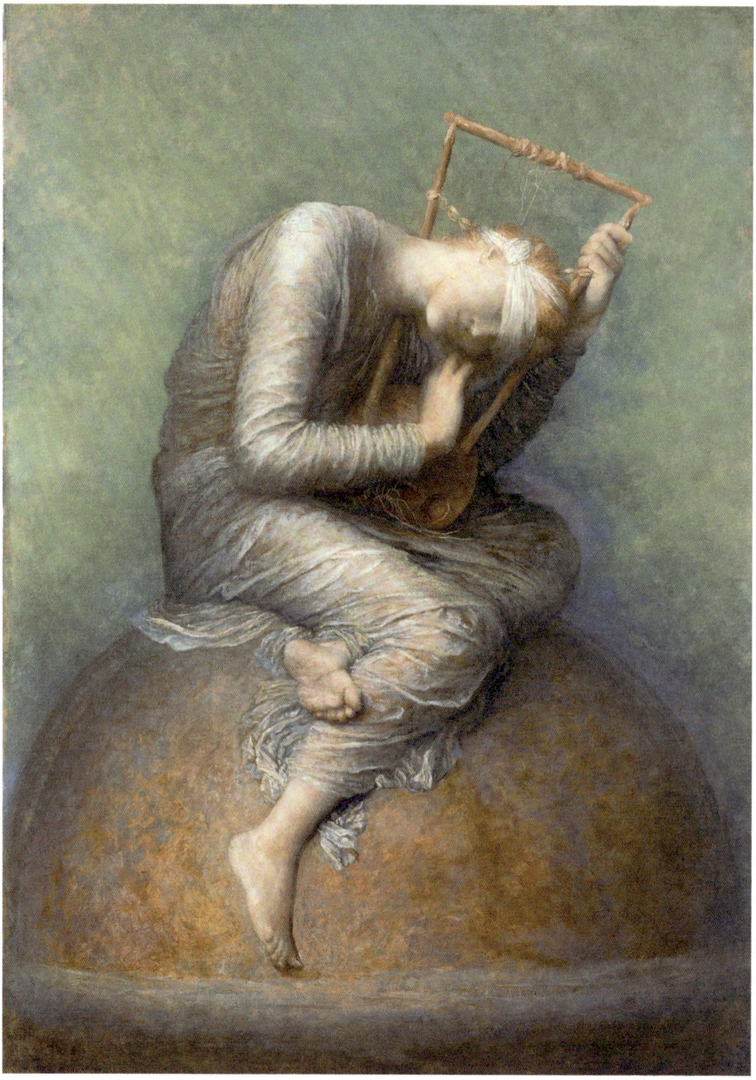

G.F. Watts, *Hope*, 1886, oil on canvas, private collection

We picked two bits of narcissus for Emma, the first flowers in Limnerslease garden.

Little Emma stuck to my side, all day, full of her plans & her future happiness & did not leave till eight o'clock, going away with Signor's wedding present of a cheque to help the furnishing.

SUNDAY, MARCH 29 *Easter Day* Gave Easter eggs to the children about. The old custom of dyeing eggs is going. My eggs were sugar! The old superstitions of the breaking of the shells that the witches might not come & make boats of them, & others, soon to be forgotten. Hanging up an egg laid on Ascension day 'saves a house from all hurts'. Hanging up eggs is thought lucky in very many nations.

MONDAY, MARCH 30 Choons writes to know if I will help Edward with something. A painted reredos she suggests, for the workhouse chapel which he is beginning to get money for. I shall propose doing it in gesso.[1]

Our little household walked off looking very happy, to see some sports at Godalming, Signor having allowed me to say they might drive back. The two pretty little maids, & Lily with her golden hair down her back; they looked so nice as the little party started.[2]

WEDNESDAY, APRIL 1 James[3] let the fires go out in the studio which deprived Signor of his afternoon's work, a loss to him like the failure of a bank. It veiled our evening for us, for he cannot be got to think lightly of such a loss, & he had no work he could readily put his hand to in the warmer library.

FRIDAY, APRIL 3 *Pelican* & *Phoenix* both finished.[4] I have my 3 trees to do, & then only 2 more to complete the ceiling. The 'Signor Bay window' has then to be considered.[5]

---

1. This was Mary's first piece of work for a public space. She worked on it in August and September 1893 at St Albans. **2.** This is the first mention in the diary of Lily Mackintosh, an orphan, later to become the Wattses' ward. **3.** James Miller, a servant at Monkshatch. **4.** The ceiling in the red drawing room has four birds at the corners of the central panel, illustrating renewal (the phoenix), love (the pelican), truth (the owl) and alertness (the cockerel). **5.** Mary was proposing to design a ceiling decoration above the bay window in the red drawing room, to be full of references to Watts's own interests.

SUNDAY, APRIL 5 The Census[1] is being taken today. A landmark. It seemed to make the half hour a grave one, as we sat in the library, a cosy party, Andrew writing. The scene of my life so shifted since the last census.

Where shall we all be the next time?

MONDAY, APRIL 6 A spring day, Andrew's birthday. We spent a long time at Limners, went round marking out the line for the fence of the wood. Signor & May paced up & down in the sunny path of the garden. I think we shall often go there for shelter & warmth on spring mornings if all is well.

Hope was put into a frame which came from home. It is beautifully finished & the iris round it such a charming touch of poetry & colour & idea.

WEDNESDAY, APRIL 8 Photographed my panels, walked early to the little house & did what I could there, but the central & owl panels are already up.[2]

THURSDAY, APRIL 9 Days of work make us silent, I find. Signor has nearly finished *The Conscience* in chalk, beautiful thing, more beautiful than any to my mind. Chalk is the material for making a spirit in! Especially as he uses this red chalk.

FRIDAY, APRIL 10 The day cleared & was pleasant as I drove out to Knap Hill nurseries. I found young Mr Waterer waiting to go round with me, & we spent 3 quarters of an hour very quickly choosing yews, hollies, Junipers, laurels, rhododens, azaleas, rejecting all arbor-vitae! I don't like their leathery foliage which looks as if so much pains had been taken with the detail of the leaf, that all simplicity & breadth has been lost, like an over-elaborate drawing stippled up.

SATURDAY, APRIL 11 A telegram from Charles Hallé, apparently Signor had written to him to say the *Naples* could not be finished and offering the *Deluge*.[3] He telegraphs accepting it.

---

1. Those who were at Monkshatch were: Andrew K. Hichens (head), Mary E. Hichens (wife), George F. Watts (visitor), Mary Watts (visitor), James Miller (servant), Arthur Stock (servant), Caroline Potter (servant), Lillie Potter (housekeeper's child), Helena Collins (servant). **2.** The central ceiling panel was the Egyptian sun, with winged rays. **3.** For the spring exhibition at the New Gallery.

Surely my dear one is more inconsistent & lawless about his exhibition pictures than anyone else. No entreaties would induce him to send the fine finished portrait of Tennyson, from Cambridge, painted this last year, because the replica is unfinished, & in peers' robes, therefore with an altogether different aspect, & because a few newspaper critics had seen it at the Brit. Artists in autumn, where the smallest possible public go. Now he sends a well known work, wh. has been seven years in his Gallery, which he refused to exhibit at the New Gallery four years ago.

SUNDAY, APRIL 12 S. wrote out some rough outlines for the little booklet for Agnew's exhibition of his red chalk drawings.

Went to Tyler's about the planting of the garden tomorrow & ran round the little place to have it & the trees together in my mind. Tomorrow's work will leave its mark in the making or marring of the little house, & I feel anxious.

MONDAY, APRIL 13 Signor woke very well & got down to the library after breakfast where he did some good work on the *Faith* & the *Conscience*. He is much inclined to like his youngest child best, he thinks, better than the rest he has done. I am not sure that he is not right.

I went out to have my first day's gardening. The trees arrived from Waterer's at ten o'clock & soon after the roots of the first yew were in the ground, & I stood by & felt I must be the Priest for the moment, swinging a censor of praise & prayer & holding out the blessing hand upon the planting of our vineyard. Peace seemed all round, & afterwards when the trees were in, the men gone to lunch near the house, I had two quiet hours there, sowing my few annuals, that the border may be not quite bare in the summer & autumn.

WEDNESDAY, APRIL 15 A lovely day, but Signor had the finishing of *Naples* on his mind & would not go out. No trees today for me so I was able to give all my time to the last few panels.

I worked till 9 o'clock but could not finish these ceiling panels. I have begged Signor to get everything for exhibition done this year, & never to have pictures on his mind again during the last days.

THURSDAY, APRIL 16 Signor came down to Limnerslease in the morning, & saw all the changed garden, & liked it. It promises, I think. Primroses & anemones star in the little copse at last.

FRIDAY, APRIL 17 Last panel disappeared down the hill in the embrace of Mitchell's man by eight o'clock. Up early & photographed it before it left.

We went to meet Mr George who walked out to see what had been done. I think he was pleased with the little house.

The ceiling was all up & I saw my work for the first time complete, though I would like to begin it again & do it better in every way. I think it is not undecorative, certainly interesting if people like to make it so.

SATURDAY, APRIL 18 Work now all day long at Limnerslease.

Steps today made there were, first, the furniture coming down from L.H.H.[1] & being stored, & then the planting of long trails of ivy over the oak fence.

SUNDAY, APRIL 19 Andrew bent on primrose hunting for his button, only thought of 'primrose day'.[2] In the village they don't think much of primroses, as the nearest thing we could find either at Eastbury or in a cottage garden were the washy sham coloured pink things of cultivation, till just by the church yard gate, I saw some & made bold to beg.

MONDAY, APRIL 20 *Little Holland House* Goodbye to darling little May & Andrew, the dearest of people.[3]

What could be more delightful than they are to us both, always, & unvaryingly. How much of the happiness of our life we owe to them, two winters of health for Signor, from the comfort & pleasure of their beautiful home, our little own home, & so many other things. We left in sunshine, our tiles looking very red over their goodbye to us as we drove past.

Thompson described me to Andrew as 'a very ingenious & industrious woman', a character I am very proud to have.

TUESDAY, APRIL 21 Red drawings are now arranged round the studio. Signor relieved at the pictures going. He was miserable, felt they were

---

1. Little Holland House. **2.** 'Primrose Day', in memory of Benjamin Disraeli, who died on April 19, 1881. **3.** It was the end of the Wattses' winter stay at Monkshatch.

bad, wished they had never been done, & were not going to be exhibited. He said 'I feel it is so unlike myself, I wish I could just work on quietly & never show anything.'

WEDNESDAY, APRIL 22 A quiet day, & I worked at housekeeping & letters, arranging our Saturday's wedding feast.[1]

THURSDAY, APRIL 23 Darling's early day of social dissipation, varnishing at the Academy[2] & luncheon at May's. Called at Agnew's & saw to the titles of pictures. Private view on Wednesday next.

Signor says Millais is superb this year in landscapes, and a good exhibition. On the whole he enjoyed it much & went back after luncheon.

Signor pleased by the way Millais, Briton Rivière & Tadema spoke to him of his work with intense appreciation, not (from them) flattery, which makes one care a good deal.

FRIDAY, APRIL 24 Some flowers at Covent Garden & hastened to luncheon & to arrange about our feast for tomorrow. Thompson made a table with planks in the gallery, & was very nearly being cross over it. I so well understand that he dislikes the little fuss. Emma on the other hand is rather proud it should be made, & sees it gives them a cachet of value, especially the bridegroom, who her friends rather look upon as a misalliance for Emma. A tiring day but all looked so nice when it was done. She came up with the hot water for the last time, & talked, quite happy & quite certain her lot is a good one. She has been a good & faithful servant to Signor many years & we shall not see her like again, but we do not feel that they are going away at all! Thompson always with us, & both in the winter.

SATURDAY, APRIL 25 All up early, the sun shining on the first hours of the wedding day. We had everything ready in good time. Thompson's dressing was the most serious function of all, the finishing touches at least carried out by five hand-maids, all exclaiming over his beauty. I was

1. Emma and Thompson's wedding. 2. Varnishing Day is the day when artists and the haute monde have access to a private preview before the Royal Academy *Summer Exhibition* opens. Artists have an opportunity to varnish their work in situ, and to put finishing touches to it, and for their friends and supporters to see it in advance of the private view.

making nosegays for the party in my room & could hear what an amusing scene was going on upstairs.

'Now, doesn't he look nice? Don't you feel happy, Thompson?' – but no reply that I could hear came from the victim. Then Emma in a distressed voice 'There now, what a nasty crease, those trousers have got to be dealt with.' However, when he at last broke away & came hurrying downstairs, in spite of the drawback, he looked magnificent, & I added his white Camellia button hole, & had a moment's word with him, explaining that though he did not like the little fuss we had made about the wedding, he must look upon it as a little token of the regard we held them both in, & with tears in our eyes we grasped each other's hands, in, I hope, as true a friendship as any can be. We were at church by a quarter past nine. I had not heard the service since our own wedding. My dear one came down & received us in the gallery, & all was ready. They fell into their places at the Breakfast table, & all went well as possible until, pelted by rice, they disappeared in their cab, for Bournemouth & a week's holiday.

SUNDAY, APRIL 26 Sir Frederic, our first & faithful visitor. He & Signor had much to say about mediums. Macbeth & Fildes have been using Petroleum, Fildes the common kitchen stuff & Macbeth the rectified, prepared by a man in Great Queen Street, where their colours are ground with it. Signor has long used Rock oil, prepared by Bell in Oxford Street, & a small quantity of Linseed oil, to prevent its too rapid evaporation. Millais they think uses Spike oil, & Sir F., rectified spirits of turpentine. Sir Fred. is sorry & angry with Mr Richmond for having abstained two years from going near the Academy, at this time of friendly meeting. It is a pity that men who think that they regard art from a more serious point of view than seventy members, should not feel bound to go & mix their light with the lamp, & try to support Sir Frederic, who said today, wearily, that it was no sinecure.

MONDAY, APRIL 27 Varnishing at the New Gallery. Went early & had it all to ourselves, almost. Mr Poynter, Mr Hallé. *The Deluge*[1] looked remarkably well. The Burne Jones are not as fine as usual.

1. *After the Deluge (the Forty-First Day)* (1885–91, Watts Gallery): Watts's impressive painting of power and light re-entering the world on the day after the rain stopped in the great biblical flood of 40 days.

WEDNESDAY, APRIL 29 Private Views at the New Gallery & Agnew's. To neither did we go but hear Agnew's was successful. *The Pall Mall* this evening suggests that the drawings should be secured for a provincial gallery. That is what would please us both most, having them together. At half past nine we were surprised by Andrew's voice. Gerry & I in our nightgowns. Signor already in bed. Gerry made a rapid & becoming toilet over a nightgown & went down to see him. He had been at Agnew's, & came up to tell Signor about the business part of it. Signor had a talk with him. There seems to be a promise of them being successful, as bricks for the little house.

THURSDAY, APRIL 30 Times are very bad, but still Agnew writes most hopefully of doing well for Signor with the drawings. He values them about twice as highly as Signor did.

FRIDAY, MAY 1 Thompson came back & the house seems to have had its chief pillar restored. It makes all the difference to Signor in the world. They have seen the Briary, spending a day there from Bournemouth. They told Signor they were leaving the Somers-Cocks,[1] so I hope there will be no difficulty in the way of our having them for Limnerslease.

SUNDAY, MAY 3 Agnew came, and I went down to tell him that S. could not see him. Agnew much disappointed, said he was sure the good news he brought him would do him good. I ran up & persuaded Signor, who was feeling better, & Agnew sat beside him, & told him the Whitworth Gallery at Manchester had decided to buy the red drawings for two thousand pounds, news most exceedingly good for us, as it relieves us both from anxiety, & also accomplishes what we wished for greatly, that the series should be kept together. Dear one very pleased & very grateful. Agnew has been most kind & said he would take no percentage, so there would be no deductions.

---

1. Blanche Somers-Cocks née Clogstoun, Watts's ward, one of three sisters taken into the old Little Holland House household by Sara Prinsep. She later lived at The Briary, Watts's house at Freshwater on the Isle of Wight, with Rachel and Laura Gurney, for part of her childhood. Watts gave her the house after her marriage to Herbert Somers-Cocks, in 1883. She and her husband both died young.

WEDNESDAY, MAY 6 Thompson went to Limnerslease to see about the picture slot,[1] & to look over the furniture by my list. He came back having done all that was wanted, & having besides looked at my little sycamore tree & brought a good report of it, a little act which is just the very character of the man. The fineness of feeling, & the activity of mind which made him remember our interest in our foundling & take the trouble to ask for it, & pay it a visit, is not easy to find. The post brings Signor a pleasant letter from Mr Budgett, so pleased & grateful for *Hope* & forwarding the price which we had not liked to count upon. Fortune at my door, my darling getting well, & his money anxieties entirely over.

FRIDAY, MAY 8 A kind letter from Agnew, who is showing the pictures without charging, an act much appreciated by Signor. He writes that the Duke of Westminster went round the gallery with him, & was so much struck he thinks he could have sold them all to him. Lord Lymington too, he thinks, 'would have been a candidate'.

SATURDAY, MAY 9 Signor had been awake a good long while last night. He thinks out designs & subjects, & says there is no time when he can do it so well. We spent our evening in the studio, in the dark. I love that room in the half-light, the roof looks so high & the shadows throw shapes, so strange. The pictures are like spirits silently standing all about, & my dear one sits resting in their midst, having worked while it was day.

From Sunday, May 10, until Thursday, May 21, Watts was in bed with influenza so Mary did not write in the diary, but he recovered well.

FRIDAY, MAY 22 Dr Bond rode up by a quarter to eight, & brings in the spirit of health, bespattered with mud, & riding boots & spurs, fresh from his gallop. There is a kind of manly vigour that is like fresh air in the sick room. How kind he has been, all thro' these anxious days. 'Now look at my face, Mrs Watts' he said looking brightly at me, one morning when my heart was failing me, 'I'll be in tears when there is any need for it.'

---

1. The slot built into the floor of the studio at Limnerslease so that when Watts was working on large paintings, they could be raised and lowered to whatever height he wanted.

SATURDAY, MAY 23 I had a few delicious minutes with S. when he talked of his illness. One can talk of it now, a danger past.

'I fancy it was near' he said quietly, 'but I have never had any fear of Death, it has no horrors for me, beyond the pain of leaving those who will grieve for me. I think I have shown in my work what I feel about death.'

'Yes, they will send a beautiful messenger when they want you, darling' I answered, 'but they are not going to take you yet, I think, not for years & years, when we are once safely among our fir trees & in our little darling home', but I added that only one thing grieved me that he had left undone, '& that was the letter you were to write to me to leave with your will'.

'Ah' he said 'you know all I want, only 3 things, first that you shall have enough, then the carrying out of the monument to heroes. I feel as I lie here more than ever how much art needs a great direction. I should like to live to see this monument sorted out, a beautiful semi-circular cloister, or triangular building around an open space, decorated with one fine group such as Gilbert[1] can do, & on the walls the names of those who had done heroic deeds to be inscribed. The last wish is to dedicate what money there is besides to the Home Arts & Handicrafts.'

My darling sat up in bed & scolded Emma for being unpunctual with his panada[2] – a great step forward, that means. He kicks against the brandy, which he is going to be allowed to leave off.

Dr Allbutt came in to see him, & was very pleased at his improvement.[3] He is a delightful doctor-friend to have so close by, & is so inclined to love Lamb. He tells me his drawings at Agnew's have made a very great impression, he hears them much talked about at the Savile Club. Yesterday Thomas Hardy (*Far from the Madding Crowd*) was breakfasting with them, & said he felt after seeing them that he must begin

---

1. Sir Alfred Gilbert (1854–1934) was a highly acclaimed sculptor in the New Sculpture Movement in the late 19th century. His work included the Shaftesbury Memorial Fountain, commonly known as *Eros*, in Trafalgar Square. He modelled a bust of Watts in 1888–9. **2.** Panada is a bread soup. The English version included currants, sugar and nutmeg. **3.** Sir Thomas Clifford Allbutt (1836–1925) was the model for George Eliot's Dr Lydgate, in *Middlemarch*. She wrote of him 'a good, clever & graceful man, enough to enable one to be cheerful under the horrible smoke of ugly Leeds'.

art over again.[1] 'I must begin Watts again, too.' The Allbutts had told him that this was Melbury Road & that we were all more or less fanatics here.

MONDAY, JUNE 1 Edith here, & later old Ted.[2] He grows very like my father, & though there is a grave look that has never left his face since Sonnie's death, he has a great deal of fun in him. He described Edith's fright of influenza. Directly she arrived at their lodgings, he was sent out to see if [he] could hear or see anything of it. He came back having had a peaceful pipe for ten minutes, & answered Edith's anxious questions about what he had seen with 'I saw nothing but the dead-carts, the houses are all shut up, & most of them have black crosses on the doors'!

WEDNESDAY, JUNE 3 Signor is up & working at the red chalk *Court of Death*, but the nerves are all on the quiver, the least thing makes him excitedly anxious, or vexed.

FRIDAY, JUNE 5 Dear one is carrying out in chalk a new version of the *Court of Death*, *Death* with young *Humanity* in her lap, as before, but *Love* only is at her feet & holds up in triumph the rose as symbol of incorruptibility. 'You have no power here' he says.

MONDAY, JUNE 8 Thompson brought back my purchases from the H. Arts. Signor pleased with them especially with the copper hot water jug, 'the first really useful household utensil I have seen made by the Home Arts' he said!

SATURDAY, JUNE 13 'A day out of heaven' of summer weather. Dear Mrs Jackson came with Julia.[3]

SUNDAY, JUNE 14 The afternoon was very restful, for we had only pleasant people. Edith, whom I had asked to luncheon & said 'Write, as, if not, you will find nothing to eat but mince in the studio' – arrived without notice with Ted at a quarter to two! She was so pretty & penitent one has to forgive her. I fortunately had something to give them, & we

---

1. Thomas Hardy's *Tess of the d'Urbervilles* was published in 1891. **2.** Ted Fraser-Tytler was Mary's half-brother, and Edith was his wife. They lived at Aldourie Castle on the shores of Loch Ness. Their two children, Hester and Neil, often stayed with the Wattses. **3.** Maria Jackson née Pattle, and her daughter Julia Stephen. Julia married Leslie Stephen after her first husband's death.

enjoyed a little quiet in the garden, & then went round to see Sir Frederic Leighton & his beautiful house. He was charming, of course, took my hand before them & said 'This is a lady to whom we are all very deeply grateful.' He talked to Ted of deer stalking & they thoroughly appreciated him & his house. Mr Burne Jones here & I told them before they left it should be a red letter day, for they have shaken hands with Sir Fred. Mr Burne Jones kissed Signor, & afterwards Sir Fred.

TUESDAY, JUNE 16 *Monkshatch* A nice day for our journey down, little Emma came with us for the day to teach the cook how to make the mince. I went down to 'Fair Rosamund's house' as it might be now the wood is such a close thicket all round about.

The house finished from floor to ceiling, & dry as bones.

WEDNESDAY, JUNE 17 Andrew's birthday. We were out as soon as our eight o'clock mince was over, & called up benedictions to him under his window.

We had settled last night to keep Andrew's birthday by christening the little house, with kitchen & fire, & breaking bread there, so I went down as soon as I could & had the furniture, such as it is, lifted out & put a little into place, brought in some branches & bits of flowers from the garden & made it look wonderful by the time Andrew drove up with luncheon, May & Signor walking. Anything more successful could hardly have been. May managed luncheon so beautifully, bringing it down, hot & steaming. We drank Andrew's health in the little house in champagne, Signor carousing too, & looking so well. They all felt it to be a good beginning.

SUNDAY, JUNE 21 Andrews[1] came for the day from the Briary, & I think he was pleased with all he saw, & went back saying he should now be anxious to be here to begin the walks & garden.

---

1. George Andrews (1838–1924) was first known to Watts when he lived in the gate lodge of Holland House with his wife, Mary Ann, in the late 1860s, as a police constable in the Metropolitan Police. Watts employed him as gardener at the Briary when he retired in 1885, and then as estate steward at Limnerslease in 1891. 'There for thirty-three years he gave his efficient and varied services' (M.S. Watts, 'Portrait cat.', p.3).

WEDNESDAY, JUNE 24 *Little Holland House* Signor awoke, grieved to think of the hours of daylight he had lost, & begging me to arrange for his having coffee & sandwiches in the studio that he might begin. I am glad, yet I dread it for he is generally knocked up by it after a few weeks. Not a touch on the horse yet.[1]

FRIDAY, JUNE 26 I traced out his beautiful shrouded figure this morning upon Thompson's canvas.[2] Went to see Lady Leighton.[3]

Lady Leighton gave a friendly reception. She talked much of Lady Waterford[4] & it made me glad to hear that the softening of that fine brain was not a darkening such as one pictured, but rather a stronger initiation into further beauty.

SUNDAY, JUNE 28 A lovely Sunday, & my darling persuaded to come & sit out under our green branches.

In talking, Signor said 'The difficulty is that Christ does not now speak to us himself. He does not come into the garden & say "you must do this or that". What he does say comes thro' interpreters who have played the dickens with its real value. However, we need never be much in doubt, for the principles are clear enough. Leave off puzzling. The idea of a personal Deity is a delightful one but it is a delight for the child's mind only' he said.

MONDAY, JUNE 29 Signor & I met before breakfast in the Gallery, a spirit in our feet had made us both think of going there. I was having five minutes peaceful joy when my darling came in & made it greater. He was pleased with his *Fata Morgana* & *Mischief* wh. have been hung lower than usual.

WEDNESDAY, JULY 1 Went to the Academy, where I spent my morning. There are some really good pictures & none really bad.

---

1. The sculpture, *Physical Energy.* **2.** The figure of death in the painting *Love and Death.* Thompson prepared Watts's canvases for him. **3.** Eleanor Leicester Warren (1841–1914), married to Sir Baldwyn Leighton, 8th Baronet. **4.** Louisa, Marchioness of Waterford (1818–91), artist and philanthropist. She had died on May 12, 1891. She redesigned the village of Ford on her land in Northumberland. A friend of Watts, who had great admiration and respect for her, and painted her portrait as early as 1848. He designed the headstone for her grave in 1891, and Mary designed the grave slab. This was one of the few designs on which they worked together.

Home to find my love finishing his morning's work & expecting luncheon.

Mr Aidé came. He tells us much of America & Americans. He was struck by the entire absence of English art. Only at the Hutchinson in Chicago did he find pictures by Englishmen. As a rule every collection is the work of the same Frenchmen. He went to see Walt Whitman, who looks like King Lear. He spoke almost with tears about the little hold he had on the Americans, all appreciation is from Englishmen. He was sitting in a room inches deep in dust, & papers scattered all round him.

SATURDAY, JULY 4 Our day marked chiefly by a visit from Mr Arthur Leake, a man who had written to tell Signor he had an album in wh. a drawing of his, Signor G.F. Watts, 1829, was.

He came, & Signor was not only able to identify the drawing after Rembrandt, a careful pencil copy (with an accomplished touch for 12 years old), but also some other drawings, one a portrait of himself! One or two from Hogarth or some comic paper, & several little originals! Some on stone by him, he thinks before he was twelve, & when he was first reading Sir Walter Scott & had his mind full of knights & riders. The little owner who looks like a boy, though he has a wife & an album, was perfectly enchanted. The book is full of keepsake pictures & drawings signed by E.A.A. - very amateur.

Mrs Percy Wyndham[1] came later. She was talking of Lady Waterford & we told her how happy she had been these last months.

MONDAY, JULY 6 A visit from Mr Oscar Wilde,[2] to whom I felt very much drawn, not having expected to be so. Enthusiastic about the pictures & portraits.

---

1. Mrs Percy Wyndham (1835–1920) married the Hon. Percy Wyndham in 1860, and had five children, who all became members of 'The Souls', the intellectual and satirical group of which Watts was a founder member. He painted one of his best full-length portraits of Mrs Percy Wyndham, and John Singer Sargent copied it in the background of his much admired painting of her three daughters. 2. Oscar Wilde (1854–1900) was 35. He had published *The Picture of Dorian Gray* in novel form in April 1891. Watts's earnest character, devoted to his art, renowned as one of the great portrait painters of the age, was similar in some ways to Basil Hallward, the painter of the portrait in Wilde's novel.

THURSDAY, JULY 9 A day with my beloveds[1] at St Albans. Found them both wonderfully well. Edward thinner & looking so nice, his eyes so blue & less congested.

FRIDAY, JULY 10 The van packed with furniture went off to Limnerslease, a new step towards the new home.

'Julia Cartwright', Mrs Ady,[2] came to pay Signor a visit. She has written on Mr Burne Jones. Signor said to her 'I am glad to have the object of my work made known' & she told me he talked to her delight. She only hoped she could remember all the ideas he had now given her. I left them alone as I thought both would prefer it, but I did want to stay! I could have made jottings of much that would be said.

SATURDAY, JULY 11 Today Signor consecrated my poor studio,[3] so long a luncheon room, by beginning his *What I Had I Gave* in it. A lovely day. My old things from St Albans came[4] & little Thompson hearing at a word from me that a certain pedestal was wanted for Signor's room by Saturday next, went to work at once, scouring off all polish & dirt, & till half past six at night (when the gallery was shut & he was free again) I found him hard at work painting it, generous earnest soul. What a service he gives his beloved master.

WEDNESDAY, JULY 15 He is at work upon 'The Epitaph', in my studio, with the door open. The days are lovely & the sweet soft air helps him.

THURSDAY, JULY 16 Dr & Mrs Allbutt came. They brought Mr & Mrs Hardy (*Far from the Madding Crowd*)[5] – who wished to 'begin Watts' as he said to them some time ago, so the first chapter in the grammar was to see Signor himself. They went round together & talked a good deal. Mr Hardy does not care greatly for art, Signor gathers, & he cannot tell me that he left much behind. I was with the others & hardly had a

---

1. Edward and 'Choons' Liddell. **2.** Julia Cartwright Ady (1851–1924) was an art critic who wrote on Renaissance artists, then on the Pre-Raphaelites, and other contemporary artists, including Watts (Julia Cartwright Ady (Mrs Henry Ady), *The Life and Works of G.F. Watts*, Art Journal Easter Annual, London, 1896). **3.** Mary's studio in Little Holland House. *What I Had, I Gave* is also named *The Epitaph*. **4.** Mary had been staying with Edward and Choons in St Albans a couple of days before. **5.** This seems to have been a disappointing meeting, with Hardy failing to be enthusiastic about Watts's paintings, and Mary retaliating.

word with him. I read *Far from the Madding Crowd* when it came out & thought it was over-rated. Now I think I shall have to 'begin Hardy'.

SATURDAY, JULY 18 Afraid of the intense heat, we settled to travel down by a train leaving at 7.7. Of course, in consequence, the day was rather cold. As we walked away from Little Holland House a ladybird lighted on my hand, to come down with us to the station, saw us safely in the railway carriage, & then suddenly opening her little scarlet, spotted box, took out her wings & went. Two superstitious people thought her visit a good omen for the new lease. The sweet blessed air as we drove out most delicious.

Emma's beaming face was bubbling over with news & happiness, our pillar Thompson following in a cab behind. We stopped the cabs & walked up from Boulter's cottage,[1] Signor stepping in by the drawing room window to take possession, & I following. The blessing hand of the ceiling was over our heads in an instant.

Then hard work began, & went on all day, & by five o'clock we had something like order. Last week's van load in the Hall was unpacked & put in its place, & today's unloaded & unpacked. Darling May came, & we planted the gentians & had tea in the drawing room. About seven Andrew came, dear old fellow, welcoming us & almost hugging Signor in his arms. He kissed my hand & I kissed him. The beginning & end of all our reason for building and rooting here. They have been like the <u>dearest</u> children to Signor.

SUNDAY, JULY 19 Awoke to find ourselves in our little home. We ought to have been in wild spirits by rights & I wish I could make up history, & say we were, with very thankful hearts. I was overtired, the darkness of the green wall of oak trees depressed me & the general look of things, as if I never could make it all lovely as I hoped. I was cross & ungrateful.

The dining room is very sweet, partly because it is not quite so shut in.

We did not make much attempt to make things right, but took Sunday as a day of rest. I tried to read but fell asleep instantly, before lunch, and after it.

MONDAY, JULY 20 One delightful part of Signor is he was never taught to 'bear'. I am sure that is often over-done. It makes it far easier to make

---

1. The carpenter's home.

him happy, as he snorts & kicks out directly if something in the daily harness of life rubs or galls, no, threatens to gall. Then it can be altered. He worked in his studio for the first time. The first dabs I was called in to see were on the *Sunset Alps.*[1]

Hanging the dressing room with a rosy red muslin I had lighted on. Thompson & I working hard, Signor very pleased with the effect.

TUESDAY, JULY 21 Thompson and I busy all morning hanging the walls of the dining room with red. 'A blind man would be very glad to see it' he said surveying his work after we had finished, with satisfaction.

WEDNESDAY, JULY 22 Signor must needs be up at four this morning, though no fire had been got ready for him. I foraged for coffee & bread, being scolded all the time for running about in my dressing gown. But he came back to dress at 7, very happy & tried to atone for his scolding by a kiss.

Breakfast early, & Thompson & I got the hall done with green before Field came to hang the *Court of Death*,[2] which rose, mounted on its pulleys & working perfectly. My love pleased to see his great work ready & under his hand as it has never yet been, the light perfect, & it drops down, until one can easily put one's hand on the top edge.

May & Andrew stayed for luncheon, Emma coming to the rescue with beef made nice, as she only can, in a scramble.

SATURDAY, JULY 25 *Little Holland House* A lovely morning, to spin out my day at Limnerslease. Left with a burden of sweet peas & wild flowers, Field & others standing at the gate.

---

1. *Sunset on the Alps* (1888, Watts Gallery): 'On the journey to Monnetier from Aix-les-Bains this scene suddenly came into view, as the train drew up at La Roche sur Foron, at the hour of sunset. On a gilded canvas this picture was afterwards painted from the impression made that evening upon the painter's memory' (M.S. Watts, 'Subject cat.', p. 139).
2. *The Court of Death* (1871–1902, oil on canvas, Tate). Watts regarded this painting as his most complete design. It shows Death as an angel commanding tribute from all humanity, at every level, as an inevitability. The great canvas, 4.28 x 2.98 m, includes figures representing a nobleman relinquishing his crown, a soldier giving up his sword, a sick young woman (modelled by May Prinsep), a cripple, a child and, in two versions, a black slave. The arrangement for its hanging in Watts's studio at Limnerslease includes a 'picture slot' so that it could be raised and lowered for the artist to work on parts of the painting at whatever level he needed it at any one time. In 2016 it was put back in position in Watts's studio at Limnerslease, on loan from the Tate.

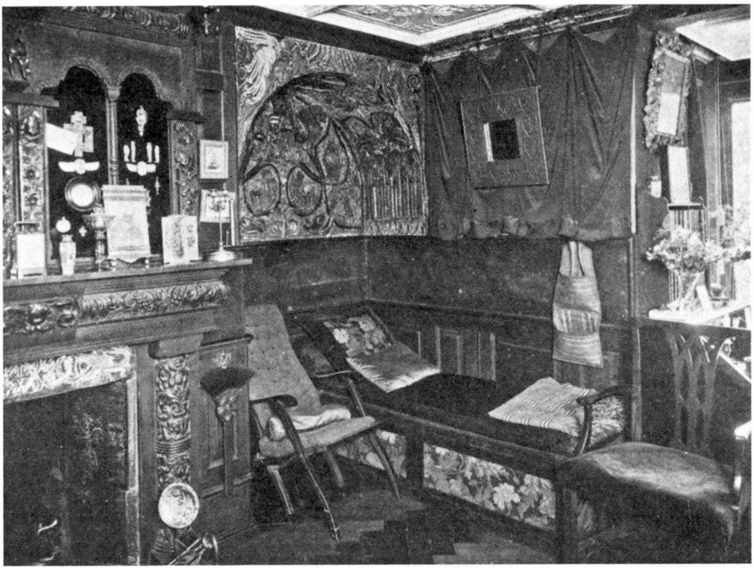

The Red Room at Limnerslease with niche designed by Mary Watts

Back to our little London home. A hot morning. We walked up the hill to save the poor village horses, snatching at more wild things till my 'Mary Anderson' basket was overflowing.

WEDNESDAY, JULY 29 Signor had a visit from Miss Margot Tennant.[1] I don't think she charmed him as much as he expected. She called Leighton 'a bore' which was not pleasant to him. I was out.

THURSDAY, JULY 30 Dear one working on his small *Faith*, pleased with the quality of technique which reminds me of Veronese in its fresh gem-like touch, at present. Will he be able to keep it?

SATURDAY, AUGUST 1 *Limnerslease* Off to Limnerslease by Waterloo, for fear of crowds at Clapham. Our train a little late. Signor full of anxiety, Emma with us, & no luggage. Even an umbrella costs him worry. I had

1. Margot Tennant (1864–1945), with her sister Laura, became central figures in the group, 'the Souls'. In 1894 she married the politician Herbert Asquith, Prime Minister in 1908. She was a great wit and society hostess, also a writer.

allowed more than a quarter of an hour at Waterloo, but he wished it had been three, &, as bad luck would have it, we were pressed, for the crowds were enormous. As we were looking for seats, Princess Louise[1] caught hold of Signor, & shook hands with us, begging him to get into their carriage, but he did not feel inclined to obey.

Down here safely by luncheon. Andrews had the garden gate open & was standing ready to greet us. We feel we have gained a new prop, a cornerstone for Limnerslease. Darling Signor today said quietly from a full heart 'How I do enjoy this life.'

SUNDAY, AUGUST 2 Our little home seems peace itself, we walked for some time with Andrews planning so many things that oh! we need a long lease to carry them all out to perfection. Andrews is delightful.

THURSDAY, AUGUST 6 This morning I wrestled with an idea for S.'s niche[2] to a design I have, to be 'peace of mind, rest of body, communion of thought, suggestion, & over that sun, earth, moon & planets, & over that again the final end of a shaft of light – *Lux Mundi* – & two angel figures veiling their faces. Stars on one door & yet more near. That only will record the joys we have in reading together.

Then for the fireplace. I set to work & think I feel my way to working out a design from the story of Prometheus.

SUNDAY, AUGUST 9 *Little Holland House* Two sweet & beautiful women came, Lady de Vesci[3] & Lady Lothian. I am very glad to have seen Lady de Vesci. She quite comes up to my idea of her, & I think she was inclined to be very nice to me.

WEDNESDAY, AUGUST 12 Sir Robert Morier[4] came to luncheon. He had not seen Signor for about 40 years, but the friendship seemed fresh, & he declared that Signor's face was unchanged. He had founded the

1. Princess Louise (1848–1939), Duchess of Argyll and daughter of Queen Victoria. She was sympathetic to many of the reforming movements, and was a sculptor and artist. She was considered a rebel. **2.** When Watts and Mary were in Little Holland House, she noticed that their evening readings were made more audible, the niche in the drawing room acting as a sounding box. She was determined they should have one in the drawing room at Limnerslease, for the same purpose. **3.** Lady de Vesci (d. 1939). Lady Evelyn Charteris married the fourth Viscount de Vesci of Abbeyleix in Ireland, and became a close friend to Watts and Mary. **4.** Sir Robert Morier (1826–93) was a British diplomat. Among other

Cosmopolitan Club, which grew out of small meetings of friends in his rooms in Bond Street. They were Mr Chichester Fortescue, Mr Vernon Harcourt, Spedding, John Ruskin, Layard & Signor. When Mr Morier was leaving London for some foreign appointment he said 'What a pity you fellows should not meet sometimes.' Signor then proposed his rooms in Charles Street, & so the foundation stone of the club was laid. When Signor left Charles Street for Little Holl. Ho., the studio became the club, & he left there for many years both *Echo* & the *Theodore & Honoria*, which later the club bought from him for not a very large sum. The club became large, & late hours prevented Signor going there, so he seldom went. Sir Robert told him today, that when a considerable sum of money was necessary some years ago to carry on the Rooms in Charles St, they thought they could not afford it, & moved out. They so missed the surroundings, associations, & the picture, that it began to fall to pieces altogether. To use it they paid any amount of money to get home again!

Sir Robert tells me Signor's face is singularly the same. How much I like to know this. How I should like to hear more, quietly from him. He promises to come again.

THURSDAY, AUGUST 13 Signor at work on the horse, made a very radical change by taking off the front leg, pawing the air, & straightening it, so that it is now motionless. I like it better but I see it will not do unless the man is entirely changed too, the action of his figure being in keeping with the movement of the horse, not with its present attitude of rest. It is only a temporary change, he says.[1]

SATURDAY, AUGUST 15 S. had undertaken to go to see *The Nautch Girl*[2] this afternoon with Blanche. There was the usual morning of restiveness & I had to promise to go with him to the Savoy & call for him after it was over, or he would have certainly kicked over the traces.

---

members of the Cosmopolitan Club, which lasted from 1852 to 1902, was Anthony Trollope, whose club 'The Universe' in his novel *Phineas Redux* was based on the Cosmopolitan. 'The club where the best informed political gossip is heard', he wrote of it. **1.** *Physical Energy*. **2.** *The Nautch Girl or the Rajah of Chutneypore* by George Dance and Edward Solomon, a comic opera in two acts, opened at the Savoy Theatre in June 1891. 'Nautch' was a northern Indian dance style, performed by 'Nautch Girls'. Watts accompanied Blanche Somers-Cocks.

He was all smiles & brightness when Blanche got in by him & began her gay chatter, tho' he did confess to her that he had been swearing awfully.

SUNDAY, AUGUST 16 A visit from Sir Frederic to say goodbye of wh. I only had a little minute. Signor went over with him & came back humbled, he said. The work half done is always so beautiful. 'Why will he work on to the death of all texture, truth of colour, losing such a large portion of the dignity that belongs by rights to his truly noble conceptions. It is a mystery to me.'

Walter Crane[1] here for a few minutes this morning. Signor told him he wanted to make a head of him for his 'representative men', & he promised to sit, declaring it would make him proud.

TUESDAY, AUGUST 18 A wet & dark morning in the studio, & splatting sound of large drops when we got down. I went & found they were falling on the parcel containing our clasped hands which I had not opened for two years, dear blessed symbol of our double yet one life. I am sorry to see the smoke of London has seeped through the double paper & has stained them much. They must go into the country & lie under glass in my own room.

WEDNESDAY, AUGUST 19 Today Walter Crane came, & I was sent for by Signor, so I was fortunate, as it is no mean pleasure to have a talk with Walter Crane for an hour. He spoke of the possible effect on the young generation of his beautiful picture books. He seems to think that art is very easily reflected onto the mirror of the mind of a child, from its surroundings, & it is therefore difficult to predict if the talent is there by nature.

While we talked the work grew, & I was surprised when Signor got up & said 'look at this, a fine head on the canvas'.

I like it now immensely. 'One who never turned his back but marched breast forwards, never doubted clouds would break'[2] rushed instantly into my mind. Mr Crane was pleased himself.

---

1. Walter Crane (1845–1915), artist, craftsman and designer. He gave Mary technical advice for her decorations in the Cemetery Chapel. He worked to bring art to all levels of society and was a socialist. Watts' portrait of him is often cited as one of his finest. **2.** From *Epilogue* by Robert Browning.

THURSDAY, AUGUST 20 Mr Crane sitting to S. for a short time. He is also making great way with the *Epitaph* picture.

SUNDAY, AUGUST 23 Able to be downstairs again with my dear one at four o'clock. He sits with his arms folded watching his dim pictures till the light comes. Today there were clouds & it tarried. Our little feast together is very pleasant. We break bread & are thankful for both being well & together.

MONDAY, AUGUST 24 Mr Walter Crane sat to him, he thought for the last time, but he will need another sitting. I find that the correct word for plaster work, any fibrous mixture, is 'stucco' not gesso, wh. Mr Crane says is only applied with the brush. 'Stucco' has such a hideous sound to one's modern ears, I am not inclined to be correct.

THURSDAY, AUGUST 27 Lady de Vesci came up, quite depressed by the sight of the soaking harvest on her way from Brighton. She has come for her first sitting.

Signor trying to learn her face which is most beautiful in expression, worn & sad, but so full of beauty. It is a lovely nature, & I could love her if I knew her well & she would let me.

Signor found her a delightful companion. I think he feels much more able to talk to women than to men, as I am. Not sure that I am right, but he has more intimate friends among women than among men.

SATURDAY, AUGUST 29 Persuaded Signor to come out & we walked to the Walter Cranes. He has a wonderful studio full of designs, water colours, & beautiful work of all sorts. They lie about in a pig-sty of a studio, where Signor says he could not possibly work. There is a beautiful design for table linen, another for a wall paper, for brasswork, for leather, & heaps of tender landscapes in water colour. Signor wonders how Mr Crane can produce such things in such surroundings. His mind works independently of all, & seems full of endless combinations of lovely lines & ideas.

SUNDAY, AUGUST 30 Walter Crane sat again. I was out at church. I came in for the last half hour, & had some pleasant talk with him. He has told me of several things at the South Kensington which might be of use to me as ideas for decoration. The picture is nearly finished, & I think so fine. So does he. 'I have given it the forward look' Signor said to him &

he replied simply 'Well, I always have looked to the future since I was quite a boy', & added 'I hope I shall never give up doing so.'

FRIDAY, SEPTEMBER 4 I do not know if I am wrong but I think his portrait of Walter Crane one of the finest he has ever done, as regards the character of the man. The execution is fine too, but perhaps there is now a little less delicacy of line wh. shows that he is right in saying he does not see as much as he did.

The patient courage of his nature is there, with the sadness of one who has the sorrows of a suffering world upon his heart, but who sees beyond & has hope. I have sat & looked at that picture with wonder & the man lives in it & holds one fascinated.

SATURDAY, SEPTEMBER 5 The sorrows of the artist's wife are upon me. Yesterday Walter Crane's portrait was entrancing, an epitome of his life, that was really a work of genius. Today Signor had it in and worked on it. The glory of it is dead! the soul blown out like a light. It is nothing more than an ordinary portrait. Will it ever come again?

An evening reading to Signor from the *Pall Mall*. He is interested in what Mrs Besant[1] says of Theosophy, & says mysticism, impossible as it is, is never small.

MONDAY, SEPTEMBER 7 Our early morning again. The sight of the 'last portrait' on Walter Crane's canvas, is pain to me. I was relieved when Signor sent it away to the glass house. I wonder if all artists' wives suffer as I do. I fancy Mr Burne Jones' works, not having that subtle quality of character, such as Signor's portraits, cannot come & go like some spirit as his do.

WEDNESDAY, SEPTEMBER 9 'How much I enjoy this early breakfast, more than any other in the day' Signor says, as his little saucepans sit cooking on their spirit lamps, & we sit together eating beef mince & bread.

Lady de Vesci came to sit to Signor, with her beautiful lamp-like eyes, & some sadness that shows how she looks into the graver side of living. I think there is a beauty in the very loss of beauty, that is very attractive.

---

1. Annie Besant (1847–1933) became a Theosophist under the influence of Mme Helena Blavatsky. Theosophists worked to understand the universe, and its connection with humanity and the divine, by secret and individual intuitive search.

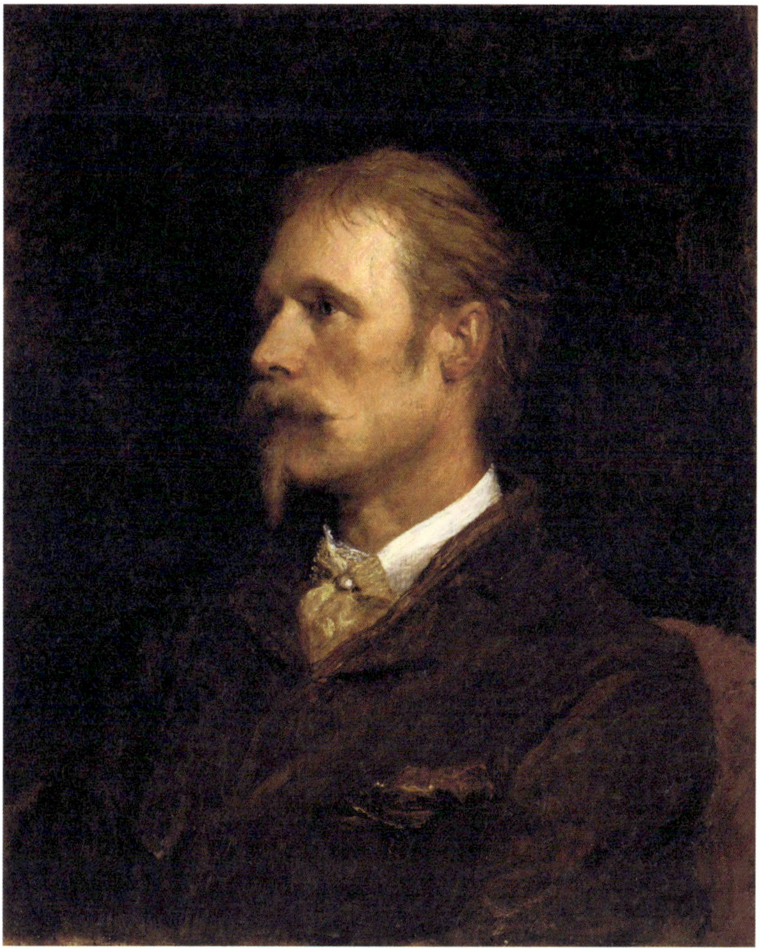

G.F. Watts, *Portrait of Walter Crane*, 1891, oil on canvas, reproduced by kind permission of the National Portrait Gallery

Before she left she & I had a few minutes alone, & as she got up to go she lifted her veil & said 'will you?' half shyly, from heights above my head. I could only say 'Thank you' as if some beneficent angel has stooped down & kissed me.

A picture of Signor painting Tennyson today in *The Graphic* – rather amusingly imagined.

FRIDAY, SEPTEMBER 11 In the evening about seven Lady Somers drove up.

She only came to town yesterday, so it was good of her to hurry here. Signor rather left her to me, purposely, I think, that we might know each other, & I found her very charming. 'I have never been dazzled by anyone else, I am thankful to say. All other brushes are like boot brushes to his.'

As she went away Signor & she chaffed each other 'You don't care for my work' he said. 'Signor, I'll kill you', she said, rushing back upon him as if she was a girl again.

SATURDAY, SEPTEMBER 12 *Limnerslease.* Dear little home. Bless you, though you are still a troubled sea of pictures on the ground & furniture aggressively at every point, waiting to be subjugated, & needing so much puzzling out. We have some clocks now & life seems to come in with them.

I had to make Signor a comfortable corner on the north side by the door, the only cool place for a seat outside or in. Thompson & I wrestled within with chaos.

We had a few minutes reading in the evening, & realised what the niche will be. Just room for us two & the walls will help my voice to carry straight to Signor's ear. It will be a very dear little place.

TUESDAY, SEPTEMBER 15 It had to be a hard working morning still, for we hung our room with muslin, but after luncheon I had time to enjoy my dear ones. Edward with Signor in the studio where he began a sketch of him, trying the effect of the light, a diffused one with no shadows. Signor is pleased with it.

In the afternoon we walked to the village, saw the church, as I had never seen it before, & also to Monkshatch. The household were all out playing croquet. Choons & Edward[1] said a bit of pleasure ground given up to them was what they had not seen before.

---

1. Choons (Christina) and Edward Liddell were staying with the Wattses at Limnerslease.

Edward & Christina talk much of Theosophy. She has been particularly interested by Mrs Besant's conversion & much that has been written. I like so much of it, that I feel angry at their assertions (which they will not allow to be tested) regarding precipitated letters.[1]

WEDNESDAY, SEPTEMBER 16 Choons sits there, the lamp light falling softly on her sweet face, & the pretty artistic tea gown she is wearing. Much of the old beauty shines there still.

Edward sat by Signor. I do not remember a happier evening in my life. This visit has been a real consecration of the little home. Edward & Choons both, in spite of the prison walls that have hedged them in for all these years, are rising with their strong intellect back to all the brightness of mind & heart natural to them. Edward with no loss of memory, can be turned over like an Encyclopaedia. 'May enquire within upon everything' I call him.

THURSDAY, SEPTEMBER 17 The sunshine & the robins sang. Thompson & I at work upon the preparation of the canvases of the hall ceiling, if all goes well, my winter's work. Choons brought out her work.

Amusement by us laughing sometimes at Thompson's funny speeches. I say he has the Karma of a King's Jester. 'Is that all right?' I asked him about a completed panel set up to dry. 'That! Why yes madam, it's just as square as a daisy.'

My heart's desire seems to be given to me now. They[2] & Signor are to be much to each other. He will call out all the noble largeness of both their minds, will give the intellectual tonic they both must be the better for now, just coming back from that sick room, which to most minds would have been a chamber of intellectual death.

MONDAY, SEPTEMBER 21 Signor walked with me along the sunny lane to post our letters, enjoying the colour at every step, there in the rich fresh green of the aftermath in the fields, & on the cottage walls the virginia creeper is turning to a burning crimson. Some with the sunshine through them more like the richest stained glass. The country has so much that is new to give him, & it is an endless pleasure to read with him in this book so familiar & so dear to me.

---

1. Letters from the dead, 'materialised' by spiritualists. **2.** Edward and Christina Liddell.

The afternoon I spent with Andrews bulb planting with that wonderful feeling of hope that those brown little balls give one, as one sticks them in faith of spring days, when they will fill our eyes & hearts with delight.

SATURDAY, SEPTEMBER 26 Our last early morning hours in our dear country home. I went out to pick what flowers there are to be had now, at six o'clock, & found Andrews picking vegetables already.

We are off early & soon after eleven are at L.H.H. I always feel a certain ruffling of my feathers, in settling down in changed surroundings, & I always have. Why is it? especially as now the circumstance is so much the same, carrying my world with me in Signor!

We find a parcel of drawings by a poor boy in Glasgow who has written touchingly to Signor. 'Perhaps my mother was right when she said "leave that nonsense alone, laddie" but I couldn't & I often feel I would go mad if I didn't paint something.'

SUNDAY, SEPTEMBER 27 *Little Holland House* I was lazy this morning, but my early bird was down at half past four. As I ran to early church it was like summer. I longed for our dear little Lease with its sweet dry smell. Kensington is damp & dark almost now, the leaves falling & the garden soaking.

Walter Crane came for his last sitting. We read him the boy's letter, Louis Deuchars,[1] & showed him the drawings, which he thinks most remarkable. His advice was just what Signor has written, tho' I did not tell him so, till he had spoken. 'Don't let him give up his permanent employment. Let him stick to that & watch his opportunity. It is sure to come.' He thinks the paintings are very remarkable, very much better than any drawings ever sent to him.

The picture has become wonderfully complete & beautiful. I returned at the last to suggest a touch to strengthen the chin, he sat down at once & did it, a very great return to that former state, which I fear in spiritual beauty he never quite recovers. The eye still as before looks beyond today. It looked before into a thousand unknown tomorrows.

---

1. Louis Deuchars (1870–1927), artist and sculptor. He worked with Mary on the terracotta decoration for the Cemetery Chapel at Compton, and also taught in her classes for terracotta work, both in Surrey and at the pottery she set up near Aldourie Castle, in Dores. Deuchars modelled a statuette of Watts. Later he worked for the Scottish Arts and Crafts architect, Sir Robert Lorimer, who incidentally carried out improvements to Aldourie Castle in 1902–4.

MONDAY, SEPTEMBER 28 What does the lamplighter think when he turns out the light below the studio window & sees our light burning within? Not many studio windows show signs of life at 4.30. Thompson's account of the visitors to the Gallery very graphic. 'I never seed more, & they looked like my own sort mostly, did not look as delicate as some on em am'. We are glad to hear it.

Our one interesting visitor today was Mr Briton Rivière.[1] My dear one sent for me as soon as he came. I sometimes feel afraid that his friends vote me a bore, but he likes me to come, I think. It is not all that he thinks I like to hear what his interesting friends have to say. Mr Rivière was riveted by Walter Crane's portrait, he considers it one of the best Signor has ever done. 'That man can never die' he said to me pointing to the portrait. The tribute was to Signor, for he considers Walter Crane 'very mischevious on his social side'.[2] His artistic gift he spoke of delightfully, 'there is a certain felicity & beauty in his arrangement of line that is quite "sui generis"' he said, which pleased Signor.

WEDNESDAY, SEPTEMBER 30 Autumn days, each more lovely than the last, Signor working outside & I working in the Iron House,[3] sketching out in the clay for my group of *Love & Death*. It is darling father's birthday, so it seemed appropriate to be working for him.

THURSDAY, OCTOBER 1 Signor wrote to Mr Stillman,[4] calling me now & then to read over what he was saying. I am glad he did. Writing hurriedly he said he 'never used the model'. 'How did you study?' I asked, feeling that the words would convey a false & mischievous meaning. He replied 'I never drew from the naked model. I studied anatomy, going sometimes to the College of Surgeons. I studied Phidias. I referred to the model more than actually painting from it. I have books full of my studies from "Long Mary" as we now call her. For the lines I saw in her were useful to me, but I never painted from her when I was painting a picture.'

---

1. Briton Rivière (1840–1920), principally a painter of animals. He and Watts had great respect for each other's work. **2.** The spelling 'mischevious' may have been intentional to mimic Rivière's pronunciation. **3.** Mary was working on one of the side panels for her memorial triptych to the three Charles Fraser-Tytlers. *Love and Death* commemorated her father. The Iron House was a shed in the garden at Little Holland House for sculptural work. **4.** William James Stillman (1828–1901), critic, artist and photographer, married to Marie Spartali, the Pre-Raphaelite painter.

We begin our mornings so easily together, he always a few minutes before me. I come to find the coffee hot, & the little low bed chair searched & set for me, because he has found out I like it best.

MONDAY, OCTOBER 5 He sent a note to Walter Crane to ask him to give him five minutes, to look at the eye again, because I still want him to try for the touch of far-offness they have in nature, that Signor had once given, & then took away. A breath makes or unmakes the spirit in a face.

TUESDAY, OCTOBER 6 While S. was busy, Andrew came. When he saw Mr Crane's portrait he seized Signor in his arms with pleasure, & began a sort of dance of joy. 'You are painting better than ever' he said. He also liked Lady de Vesci's sketch greatly. He says she has been so often painted & no one is satisfied.

I am much interested in Lady Brownlow's[1] letter asking Signor to advise her about a gravestone for Lady Waterford.[2] I should like to do something like it in clay. I am interested because I do share Lady Brownlow's feeling against anything ugly being set up over her. I wonder if they will at all enter into my feeling, about the treatment, beauty, simplicity, architectural conventionality of design & as much beauty of symbol as is possible to put into it. No sculpture. Figures of angels look well in our climate, or in our simple English church yard.

Mr Crane came & Signor gave the eye quite half an hour's work, & got back much of the old beauty. I am glad, but he will never recapture what he once had. I only know it wh. is a good thing, & all those who have seen the portrait are delighted with it.

TUESDAY, OCTOBER 13 Signor at work on a new picture *Neptune's Horses*, the team we used to watch on the green Malta seas, when Signor told me it was Neptune's gift to Athens, when Pallas Athene gave the olive, which they loved better. So do I! The horses must be pretty rampant now, & I turn my thoughts gratefully to our little peaceful winter home with no seas between us & it.

---

1. Adelaide Chetwynd-Talbot (1844–1917) married 3rd Earl Brownlow, Conservative politician. They were active in the Home Arts and Industries Association. Watts painted both their portraits. **2.** Lady Waterford, see note 4, Friday, June 26, 1891 (page 84).

We shared our evening with Miss Austen. Signor says *Cranford* comes near it for charm, but I feel that there is conscious art in *Cranford*, the absence of which in Miss Austen makes her work unique.

WEDNESDAY, OCTOBER 14 The Lawrences[1] have now 3 houses & 60 girls to look after.

Mr Leslie Ward[2] here all the afternoon, drawing Signor for *Vanity Fair*. It was not to me so much of a caricature as many portraits done of him seriously. Anyhow he looks the anxious-minded artist, not a fat Alderman.

SATURDAY, OCTOBER 17 *Limnerslease* What an idle happy day, in & out of the garden, planning, planting & cutting here & there & watching work going on all round.

Signor & I ourselves dug up a bit of ground in the wood, took out sand, & filled it in with leafmould, & planted the potsful of white heather, brought from a London stall of flowers!

SATURDAY, OCTOBER 24 I am deputy head gardener today, Andrews has gone to Woking with Boulter to dig up the rest of the trees, so I had to pay the workmen in the garden a visit before breakfast, as Andrews had not left their orders. The air was sweet, like orange blossoms, some delicate combination of dear dying leaves, giving up their souls odorously. The two men looking so clean & healthy, fresh as the morning, & such children of nature, their very clothes stained like the leaves & the brown earth all round them, beginning their day with the vigorous prod of their spades, & all the contentment of strength, absence of care, absence of haste. Signor quotes 'but the bold peasantry the country's pride, when once 'tis lost can never be supplied' – from *The Deserted Village* by Oliver Goldsmith.

TUESDAY, NOVEMBER 3 Signor working at *Eve*. He seems to have been re-inspired about that picture, & I think he will finish it now. I had got hopeless.

---

1. Three Lawrence sisters, Penelope, Millicent and Dorothy, founded and ran Roedean School, Brighton. At one point, eight Lawrence sisters were teaching there. When Lily Mackintosh became the Wattses' ward she was sent to school there, as Watts had been one of its co-founders (see diary entries for 1898). **2.** Leslie Ward (1851–1922), also known as 'Spy', caricaturist for *Vanity Fair*.

He was out brushing up the fallen leaves with great vigour between whiles.

FRIDAY, NOVEMBER 6 Signor sat by the fire today toasting his cold toes, a very unusual thing for him to do, & I sat by him while he told me the whole story of Achilles, Paris, Helen & Troy, in a way I love to listen to. It is so simple & so fine, dwelling on the beauties of character in each, especially his favourite Achilles, till I felt a child again, listening to stories from someone great & wise, where we give unbounded unquestioning confidence, & have all love & care & guidance.

WEDNESDAY, NOVEMBER 11 A great storm, the wind whirling our fir trees about in a most alarming manner; & while we were watching it the tall one close to the studio window, a ship's mast, with a mop upon the top, went slowly & gracefully over, its fall taking about half an hour, & doing it with as little damage to other things as possible. It went into the small arms of a young fir & there it lay, & Signor immediately proposed leaving it. Its roots were not out of the ground, & Andrews instantly propped it.

THURSDAY, NOVEMBER 12 We had a most delicious hour, when Signor had done his work for the morning, & I had finished mine, & we went out to garden round the fallen tree. Signor has settled to give it a chance for life, & let it live, & we have had it propped, & have planted round it, stolen ferns at the roots, emerald green cushions of moss, dogwood, & spindle, Andrews, Signor & I making excursions into the wood with barrows & spades.

FRIDAY, NOVEMBER 13 I went up to London to look out portraits for the Victorian Ex. at the New Gallery, & had a busy morning.

Dear little Holland House tho' empty, all in its curl papers, yet looked very sweet, & though I love this, I won't have my affections parted away from that, nor my gratitude for the golden days I have had since I came under its roof.

SATURDAY, NOVEMBER 14 *Limnerslease* Mrs Guild[1] here to do this bust of Signor for the Whitworth Gallery.

---

1. Emma Marie Cadwalader Guild (1843–1911), American sculptor from Ohio, living in London. The bust was first shown at the *Autumn Exhibition* at the Walker Art Gallery, Liverpool, in 1893.

SUNDAY, NOVEMBER 15 Mrs Guild talked much of her work in the evening to Signor.

MONDAY, NOVEMBER 16 Mrs Guild began Signor's bust & worked on rapidly, making it really very correctly. Will she make it him? So far it promises, and she is very nice about everything, & I like her, & so does Signor.

TUESDAY, NOVEMBER 17 Mrs Guild is enthusiastic about Signor in his smock. She said this afternoon she would do him full length, as he sat there, his arm on the table, his hand under his head, the little oak stool, & feet crossed behind it. It was very beautiful, the lines of the smock falling so exquisitely. She is wildly enthusiastic about him altogether, & says he is the rarest type she knows. No one like him. Even I may be satisfied with what she sees him to be, & if she can carry it out in the clay I shall insist she sees him differently from those that have already tried, & more as I do. Mr Gilbert saw all that was noble & strong & humble,[1] but not that. Some have missed all. She loves her mornings now with him, she is getting over all fear of being in his way, & he is happy with her. She is good & pleasing, has been very pretty, & so no difficulty in making him feel at home with her. Little by little we find she has a story. We think her husband lives, & she has not had love or happiness, but she has her daughter, a beloved friend & mother to her as well as a daughter.

FRIDAY, NOVEMBER 20 Our 6th wedding day, & we began to keep it at one a.m. when Signor spoke to me, & I told him it was the morning of the 20th. Half waking, we blessed each other, but later, after I had been up some time at my writing table, he came out with my cup of hot drinking water, & stood smiling at me with a sort of supreme & sudden consciousness of my happiness with him, & said 'Well, are you pretty happy?' I had to tell him that he was too stuck up & full of pride, & that I was on the contrary a very miserable woman! On the breakfast table were two books & a dear letter from Choons with hers & Edward's blessing.

He & Mrs Guild worked silently side by side from luncheon time till half past four, forgetting each other, till she, poor thing, over-tired, was

1. Gilbert's bust of Watts (1888–9) is in the Tate Collection.

overcome by an access of fear, & mistrust of Agnew's promises, & Signor was disturbed, & not able to comfort her.

SATURDAY, NOVEMBER 21 Ethel[1] & I left the workers in the studio alone all morning, & when luncheon time came we found they had been on each others' nerves. Mrs Guild could not come to luncheon, being in tears, Signor not being able to refrain from urging her not to lose her clear edges, & she in her highly nervous state having wept at his saying 'it makes the difference between refinement or vulgarity in work'.

SUNDAY, NOVEMBER 22 Phoebe came in & told me Mrs Guild was staying in bed & had been much disturbed in the night by noises. Later when she came down she was full of the idea that her room was damp over the kitchen & hot pipes running up the wall in the dressing room. Used and enjoyed as it has been I cannot believe it, but think she shifts the shadow over her from day to day. Friday, Agnew, Saturday, Signor's criticisms, tears over each, today it is health & this damp room doing her the mischief. I could only consult with Ethel & ask her to change her room wh. was surlily done.

WEDNESDAY, NOVEMBER 25 Signor worried by the thought that since Saturday Mrs Guild had scarcely worked upon the bust at all, & was still proposing to do the two hands. He got out of bed while I was writing in the early morning & began to pen a letter to her telling her he absolutely must have the clay out of his studio by Saturday next. I thought there would be something. I have been shaking & worried since the morning, & he was, all the afternoon. I long for her departure. She came to dinner & talked to Signor. He had in the meantime paid her a visit, & reasoned with her quietly with some effect, as she listened quietly. Dinner went off fairly well, thanks to Signor's efforts. She talked a good deal about artists generally being killed with worry, & Signor said generally that was not the case as they were generally long-lived. Of course she has not improved the bust today. I see little likeness, but she has given up the hands, & goes tomorrow.

---

1. Ethel Fraser-Tytler, Mary's eldest sister.

FRIDAY, NOVEMBER 27 The bust goes on well, & the Sculptress is smiling & has returned to her usual pleasant & even fascinating way. She can have no reason to feel we bear any resentment. Signor asked me yesterday if I could be generous & ask her to stay till Monday, & I have done so without effort today. Yesterday, dreading more scenes, I did not feel equal to being very generous.

SATURDAY, NOVEMBER 28 The bust had its last finishing touches, & I am sorry to say Mrs Guild put in again a wrinkled forehead that is not Signor's. He has no one particular wrinkle at any time, only general very mobile ones, accidents that fly across his brow now and then but the habitual expression is serenity. I think she has done the bust no good by this morning's work on the forehead, but I have said what I could to try & save it. Much of it is very good. The shape of the head, the nose is really more literal in form than Gilbert's but there is a characteristic distinction about Gilbert's which this has not, though it looks like a refined man.

She left in a happy mood, & we felt as if a little skip round the studio was the only way in which, in spite of age, we could express our feelings. What a pity a nature so much endowed with the power of pleasing should have also the power of making so much unhappiness.

SUNDAY, NOVEMBER 29 We woke with a feeling of rest, being alone. 'My selfish happiness' I called it, & Signor said 'Oh, don't call it selfish. I don't think it ought to be that.'

TUESDAY, DECEMBER 1 I had an affectionate and grateful letter from Mrs Guild.

MONDAY, DECEMBER 7 *Cranford* came this morning, a charmingly illustrated edition with preface by Anne Ritchie, very dainty & appreciative. Signor is delighted. *The Crown of Wild Olives*, by Ruskin, his Christmas present to me, has come also.

We have a charming evening, carried to *Cranford*, living there among the joys & sorrows of that delightful little place, rose leaves & lavender, it all seems. How good for one to be in such sweet placid company. My dear one lay & listened with all the old delight, tears for the death of the good captain, still more ache of heart for the love griefs of dear Miss Matty, so sacred & so deep.

WEDNESDAY, DECEMBER 9 Lady Lilford's[1] death reminded Signor of days at Holland Ho. I dare say I have written down before how he & Lord Holland travelled back to England together in 1845, & how Holland's mother being then alive, he offered to show him Holland House, & had to take him in at the back door, telling him his mother allowed no-one to go in, & he had to do it sneakingly.

Holland told him that he was sorry to say his mother had asked Signor to dinner, adding 'I'm very sorry, for she makes a point of being very rude to all my friends.' Signor went, quaking, but the capricious lady was extremely civil.

FRIDAY, DECEMBER 11 I have had to laugh consumedly. Signor's legs I have always known to be the most imaginative people, but did not know how far they could be so. I have had to order new Jaeger wool drawers for him. I showed them to him & he immediately said that they must be a size too large. They were measured & found they were only larger by the difference of being unwashed. Yesterday however he was under the impression that he had them on & came to me with a distressed face to say they were 'quite unwearable', they were too large. When I tried to argue in their favour a little, he said pathetically 'I can assure you, I can hardly waddle'. On asking Munro, I find the new drawers are still in their box. My light-stepping thin little man, scarcely able to waddle, was a sad picture, but I could not stop laughing for a long while.

THURSDAY, DECEMBER 17 Christmas books have come, Caldecott's 4 vols, amongst them. How wonderful in pathos & in wit every line, almost, is. Signor & I spent hours over them. *Atalanta*, for the children, Walter Crane's new poetry book. We had our Christmas looking over them. Of course he knows *The Great Panjandrum* by heart, better than Caldecott, & tells me it was made by Foote for a man who boasted he could remember anything once repeated over to him.[2]

---

1. Lady Lilford, sister to Lord Holland. 2. Randolph Caldecott (1846–1886), painter and illustrator of numerous children's books, including *The Great Panjandrum* by Samuel Foote ('the great Panjandrum himself, with the little round button on top').

TUESDAY, DECEMBER 22 Tolstoi's[1] *Peace & War* continues to interest us much. It is a fine delicate work, without any touch of coarseness or hideousness. He makes war horrible to one, all the glory & glamour is removed. We see the plain fact, horrible, senseless, barbaric. A novel like that must be helping greatly to 'ring out the false ring from the true'.

WEDNESDAY, DECEMBER 23 Our living room was decorated so prettily for Xmas, & Andrews was hanging a bunch of mistletoe in the Hall, under which he means to have some diversion. The 'Room'[2] has been hung with pictures, & decorated. I went in & found Munro & Andrews at work, Phoebe, Maud & Ellen all grouped together admiring our pictures. Such a pretty picture they made.

Our evening was a little cheered by Tolstoi. Certainly he is a great artist.

THURSDAY, DECEMBER 24 The white mists again & the fairy world of Rime. Our trees are as thick as summer, only the leaves are crystal.

FRIDAY, DECEMBER 25 *Peace & goodwill morning.* I awoke & the embodiment of peace was at my side sleeping peacefully.

Signor woke. 'This is Christmas' he said turning to kiss me. 'Day of all days to keep!' 'In England here you need not complain of that' I said. 'We keep no saint's memory, only Bank Holiday!' 'Ah, yes. St Mammon' Signor said sadly.

On our breakfast table were a number of little presents, a pot of blackberry jam from Mrs Andrews, a carved clock case, & a little basket with ingenious little birds on it, from his clever hand, my bag from Ethel, an old horse-shoe from Maud & Signor. He was pleased with the new binding on our *Praeterita*, & a little *Morte d'Arthur*, my present to him. *The Crown of Wild Olives* he gives me. My dearest ones, Choons & Ethel do not forget me, books & a sumptuous bag. Signor & I paid a visit to the Room, cards & holly all along the mantelpiece, & our nice little household shaking hands with Signor, & very proud of their room. Later the Andrews' dined, & spent the rest of the day helping to keep the day merrily. After Church, May & Andrew. Signor & I returned the call

---

1. They were reading the first translation into English of *War and Peace*, which credited Tolstoy's name with the Russian spelling. **2.** Watts's new Limnerslease studio.

after luncheon, the dear people walking back with us. Our happy day ended with Snapdragon![1]

SATURDAY, DECEMBER 26 We have scarcely recovered from the certain disturbance of life which Xmas with its letters, its remembrances, its toils brings. Choons writes 'Xmas, like everything else, is getting too fussy. The numbers of people one tries not to forget!'

Signor slept soundly for an hour or two in the afternoon, & then I took up *War & Peace* & we read & talked from five o'clock until bed time.

'On this earth there is no truth, no virtue, all is a lie, but in the universal scheme of creation it is truth that rules. We are, of course, the children of this world, but in eternity we are the children of the universe. I cannot help feeling that I am an integral atom in this immense, harmonious whole' are Pierre's words,[2] & we paused before them as they express so well what Signor & I believe & hold to.

SUNDAY, DECEMBER 27 I went early to the little church, thinking this last Sunday of the year I should like to drink the blessed wine, the symbol of God with us of all that is light, love & truth. But the doors were closed, & I had, instead, to make my worship in the lovely outer world, with the rising sun for chancel, & the blue heaven for roof. The world was beautiful, so fresh, the frost just making a delightful edge to the sweet, still air. I scarcely missed the service. The music of the universe seemed so divine to me. I was so glad to have been out. I walked to Monkshatch, where with May I had a little talk. A letter from the never unmindful dear Sir Frederic. 'The less said about Xmas the better' he says, writing that day in darkness.

MONDAY, DECEMBER 28 Sweet May was busy practising dance music for her servants' dance wh. comes off in the dining room tonight. Our little maids are kindly invited to the dinner, & dance. (They came in at five o'clock, to show themselves, before they went up, & a pretty little pair they looked.)

---

1. A parlour game in which heated brandy was poured into a shallow heated bowl. Raisins were tipped in, and the brandy set alight. The game was to snatch the raisins out and eat them without burning oneself too badly. 2. In Leo Tolstoy's *War and Peace*.

May, in a loose sort of velvet tea gown which had been a lovely gown, & is now a scrub, looked a picture. She was soon busy helping to carry in an unmanageably long table from the hall to the kitchen. I think she has the prettiest hands I know, because, with all their beauty, they are hands that can work. Talking of her today, Signor said 'she is without a flaw', & I do not know of any in her character.

We came back to the fascinations of our Tolstoi. Only yesterday we were agreeing that as far as we had gone, if it were not for the Russian women, the whole thing might have been in London, certainly the social life.

TUESDAY, DECEMBER 29 This day is chiefly distinguished by Signor's having a very delightful letter from William Rossetti about his brother's picture, the replica in the New Gallery.[1]

'Will you allow me to express my thanks to you for that very beautiful portrait of my brother. I looked on it long with deep interest & satisfaction. It will continue to long distant years & represent my brother to his countrymen in the most advantageous light, & a truthful one too. Certainly in that Victorian Exhibition you have made my brother shine forth prominently among his contemporaries both for aspects of genius & for other attractive qualities of person wh. one is glad to associate with mental superiority.'

THURSDAY, DECEMBER 31 We woke this morning at five. Our year has only a few more hours. We did not speak much. It was enough to lie still, I conscious that my darling was by me.

Our last evening of the old year passed, nothing to distinguish it but a feeling of wonder at the year undivined which begins tomorrow, a feeling of thankfulness for the past one, which has given us our little home.

---

1. This replica of the Dante Gabriel Rossetti portrait, painted by Watts in anticipation of the Victorian Exhibition, was acquired by the collector, James Smith, while Watts presented the original to the National Portrait Gallery, with 16 other portraits of the great and good, in 1895. Smith bequeathed the second oil to the Walker Art Gallery in Liverpool in 1923.

1893

The pattern was set for winters to be spent at Limnerslease and summers at Little Holland House, although there was still plenty of coming and going between the two in all seasons. To get to London from Compton for the many private views of exhibitions they went to through the year, Watts and Mary set off at about 8.30 a.m. down the Limnerslease drive in a brougham for Godalming station (see page 63). They caught a train to Waterloo, and, if they were going to the Royal Academy, took a horse-drawn cab to Piccadilly, where they would arrive at about 11 o'clock. That journey might not be much quicker in the twenty-first century!

The year opened with a large and important exhibition of Burne-Jones' work at the New Gallery, soon followed by the Royal Academy failing to award him a Fellowship, an omission taken to heart on his behalf by Watts. Leighton, then President, was having a hard time with the backward-looking views of the 70 Members, who still regarded some of the best painters as too avant-garde.

Mary spent the early part of the spring working on a birthday present for Watts. This consisted of symbolic decorations from many cultures for the niche in the Red Room at Limnerslease where they spent their evenings, she reading to him. He was growing deaf and the sound of her voice was enhanced there. He, at this time, painted the portrait of the novelist George Meredith, whose novel, *Diana of the Crossways*, had a popular theme for the period, a woman trapped in an unsuccessful marriage.

Meredith stayed with friends in Compton for his sittings, and Mary, who always enjoyed detailing in the diary interesting conversations between Watts and his sitters, gives us a picture of the few days of

Meredith's visit. Among other notable sitters and conversationalists was William Gladstone, four times Prime Minister, and he and Watts enjoyed each other's company over many years.

The Wattses were Liberals, sympathetic to Gladstone's ideas for reform, particularly on the question of Home Rule for Ireland. He had recently started his fourth term as premier, and they spent a memorable day at No.10 when they went to congratulate the grand old man. For most of the time they sat and discussed one of Watts's drawings of Theseus with the Prime Minister and his wife. Watts had many friends with whom he discussed Greek mythological stories and their meanings. He had plaster casts of parts of the Parthenon frieze on the mantelpiece in his studio, and painted many subjects from Greek antiquity.

In London Mary worked at the British Museum, exploring her growing interest in symbols and how they are adopted from one religion or belief system to another. She was to use what she discovered when she came to design her plaster and terracotta murals at Limnerslease, and then in the exterior decorations of her Cemetery Chapel.

Another formative influence on Mary during this year was Conrad Dressler, the sculptor and potter, who was about to go north with his friend Harold Rathbone to start a pottery in Birkenhead. The conversations she had with Dressler were to affect her decision to start her own pottery at Compton in 1898, at a time when several years of running terracotta classes gave her a well-trained workforce. She and Watts kept in touch with the Birkenhead venture, and the idealism behind it, which was to give craftsmen and women the free opportunity to be creative, while making use of well-tried and almost forgotten techniques.

A great happiness, and a surprise, came to them when nine of Watts's friends and admirers clubbed together to give him a present of a grand piano. They included John Ruskin, who they greatly revered, and who had been a long-standing friend. The Wattses intended to pay him a visit in his retreat on Coniston, but, sadly, Signor did not feel well enough to go.

Towards the end of the year, he worked on his painting *For He Had Great Possessions*, his portrayal of the rich man who could not give up his wealth and follow Jesus. The man turned away sadly, and Watts did not show his face, which Mary thought showed great restraint, and counted it among her favourite paintings.

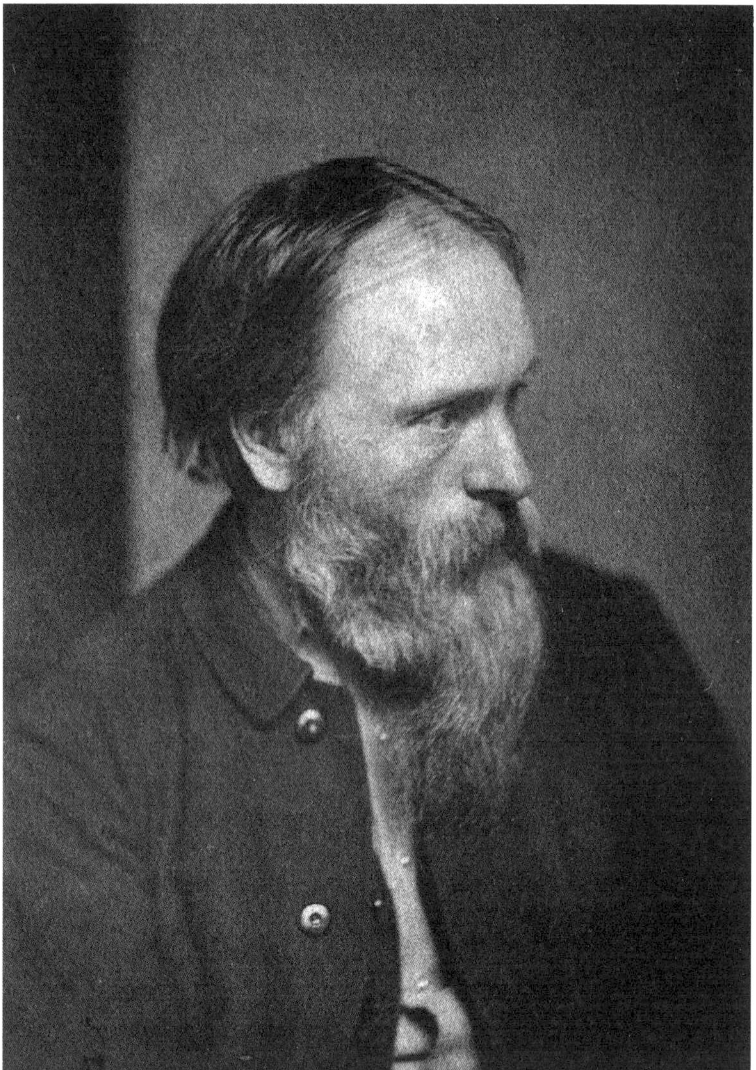

Edward Burne-Jones, photograph by Frederic Hollyer, undated,
Rob Dickins Collection, Watts Gallery

SUNDAY, JANUARY 1 *Limnerslease* Happy together, & in our little home. We awake, & dear one gives me his blessing.

Andrew and May had luncheon here. Andrew, no great admirer of Burne Jones, is completely vanquished by the New Gallery,[1] & says it is superb.

MONDAY, JANUARY 2 Signor came in and found me on my knees scrubbing a little carved table very ineffectually, & said 'get Andrews'. So I & table went out to the yard, ruthlessly called Andrews from his electric lights he is putting up in the studio,[2] & in half an hour the undoing was done & the restaining too, ready for beeswaxing tomorrow.

THURSDAY, JANUARY 5 Ruth & Agatha[3] came – nice dear girls, so full of work & life, & yet so gentle & so girl-like. Ruth played charmingly on her violin – such a treat.

FRIDAY, JANUARY 6 Agatha, Ruth & I walked to Loseley,[4] & skated for a few minutes, not much more.

Delicious music in the evening – Ruth playing & singing. She ended up with a specimen of 'knocked them in the old Kent Road' & others of the music hall songs, delighting Signor. He sat beside the piano looking so happy, & interested. It has been a great pleasure to have these nice girls here & I think it must be a pleasure to them to be with Signor.

THURSDAY, JANUARY 12 I would not let S. superintend the kettle he always has boiling for my bath, in case it should not be hot but 'I have swept the hearth' he looked up & said when I took the kettle off & found a clear space to put it down.

'I should be very sorry if I did not think of things for you' he said the other day when I thanked him for some little particular care.

MONDAY, JANUARY 16 'Are you there?' he calls up to my studio sometimes, & then he asks me to look at something he has done. Once, today, it was to see the little boy *Promises*. 'What do you think of it?'

---

1. The major retrospective exhibition of Burne-Jones' paintings at the New Gallery, winter 1892–3. **2.** The first electric lights to be installed in Limnerslease. The house was not entirely electrified until the 1920s. **3.** The children of friends in London, many of whom visited the Wattses in Compton, with and without their parents. **4.** Loseley Park, the residence of the More-Molyneux family for more than 500 years.

I said 'You have made the wings too real, & have lost the dignity of the work. It is more sweet but less noble.'

TUESDAY, JANUARY 17 I dare say what I think & mark as he is too much in earnest not to wish me to do so. He has lost colour & quality in the wings & the picture is much damaged by it. He told me he had taken out a real wing, & had been working from it. An hour afterwards & he has much restored the quality, the danger of finishing is that dignity is easily lost.

SATURDAY, JANUARY 21 Edward & I drove to see Miss Jekyll.[1] A long drive, too far for Dot.[2] It grew dark & I suffered from nerve tension all the way home, afraid Signor was fidgeting, & that Dot would have bent legs tomorrow.

TUESDAY, JANUARY 24 My little Brenda went very nicely today. I've ridden her for the second time only. We both loved it.[3]

I had a nice letter from poor Lady Tennyson living in her journals & journal letters. She says 'We would leave him embalmed in his own poems, but they say such cruel things of him, we must answer them, by trying to write of him as he really was.' She & Hallam must be much absorbed by it just now.[4]

WEDNESDAY, JANUARY 25 I went up early to London & managed to have an hour at the New Gallery.[5] The light was dim & I can't see how much I lost of glowing colour & glorious light from every one of them. It is great art, beautiful in all ways, spiritual, ideal, poetic.

Georgie[6] tells me he is very sad & humble over it & says he was never 'brought up to believe that there were two Days of Judgement for him to go through'. She must be very glad & proud to see such a lifework spread out before her & yet it does not represent much more than half, nothing

1. Gertrude Jekyll (1843–1932), horticulturalist and garden designer, and a friend and neighbour of the Wattses. She helped with the design of their garden at Limnerslease, and gave them plants. Watts was particularly interested in her collection of traditional tools. **2.** The Wattses' old mare. **3.** Mary's new mare. **4** Alfred, Lord Tennyson died in October 1892. The Poet Laureate was an old and valued friend of Watts; Hallam was his son. Watts painted Tennyson's portrait six times between 1864 and 1890. Of the last painting, Watts described the grandeur of the head as 'the half unconscious insistence upon the nobilities of the subject' (M.S. Watts, 'Portrait cat.', p.158). **5.** The Burne-Jones exhibition. **6.** Georgiana Burne-Jones.

of the glass windows, which Signor thinks his greatest work, for he made that art, nothing like it having gone before.

Georgie picked me up after four at L.H.H. where in the dim light I had been seeing my dear one's pictures hung again. *Found Drowned* & *The Irish Famine* & instead *the great sun*[1] & *Sic Transit*, flanked by those.

THURSDAY, JANUARY 26 *Limnerslease* We rode together, he on Brenda, liking much to train her to go upon the weight of the bridle,[2] & I think perhaps by & bye we may break her of that habit of wanting to break into a gallop.

SATURDAY, JANUARY 28 *Limnerslease* We rode to see Ethel, Signor on Brenda, much enjoying it, I on the old mare. Had a lesson in opening gates. I was sadly out of practice, but managed them all at last with some nervous excitement!

Found Ethel well – 'turning out the nursery'. She is looking forward to having Neil & Hester.[3]

MONDAY, JANUARY 30 My hand is almost upon my plaster work.[4] This week I begin to design & think.

TUESDAY, JANUARY 31 My niche back cut & fitted, & I have thought it out & begun designing. I study rather purposely & carefully the Book of Kells & other Celtic work, but I must not copy or it will be worthless. The Celtic seems in character, the most decorative & symbolic style there is. You draw men, women, angels, hearts & birds all twisted & knotted in with pattern, an integral part of it. The fault of the Celtic is that it is unrestful & 'too busy'.

Walter Crane advises the decorator to put away all styles from his mind & look at nature & trust in his own invention. Signor agrees with me that it should be an outgrowth of some style particularly sympathetic for the expression of his idea. Walter Crane's decoration is very pictorial & it is fairly easy to decorate in that style, but to tie yourself to pattern making, which is my ideal, tho' I can't reach it, is much more difficult.

---

1. *After the Deluge.* **2.** Watts had always been a fine horseman. **3.** The children of Ted and Edith Fraser-Tytler, Mary's half-brother and his wife. **4.** The plaster decoration Mary was planning for the niche.

WEDNESDAY, FEBRUARY 1 Signor asked me what I was designing for the niche. I said I want it to be descriptive of the time we pass there, the things we think of chiefly. Therefore I am trying to make my patterns express the whole range. Flowers, trees, birds, beasts, & man in his double nature, spirit & flesh. Sun, stars, moon, angels, & a light beyond from whom they veil their faces! But that is not all. Papyrus comes in for books, poppies for rest, & then I am trying to get in painting, art, science, religion, history, fiction.

He laughed. 'Oh, you are greedy' he said.

My present idea is to make it a kind of illumination if I can.

THURSDAY, FEBRUARY 2 Signor gets up very early. Soon after four he is awake & I must needs give him his little cup of coffee, which he longs for. He gets up a few minutes after & arranges a screen to keep the light from me, to let me sleep as my hog nature requires, & sits writing till six.

His old step-sister has passed away at 90. He had not seen her for 30 years, he says, not much, I suppose, since he came back from Italy. A prayer book came today, a nice old book with 'George Watts of Hereford' in the book plate & dates of father & grandfather back to 1775. He remembers the prayer book & patiently copying the plates, St John, perhaps ten times. He thought it was a large book! His birth is entered & that of 2 brothers younger. They are all dead but him. The sisters he remembers were kind, but of very weak intellect, & his home seems only to inspire him with the memory of pain & struggle. He says he attributes his nervousness entirely to that early time when as a boy he lived in daily dread of something jarring happening. I am glad he is Welsh. I always felt sure he must be. He is not English.

FRIDAY, FEBRUARY 3 A lovely morning & we rode to Ethel's. We found her on the common with two little people in scarlet running by her side. Hester says she has not forgotten us. She is pretty I think, & Neil, a funny little ball, buttoned up in his red coat, seemed ready to chatter & at home at once.

The Aldourie childnoise has a very familiar sound for me, & takes me back to a very happy childhood.

SUNDAY, FEBRUARY 5 A box on the table this morning with my beloved's seal skin coat made nice for me. His own little idea, & insisted upon, so

I am wrapped warm & proud in his mantle, & was glad to be kept so comfortable. Today, east wind & frost, but it was well kept out.

We want a gentle cheerfulness this evening, & so took up *Northanger Abbey*, & we found it.

MONDAY, FEBRUARY 6 Mrs Stevenson has come this afternoon, the first model Signor has new since we married, I think. No, I am sure. I am glad he is going to refer to nature. I feel sure his work will be better for doing so. We are both working hard. I looked in at my design as I went to bed & felt very despairing about it, but I want to get it done & up by the 23rd,[1] little more than a fortnight.

TUESDAY, FEBRUARY 7 My dear one made studies of the arms & neck from Mrs Stevenson for the *Eve Repentant*, & I suppose I made a little step in my pattern, but at the last there was much undoing & I left off very unsatisfied.

Our evening quiet with dear Jane Austen. She comes to us, when no one else could soothe & amuse!

WEDNESDAY, FEBRUARY 8 It is delicious to me to have Ted's children in my arms, the Aldourie children. I suppose I am touched by 'passion de la terre'. Ethel looks very happy.

FRIDAY, FEBRUARY 10 S. is tired by the work from the model. Tomorrow it is over & he will be glad. He has made many studies.

In yesterday's *Pall Mall*, I am glad to see Signor quoted on the non-election of Mr Burne Jones to the Academy.[2] He does not give Signor's name, but it will be easily guessed at. Signor is glad.

SUNDAY, FEBRUARY 12 We are considering electric light & its expenses. Andrew says the installation would cost a £1000, & that he can afford nothing extra now. I don't think we can at present. The blessed sun will shorten our hours of lamplight soon.

---

1. February 23 was Watts's birthday. **2.** 'Signor had attended the election to record his vote for Sir Edward; the attitude of the majority in that body upon the subject was a matter of very painful annoyance to him.' M.S. Watts, *George Frederic Watts: The Annals*, vol.2, pp 233–4.

MONDAY, FEBRUARY 13 The even life today has one event, the arrival of a great packet of old pictures & drawings from Long Ditton.[1] As it was it was nearly dark, so I have still the pictures to see well again, some of which seem to be very good indeed, especially some heads of boys, though all done before 1843, & never seen since, for the rather unhappy home was never visited. The drawings & portfolios were a feast for all the evening, drawings dated 1827. Careful painstaking copies of prints, facsimiles, as one can see, for in one case the original is there. There are the cricketers, if not the complete set, a great many, some the original drawings.[2] I must order a scrap book & put them all in as much by date as possible. There is a primeval donkey wh. must lead the way! We look back on the record of work of 67 years from the first dated drawing & possibly of earlier work! I see the same thing, the love, the reverent care, the unflagging pains. He is pleased with some of the painting & with the care, but saddened at not having done more. His memory for all these early things is wonderful. I shall be able to label nearly all the scribbles! The names of the sitters he forgets.

TUESDAY, FEBRUARY 14 I had a glimpse yesterday of the portrait of an old man, whose face I could not see without knowing who it was. Today at breakfast Signor told me it was his father. I said I saw everything that was good & earnest & refined in it, & how precious the possession of it was. Signor's face quivered & tears rushed to his eyes. 'He was very refined' he said. Then he told me how interested he had been in Signor's art, drawing, himself, & having a mind fond of invention. Much time given to trying to invent some musical instrument, & growing poorer & more fragile. Failure, & many cares must have brought his grey hair the greyer. The picture is cracked & blistered, alas, because he used meguilp[3] in these early pictures.

Bad health & want of vigour of character pulled the dear father down & how much so tender a nature must have suffered. How I wish he

---

1. Close to Kingston upon Thames where Watts's half-sister had lived. **2.** When Watts was 20, he had a studio on Blackheath and often sketched in the garden of the school run by Nicholas Wanostrocht, or 'Felix the bat', where cricket was enthusiastically played. Watts was interested in the boys practising their cricket strokes, and drew them in great detail. His illustrations were later published. **3.** Meguilp is an oil painting medium consisting of a mastic varnish and a leaded oil. The paint may become yellow and brittle in time.

could have seen his son! It is sad that the breach between him & his stepsisters has made him so silent about his early days. It has been an injustice to his father & to himself.

WEDNESDAY, FEBRUARY 15 Signor has opened an old box of books from Long Ditton & we find many treasures. His own little old Ossian, his Pope, his father's Shakespeare, all very precious to have.

Miss Jekyll came & brought a great root of poet's laurel – the True one!

FRIDAY, FEBRUARY 17 I worked like a fury & got all done as I purposed, plastering the back arch. I left it to harden for tomorrow's work.

Signor at last read Mr Burne Jones' letter, & sent an answer. Mr Burne Jones says he has felt in the position of a man who had been passing by in the street till beckoned & asked to come into a house, & went in, not much thinking about it, & had been left standing in the hall ever since. Signor thinks his action right & wrote sympathetically, tho' to neither of them is it a matter of importance. Mr Burne Jones says 'nothing matters except to paint a beautiful picture' and Signor, that 'it belongs to the infinitely little'.

SUNDAY, FEBRUARY 19 Went along the Pilgrims' Way.[1] It is a glorious way today, steeped in colour & sunshine. My walk alone, to church, is more my church than inside the walls on such a day, at least. In our evening we finished dear little *Northanger*. Charmed, as ever.

MONDAY, FEBRUARY 20 Signor said to me 'the older I get the more I am aware that the only reality that exists is the spiritual'. His words made me realize what the loosening from earth world would be to him. 'Ah, but sweet' I said 'you will have with you a paint brush when you get to the new life.' 'That I am sure I shall' he said, laughing.

WEDNESDAY, FEBRUARY 22 I only finished my last bits of plastering today. Signor busy below, he has not yet seen the niche ornamentation. I ask him to wait now till it is up.

---

1. The track running along the bottom of the Limnerslease property is an ancient route between Winchester and Canterbury, considered to have been used by pilgrims. After Signor's death in 1904, Mary designed a terracotta memorial to him close beside the Limnerslease wood and the track.

THURSDAY, FEBRUARY 23 *St George's Day* 76!

My beloved wakes soon after 12 a.m. & says 'this is Thursday', asking for his blessing early.

My work on my mind. I got up soon after he did, & got two hours work done & by eleven Phoebe & Andrews & I had got it over its perilous journey downstairs, hoisted it into the niche, & had it safely screwed up, not more than a chip or two of plaster in the whole process, & considering it is on a single sheet of perforated zinc, I think it shows careful handling, & much of it is our careful judgement. I think it will look rich, & I am glad of having it over Signor's head today as I purposed, my only present to him. Nature, who he so often flouts, has paid him out by giving him the darkest day of the winter.

Kind letters, telegrams & gifts for him came, & Ethel, & Neil & Hester, the dear little people helping us to arrange the candles, & put the flowers round the cake. Andrew in great form.

SATURDAY, FEBRUARY 25 A lovely morning which we need for work. Signor hard at work upon the *Eve Repentant*, certainly a very exquisite & poetic picture, though not nec. as enthralling as *The Creation of Eve*. The niche is getting on. The colouring takes longer than I thought, but my dear one likes it & comes in with kind words of praise to help me along.

MONDAY, FEBRUARY 27 Happiness ought to be so much more common. I got a good day at my niche, tho' it was very dark, but I have got the whole thing more together now.

WEDNESDAY, MARCH 1 Phoebe was just beginning to have a field day in the drawing room when a note came from Mrs Palmer at Loseley asking if she could bring over Mr George Meredith to see Signor.[1] They came at once, about twelve or soon after, & stayed an hour. George Meredith is very much bent & walks feebly, & is much changed since Signor saw him perhaps twenty years ago, but the finely cut sensitive face, still surrounded with a plentiful quantity of wavy grey hair, is pictorially beautiful. I can see a Signor portrait, with all those delicate lines dwelt upon lovingly. It would rival his Walter Crane's portrait, I think. Mrs Palmer proposes to

---

1. George Meredith (1828–1909), novelist and poet. *Diana of the Crossways* (1885), about a woman trapped in an unsuccessful marriage (very much a theme for the 1890s), was immensely popular.

make it easy by having him to stay at Loseley. Signor & he had some little time together. Mr Meredith spoke flatteringly of Signor's place in art, but like other literary men, he did not think he himself understood it.

FRIDAY, MARCH 3 Poor dear Tennyson continues to be torn to shreds & tatters by his friends.

A niece in the *Contemporary* writing about him assures the world she is delivering herself of a solemn charge from him, when she tells it that it has quite misunderstood his attitude when he accepted the peerage & speaks of the 'enormous sacrifice he made when he yielded to Mr Gladstone's persuasions'. Signor says Tennyson was not at all the man to undervalue the honour done to himself & to literature anyhow, & to speak of 'enormous sacrifice' is quite as much over-valuing the title, as if he had grasped at it with all his might. When will they let these trifles alone, & leave him in his books & his grave at peace.

TUESDAY, MARCH 7 The window wide open when I woke this morning at six, the birds outside singing a host of morning songs, & inside, my bird has been up two hours. My dear one diligently working at a small model in wax of a leg. This morning many hours 'naked & not ashamed' he is taking his air bath modelling & studying from his own finely wrought leg.

FRIDAY, MARCH 10 *Little Holland House* We drove away to Godalming at half past eight in our two pony carriages, Signor driving one, & were at Burlington House[1] soon after eleven. On the steps were Sir Frederic, Mr Calderon, & the Prince of Wales waiting for the Empress Frederick.[2]

Signor & I slipped in after he had saluted the Prince, & we began with the water-colours & Black & White rooms – the Blakes, Palmers, & Lady Waterfords.

The Princess Louise caught Signor, saying 'I thought I saw a friend.' Once when we had strayed away from each other, she took him up to the Empress & Prince, who seems to have chaffed him about his fur coat. 'What are you going to wear when the weather is cold?' The Princess Louise sent Signor for me, & was very nice & civil. She seems well & looks like a girl.

---

1. Home of the Royal Academy since 1868. **2.** Victoria, Princess Royal, eldest daughter to Queen Victoria, known as Empress Frederick after she married Emperor Frederick III of Germany.

SATURDAY, MARCH 11 We are indeed in a whirl of life. We had just finished breakfast when Sir Frederic Leighton came in, full of life, & looking well. He told us that the Empress, standing before a picture of Vandyke, had admired it enormously, & said it made her feel that everything else was wrong. Of course he pointed out to her that it was impossible to have one form of expression in art.

He spoke of a disgusting picture in the Grafton of the *Absinthe Drinkers*, so cleverly painted that the young men are completely carried away by it, & say what does it matter what he paints when it is so 'superbe'.[1] Said his answer to them was that if you are merely designing a pattern for a carpet or a frieze, it did not matter so long as it was beautifully done. But the moment you take man for a subject then it does matter enormously what you say of him, & the emotional comes in.

SUNDAY, MARCH 12 The morning brought us Phil Burne Jones, & to Signor, Mrs Barrington[2] with many letters & newspaper criticisms in praise of her book[3] to read to him.

FRIDAY, MARCH 17 We looked into the Grafton to see that detestable picture *The Absinthe Drinkers*. Debased detestable human beings, the scum of modern life. Why is it done, except to make the painter's cleverness known? Signor says, though the painting of the head is so subtle, there is no drawing in the figures, the woman is very ill drawn, the glass is bent, the bottle as if made of a shaped lump of clay is bent, the table etc. mere daubs.

THURSDAY, MARCH 23 *Limnerslease* Too enchanting to be back in our dear little house. Just a little heaven, with earth's best incense rising up all round it on such a day, when briars & pines & all sorts of spicy scents are blowing about on a soft south wind. My love so happy.

---

1. *L'Absinthe* (1876) by Edgar Degas caused a stir when it was first shown at the Grafton Gallery. **2.** Emilie Barrington (1841–1933), writer and painter, a friend and neighbour to Watts in Kensington. She wrote the catalogue for his one-man exhibition at the Metropolitan Museum in New York in 1884, and published *G.F. Watts Reminiscences* in 1905, a year after his death. Their relationship deteriorated after his marriage to Mary when she wanted to maintain the close friendship they once had. **3.** Almost certainly her novel *Lena's Picture*, published in 1892.

Our hearts are fast rooted here, & he really seems to me to look more vigorous than he has been for many years.

WEDNESDAY, MARCH 29 Drove to Loseley in the afternoon. Mrs Palmer[1] at home. She showed us over the house.

The strange portrait of Miss Palmer by Sargent hangs now upon the old oak panels of the drawing room wall. It looks better than it did at the New Gallery, but a vacant idiot, it seems to me!

She admires it immensely.

FRIDAY, MARCH 31 We read *Diana of the Crossways* & are intensely interested now, every line tonight thoughtful, great thought too, incisive, & delicately descriptive, the men & women in flesh & blood.

SATURDAY, APRIL 1 Cowslips have sown themselves by dozens this year upon the bank. How glad I am. From two plants.

We read our *Diana* in the evening. Signor says it interests him too much! Too true, & therefore saddening.

MONDAY, APRIL 3 George Meredith's first sitting. They spoke of Tennyson as the man 'the most natural'. They both agreed.

'Absolutely natural, & so was Carlyle if he was a little less direct' Mr Meredith said. 'He had the look of Lear encountering a storm upon the Cornish coast.' Signor replied that the portrait he had made of him was a failure.[2] Carlyle was a submissive sitter, but S. was conscious that it was wearisome to him. 'I said I would sit, & so I will do so' he said when Signor apologised. 'You've made me like a road labourer.'

WEDNESDAY, APRIL 5 Mr Meredith came punctually. Signor had a few words with him first.

Mr Meredith read to me. Of course he has not the sonorous music of Tennyson, but I was deeply grateful, for a poet interprets himself to you as he reads. Mr Meredith was kind enough to say that he felt he could talk to me from the first moment that he saw me.

---

1. One of the family of millionaires from Colorado who settled in the United Kingdom. The painting of her daughter, Elsie Palmer, by John Singer Sargent, is considered one of his most innovative. **2.** *Portrait of Thomas Carlyle* (1867–8) by G.F. Watts (National Portrait Gallery).

FRIDAY, APRIL 7 Signor & I were talking this morning of the loss in beauty, which seems almost inevitable in all forward movement now, but we need that spirit to be more universal, democratic. Burne Jones, tho' a priest of the Temple of Beauty, speaks to the cultured. Morris also, & these democrats are not practical. I have always felt that Morris should have had a shop of common things, beautiful in form & colour.

SATURDAY, APRIL 15 My days slip by without a scrap of artistic work being done. Why women fail in art is answered to myself 'because of the little things in life'.

I arranged for a picnic this morning for the household, walked with the chicks to the village, was met by Signor at the door & went for a walk with him, sending off picnickers, who were slow of going, minded the kitchen fire, opened the door for Mr Martineau,[1] who spent an hour here.

My dear one talked hopelessly of art today. I told him it cut me like a knife when he does so. He knows it is an expression of the human mind which you cannot by any sort of surgical operation cut out of it. It will have dormant & active periods, but there it is & must be.

SUNDAY, APRIL 16 My life is happy, happy enough to be unhappy about his sad views on art. I told him this morning that I was in the position of an orthodox clergyman's wife who has to listen to her husband who tells every guest that comes to their rectory that the religious instinct in humanity was entirely a thing of the past, that it was a dead thing. He answers 'Ah, so the religious instinct cannot die', to wh. I triumphantly exclaim 'the artistic cannot die either'.

WEDNESDAY, APRIL 19 *Little Holland House* Our little people leaving us today,[2] Hester & I earnestly engaged in painting wallflowers, & then picking some for them to make Aunt Ethel's vases pretty. The time flew & Neil was soon wagging his head for goodbye & assuring us 'he would never turn bat'. Hester promising she would, to cover his unkindness.

Signor & I left after two o'clock. A slow train & heat intense. The sand banks of Weybridge & heat of the carriage made it feel as if we were on the way to Cairo instead of London in April.

---

1. Watts's solicitor. **2.** Hester and Neil Fraser-Tytler had been staying with them at Limnerslease. They were going on to stay with 'Aunt Ethel', who had bought a house in Puttenham, a village a mile from Limnerslease.

THURSDAY, APRIL 20 This morning at breakfast in the studio, my eyes fell suddenly on the face of my darling's father. Somehow the pathos of it came out so strongly. Was it the father's struggle in surroundings discordant with every instinct of an intensely refined nature or was it the painter's own sufferings that I felt so powerfully there! It quite overwhelmed me. I longed for the father to know that his strivings had lived, taken shape in the very soul of his son. Nothing is lost, & now I know the father struggled nobly, & that is what makes Signor what he is. I am more glad than if the blood of Plantagenets & a bar sinister had given him birth. He is the son of aspiration & of sorrow.

SATURDAY, APRIL 22 Passed old Gladstone & Mrs Gladstone, driving probably to Hampstead. His calm colourless face made a deep impression on me. Signor went again to the Academy till seven.

MONDAY, APRIL 24 Ah, if we could but work fanatically in the light of our own 19th century thought, the accumulated wisdom of so many thousand years, fight against immorality, seeing the injustice of present social opinions, against that sacrifice of sacrificing women, against intemperance, against that desire for wealth, & the hideous inequality of distribution, to living in at last the universal brotherhood! A return to our true balance, man with woman, both with nature, which means health, beauty, innocence. Raising humanity at last, at last, & living the embodied aspiration of creation.

Instead of dwelling upon things we cannot prove, let us dwell upon those which can be proved, the Divine sensibility which should make all men happy & look forward to future happiness. As for me, Mary, the 1st article of faith is to the last that there is a part of Divinity within us, & in every part of us – in brain, in heart, in flesh, in soul. But the fallible & infallible are inextricably interwoven. It is life, & the whole meaning of it, that is to labour & search for the work that brings the whole into the completest union with the Great Divine Essence. That is 'Thy kingdom come'.[1]

THURSDAY, APRIL 27 *Limnerslease* We drove to see Miss Jekyll in the afternoon, her polyanths garden in full flower, & Gloire de Dijon out on

1. These thoughts of Mary's are reminiscent of the themes in some of Watts's late paintings, *Mammon* and *The Minotaur* particularly.

her walls, a peony tree out in full blossom, & gentians too, with their heavenly blue, in one patch.[1] She has tried them in many places & they all failed but there. She cannot tell me why a banksia should not flower.

Her workshop full of interesting work, a platter of iron tempered to a beautiful blue colour with silver edges & enlargings was what fascinated S. most. It is just the blue & line in variety & surface that he feels old armour had. She has small wrought iron tongs, the pincers in the shape of hands, several sets of waggon bells, all things that remind one that the simple pleasures of life have been lost, the pleasure of a little jingle that so pleased the horses. Andrews can remember that the men did not dare touch the bells before the horses were fed, or they would not eat their breakfast. What a delicious life to live in the country, & try to bring all that back again.

FRIDAY, APRIL 28 The papers say the Americans, who first set the example, are revolting now against this continual desire for publicity of private affairs. Signor says 'vulgarity is a relative thing. If you speak of the immorality of the Romans, it means much, but if you speak of their vulgarity, it means nothing.'

I don't quite agree. In our age the vulgarity of publicity means that we would sell anything, the private, confidential talk of a friend, our own privacy! Surely it is the sign of a certain loss of character.

SATURDAY, APRIL 29 The *Daily Telegraph* critic calls little *Promises* 'unwashed, unfinished, ragged in workmanship' & says Signor has before now shown us that a rainbow can be 'grimey'. He atones by high praise of *Neptune's Horses*.

SUNDAY, APRIL 30 Newspaper critics are busy now on the art of the Academy & the New Gallery. *The Times* is favourable to the little *Promises*, at the expense of *Endymion*[2] which none of the papers praise, tho. the artist friends who saw it surprised us with their enthusiasm, Mr Burne Jones, Mr Rivière, & Sir F. Leighton.

WEDNESDAY, MAY 3 Signor regretting the effect of the yearly exhibition on art.

---

1. Gertrude Jekyll, the horticulturalist (see note for January 21, 1893) was living in her childhood home, Bramley House, not far from Compton, at this time. **2.** G.F. Watts, *Endymion*, 1893 (second version), oil on canvas, Watts Gallery.

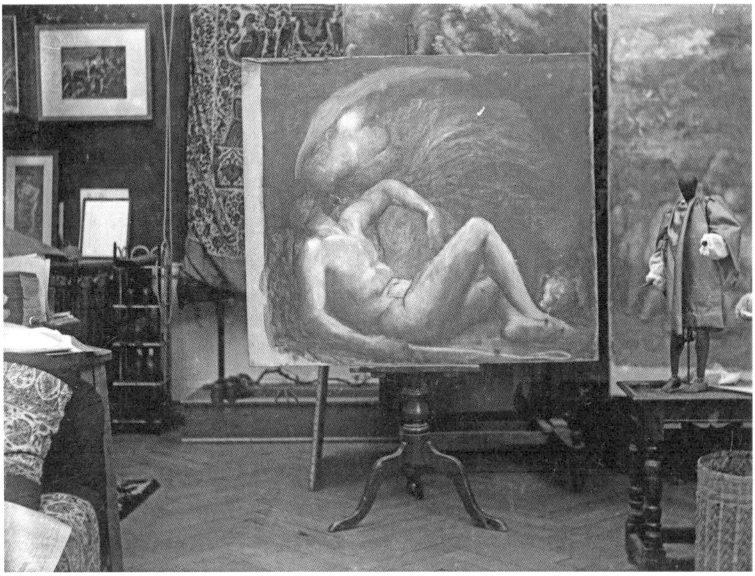

A version of *Endymion* in Watts's studio at Limnerslease, *c.*1903

'Look at Leighton's work for instance. He makes up his mind to paint certain subjects, makes his sketches, only extremely fine things, but to carry them out without loss of time, he treats them much as Andrews does his fret work. There is never anything unexpected in his work, consequently nothing that appeals to you. I deplore it, for tho' imagination is not his strong point, he possesses it, & this painting by recipe, is the negation of it.'

I get a bit of niche done & sweet works well & oh! that head of George Meredith. He has worked in that surgeon-like sharp delicate cut of his.

While I sat in the garden, *The Man who went away sorrowfully*[1] was put up in the studio window & got baked. I was suddenly struck by the

1. *The Man who went away sorrowfully* was eventually named *For He Had Great Possessions* (page 129). The painting, as Mary said, was daring in not showing the rich man's sad face, turning away from following Christ because he could not give up his riches. 'It shows that his way of expressing hesitation ceased to depend on any facial features, & all accent was laid upon the droop of the head, the bent back, and the movement of the fingers.' (M.S. Watts, 'Subject cat.', p.57.)

wonderful beauty & pathos of it. None but my little man would have dared to trust in making a picture out of it without a face!

THURSDAY, MAY 4 We both began our day at four o'clock. I worked out my firmament for the niche. Found out how I would render it Celtically, from the Book of Kells.

FRIDAY, MAY 5 Andrew is much struck by the picture of the rich man, but he wants the name changed to 'Lord, be merciful to me a sinner'. That is so easily said. One touches the pulse of the good conservative in that wish!

SUNDAY, MAY 7 Looking over Signor's child-drawings & placing them in a scrap book by date as far as possible, work from 1827 to here in 1893! What a long spell, still working, endeavouring, striving to do better. The drawing shows pains-taking from the very first, nothing for effect, a desire only to do the very best. These represent work of only a pretty early time from '27 to '38 or '40. In '43 he went to Italy, & never saw his kind old father again.

MONDAY, MAY 8 Out of doors in our garden chairs, wh. Phoebe left out, thinking it might bring rain. Any other year, it would. It shows the obstinacy of the brazen heavens!

MONDAY, MAY 15 We had both a hard day of work. Andrews & I got all the *Firmament of heaven* up (except *the sun* wh. is creating still) over the niche, & I worked on it from soon after four a.m. to half past six.

SATURDAY, MAY 20 Our usually quiet days are suddenly broken into by Nanny, Julia,[1] & the three children, Vanessa, Virginia, & Adrian to luncheon at half past one, only hearing that they were come to luncheon at one o'clock. Mr & Mrs Walter Crane & their daughter for luncheon just after. Too much for Signor, who was very tired.

Mr Crane impressed me today, with a sort of gentleness I had never noticed so distinctly before, a sensitiveness that makes him bear life, more than enjoy it, sensitive to others' wrongs & sorrows as much as to the beautiful & delightful he is always taking in & giving out again. I feel certain that if one lived with him any time, a rare & beautiful nature

1. Julia Stephen.

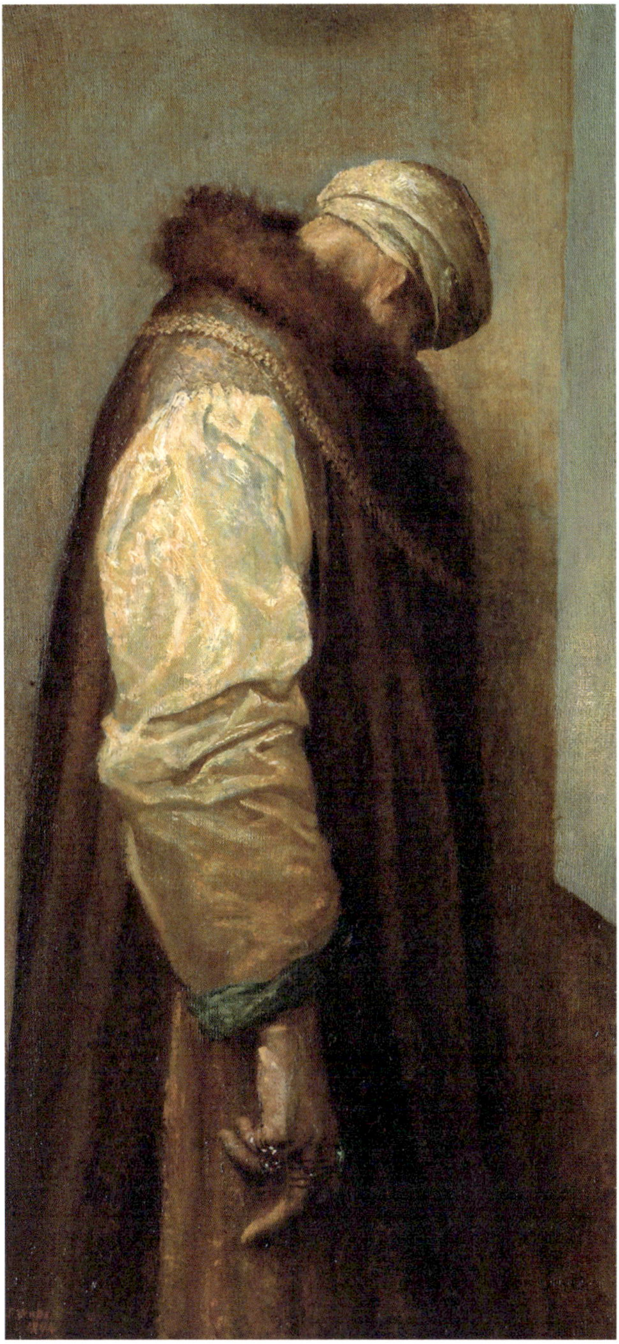

G.F. Watts, *For He Had Great Possessions*,
1893–4, oil on canvas, Watts Gallery

would be revealed. There is something in word & look which promises so much. I see good qualities in Mr Crane, & can never believe in the common assertion that he has an unhappy home.

THURSDAY, MAY 25 Mr Meredith sat for the last time. A friend came with him & it was curious to me to see how he drew out more of the cynic than had ever come out with me. He was less serious, more witty, & less generous. I told Signor afterward that if I had only known him in a crowd I should never have liked him. A soul so beautiful, deeply hopeful, generous, wise, large in his views, you would not see unless alone. It is veiled in a manner a little artificial, a voice somewhat harshly pitched & a pleasure in gibbeting people with his witty tongue.

Andrew dined at Loseley last night & was tremendously amused by him.

TUESDAY, MAY 30 Up early, & at eight o'clock, breakfast, & Lady de Vesci came. Everything is a pleasure to her. She likes our early hours even, she says. The day gloomy, & she looked too tired for Signor to attempt to do any thing to the drawing. She is very delightful to be with, the true woman, desiring to know everything that is good & great & large, dissatisfied with all that is merely conventional, orthodox, & narrow.

TUESDAY, JUNE 6 *Little Holland House* The new gardener & I met at High St. Station at six & went to Covent Garden for new bedding plants. I like him much. His name is Gerrard, & he has a refined, nice face, & looks as if he understood & loved his craft. We were late for the market. The costers were packing & flying off at a great pace, & so many things wanted by us were sold. I think I hate that wild buying & selling of these dear souls, & did not much enjoy the sight.

WEDNESDAY, JUNE 7 Rehanging our impoverished Gallery, the cruelly skied pictures have come down. I have made a sad wall of *Found Drowned*, *Irish Famine*, *Dry Arch*, *Old House*, *Song of the Shirt*!

THURSDAY, JUNE 8 At 10.30 we went off to the Academy, then the New Gallery.

Our little *Endymion* looked small, *Promises* has had all the colour washed out of it. Stood in front of Sargent's *Mrs Hugh Hammersley* & cannot admire. He & so many other young men seem to try to give the quality of coarsely used distemper, a theatre curtain quality, instead of the noble richness of oil colour. Easy to give where it is done by smearing daubs. Not easily done, where anything like the finish & perfection of nature is given. Surely such art cannot have a lasting reputation. Lord Carlisle took Signor up to it, & he simply turned away, saying 'I can't look at it'. Lord Carlisle replied 'That is what I thought you would do.'

SUNDAY, JUNE 11 Our visitor Lord de Vesci. I like to look at our beloved Evelyn's husband. A dear manly face, both strength & tenderness, all the manly qualities.

MONDAY, JUNE 12 Mr Henry James and Phil came.[1] Mr James came to see the portrait of Mr Meredith in which he is so interested. He feels as we do that Mr Meredith is two men. To the world he has the manner of the poseur! Brilliant but an actor! Alone he is simple, generous, childlike. Mr James says he never saw anyone so conscious of an audience. If a maidservant comes into the room, he begins to talk to her. Signor and Mr James had a long talk looking at many heads.

W. Morris pleased him most.[2] He says a face passed through the mind of Signor, comes out like a better self of that sitter! I told him of Lady Holland saying 'I never know my friends till you have painted them.' He looked at Thomas Wright[3] for long, saying it was the face of a saint.

MONDAY, JUNE 19 *Limnerslease* The rider has now a new head & thickened torso,[4] but I cannot say yet whether it is for the better or worse. Signor asks me & I cannot speak with authority. 'I am so discouraged about it' he says. 'I feel as if I could knock it all to pieces.'

TUESDAY, JUNE 20 Lady Betty Balfour came, with Miss Olive Schreiner[5] as arranged this morning. Signor met them & took them into the Gallery till the drawing room was empty.

Miss Schreiner is so much smaller than I expected. She is not endowed with an outer woman as great as her inner, but is in fact far from being disappointing. The face is sensitive, & her apprehension of Signor's *She shall be called Woman* is enough for me.

---

1. Henry James (1843–1916), the writer, and Philip Burne-Jones, son of Edward. **2.** G.F. Watts, *Portrait of William Morris*, 1870. 'Poet and author in prose. Great artist of decoration. A man of extraordinary power and not less extraordinary energy' (M.S. Watts 'Portrait cat.' p.112). **3.** Thomas Wright (1789–1875), philanthropist and supporter of convicted criminals. **4.** The sculpture, *Physical Energy*. **5.** Olive Schreiner (1855–1920), the South African writer admired by the Wattses. The author of *The Story of an African Farm* is often mentioned as one of the first feminist writers. Lady Betty Balfour was a society hostess.

WEDNESDAY, JUNE 28 I made the green wreath for our St Anthony. I have found the words to bind in worthily.

'In memoriam – Anthony Ashley Cooper – Earl of Shaftesbury – Fast & faithful Knight of God.'[1]

THURSDAY, JUNE 29 Darling & I went out from our little haven, where we see the great events pass in picturesque fashion, & in truer proportion, I sometimes think, than if we lived in the turmoil. We had had a vision of a long procession of grateful people bringing flowers to lay on this beautiful monument of him 'who watched & eased the burden of the world', of draperies & flags worthy of the great St Anthony from every window in the circus, & wreathed all about the base of the statue, while it was unveiled with thrilling words recounting all the good deeds of our great good man.

And, what was it? A wooden pen, covered with a grimy sail cloth, rows of respectfully hideous chains tied together where people with pink tickets could go. Outside the crowd were warned off. 'Pass along, please, pass along.' Inside, the privileged few sat for more than an hour while one dull speech after another was stumbled out, speaking for the most part of one of the greatest philanthropists of our day!

The Duke of Westminster was best, & old Sir Harry Verney paid his schoolboy friend a tribute, trailing in the little quavering voice of the 91 year old! 15 years older than my darling, standing bareheaded there, & making his voice heard. It was the only bit of poetry in the whole thing.

MONDAY, JULY 3 We passed the Shaftesbury fountain & saw the green leaves of our wreath gleaming there under the spray of the dolphins, the copper ribbon too, bright & red gold, & I was pleased. The great silver wings, are I am sure, too natural & the whole is a little disappointing, & yet it is the finest thing we have in London.

---

1. Anthony Ashley-Cooper, 7th Earl of Shaftesbury (1801–85), politician, philanthropist and social reformer. The statue in his memory in Piccadilly Circus, by Alfred Gilbert, was named *Anteros*, a nude, butterfly-winged archer. However, it has always been popularly known as *Eros*. Mary described Ashley-Cooper as 'the great philanthropist who gave a lifetime of unremitting labour to better the condition of suffering men, women and children, the coster's donkey or the ill-used horse' (M.S. Watts, 'Portrait cat.', p. 143). Mary often referred to him as their St Antony. Her wreath was to be placed beside the Shaftesbury fountain.

WEDNESDAY, JULY 5 Mr Agnew[1] here, softened by sorrow. He told Signor that when he & his wife were young they had seen Holman Hunt's *Hireling Shepherd* & Mr Agnew had said 'how I wish we were rich enough to buy that picture'. He says he saw it at Christie's the other day at one of the Baring sales & bought it & hung it in her empty room! He has given *The Harbour of Refuge* to the Nat. Gall. Good news!

FRIDAY, JULY 7 Today is eventful chiefly because of a letter from Mr Hipkins of Broadwood's writing to say he was sending Signor the gift of a grand piano 'the present of a few friends & admirers of Mr Watts'!

We went off at two o'clock to see the collection of drawings by Sambourne[2] at the Fine Art & Signor was as enthusiastic as ever. He has always said that Sambourne's line is finer than any other man's alive! He is confirmed in this opinion today.

We then went on to look at *The Daphnephoria*[3] by Sir Frederic Leighton, wh. Holman Hunt has praised in a letter to the *Times*, a letter full of enthusiastic warmth.

I can never love Sir Frederic's work (Signor only loves it by an effort of will), therefore I am not a fair judge. Beautiful as the design is & noble in line, I can't forgive it for the want of dignity or vitality of colour. There is nothing free, spontaneous, nothing that with all its faults, has a truth to give one the answering vibration in one's own soul – makes it impossible to criticize.

SATURDAY, JULY 8 The piano came. Signor is overwhelmed & unhappy. He who gives & gives never likes to receive himself! He would not believe that the letter was a genuine one & till it came, said that there were many hoaxes being played upon people just now.

---

1. The gallery owner William Agnew's wife had recently died. *The Hireling Shepherd is* now owned by Manchester Art Gallery. Frederick Walker's *The Harbour of Refuge* (1872) contrasts a group of old people in a monastery garden with a strong young man scything the grass. **2.** Linley Sambourne (1844–1910), cartoonist and illustrator. He was a satirical draughtsman for *Punch* for many years, and its chief cartoonist after John Tenniel. **3.** Frederic Leighton's *The Daphnephoria* (1874–6), illustrating the nine-yearly festival of that name held in ancient Thebes, in honour of Apollo.

FRIDAY, JULY 14 *Limnerslease* We left at 2.37 for our sweet paradise. Emma & Thompson with us. Found all right & well, though the Andrews did not expect us.

'Fatima' left behind for a holiday, poor thing!

WEDNESDAY, JULY 19 Am told of Mr Benson's *Dodo*.[1] From the description I should say it is covert libel. I cannot bear the modern way of drawing from life, & gibbetting the sitter. Miss Margot Tennant does not fascinate me, but I feel angry to hear of it being done from her, & so cruelly.

SUNDAY, JULY 23 Edie Reynolds & her mother came & played most exquisitely the new piano, much appreciated. Mrs Reynolds thinks it a fine one. They played gloriously.[2]

TUESDAY, JULY 25 Poor Blanchie[3] came, who has just been told that Herbert's lungs are affected. He is to go away to Colorado for a year. She is torn & puzzled as to how to go, and how to leave the children.

FRIDAY, JULY 28 Dear one up at four, chipping in the sculpture studio. Phoebe tells me he was singing & whistling by turn.

Blanchie here in the evening, happy that the children are going to be with Rachel.[4] She is nice about not speaking of any money need. I cannot get her to say how much they are in debt. Much that is good, much that is sad.

SATURDAY, JULY 29 Signor & I drove off to see Mr Gilbert,[5] & found him just wakening out of the nightmare of his poor wife's madness. Yesterday she went away to a doctor's care. It has been one increasing harass & increasing grief since he was with us all those years ago. Now he seems half shattered himself. Blessedly a son of 18 & a daughter of 16 will, I think, help to smooth life for him now. He has a glorious studio & such beautiful things going on. The Shaftesbury monument, & much that he did of that was all at his own expense, I am told. Signor came away saying 'well, we have one artist now!'

---

1. This was the first, and very controversial, novel by E.F. Benson (1867–1940). The character of Dodo was thought, by some, to be based on Margot Tennant, who married Henry Asquith, future British Prime Minister, in 1894. **2.** Edie Reynolds, violinist, who played Brahms at the Promenade Concert of 1895. **3.** Blanche Somers-Cocks née Clogstoun. 'Herbert' was her husband **4.** Rachel Gurney. **5.** Alfred Gilbert, sculptor.

SUNDAY, JULY 30 Sir Frederic here when I came back from church. Could one get in a word (for I always feel my breath taken away), but the rapid darting ideas fly from point to point, not unlike the movements of a hummingbird moth. We should like to know what English writing is a pleasure to him. I think his own English, fluent as it is, often too ornamental, wants strength & terseness, suffers from over-sweetness.

MONDAY, JULY 31 In the afternoon we had promised ourselves a treat, not knowing how great it would be, & set off. We reached St Paul's soon after three, & climbed & climbed, until at length we found ourselves under the roof of the Apse directly above the altar. There was our 'master builder' swung high in heaven, with a tide of prayer & music rising from below. Here in his white linen dress with his English workmen behind him (he would have nothing but Englishmen) was an artist, pure & simple, free & happy, making something glorious, good, holy, under the most splendid conditions, giving himself to the nation, art, the world, for no money, just to do the work he has lived for, been born for. At last our 19th century has broken through the fogs, smoke, market price, all the chains that bound it, & is to claim its glorious roof, all creation crying hallelujah in songs of colour. Mr Richmond[1] has found himself, has come out of the shadow of all other work, & is doing something that I think has never been done before.

TUESDAY, AUGUST 1 Sir Andrew Clark came at 8 punctually, & resigned himself to the sitter's chair.[2] A year since he was last there, & at first I found him occupied & sad. I find he too is worried by money troubles. He tells us he went to see Mr Gladstone last Sunday, & asked how he felt. 'Mal' he replied. 'I'm very deaf & rather blind, otherwise, I'm not conscious that I have a body.' The physician had to admit that he was never unconscious that he had one!

WEDNESDAY, AUGUST 2 Lady Constance Leslie came, & I went to her in the drawing room. She began very kindly saying something defending herself if she seemed to be rushing in where angels fear to tread. She

---

1. William Blake Richmond (see note 2, Saturday, July 9, 1887, page 35). **2.** This was the final sitting for Watts's portrait of him, very shortly before Sir Andrew Clark's death. He was a friend and medical advisor to Watts (and to Gladstone), 'his observation and knowledge made him a most interesting talker' (M.S. Watts, 'Portrait cat.').

then told of a letter she had had from E T,[1] in which she felt there was a second message she must deliver herself before she left London, I to bury it in my heart if I like. She then gave me this to read.

The end of a letter written before leaving for America under a strong impression she will never come back. '& if I don't, now this is very private, please see Mr W, (the dear Signor) for me, & to him present my devotion & say, he, from first to last, has been a beautiful influence in my life, & that I pray God bless him, & she too I bless, for going into his life & cheering it. I have always had a great desire to tell her so, but feared it might not be seemly to her. Farewell, sweet Lady Constance.

Yrs affectionately, E T.'

I told Lady C of the sacred silence between him & me.

THURSDAY, AUGUST 3 I wrote a letter to Lady Constance, & pondered over it much. I wanted some of the peace of his sweet & holy life to go out in the letter & yet to say that I cannot break the silence with Signor now, but that I will, if her presentiments of illness or death in America are fulfilled, or before he goes away from us altogether.

I had to go out in the afternoon to see Mr Dressler,[2] who lives in a little nest of studios in Glebe Place. He interests me much. He has got hold of the right idea, & wants to found a confraternity of artists in Liverpool, starting a workshop, where the artist is to be backed by the Liverpool merchant, that is, given enough to live upon, & work without anxiety. They are to train apprentices, to have no machinery that is not turned by water, or by a donkey. They are to graft an English art upon a Luca Della Robbia ground. At present the confraternity consists of Mr Dressler! It is wonderful to see this new spirit rising about one. In one short week we have found it in Gilbert, Richmond, & this man, & yesterday too a feeling of it in Mr Ward's desire to train English hands to reproduce, mechanically, perhaps, the electro gravure, instead of sending all our pictures abroad to foreign hands!

---

1. Ellen Terry (1847–1928), the actress, Watts's first wife. He and Mary had a pact never to speak of her to each other. 2. Conrad Dressler (1856–1940), sculptor and potter. He visited the Wattses, describing his and Harold Rathbone's plans for an Arts and Crafts pottery in Birkenhead, to be named the Della Robbia Pottery. It opened in 1894 and lasted until 1906.

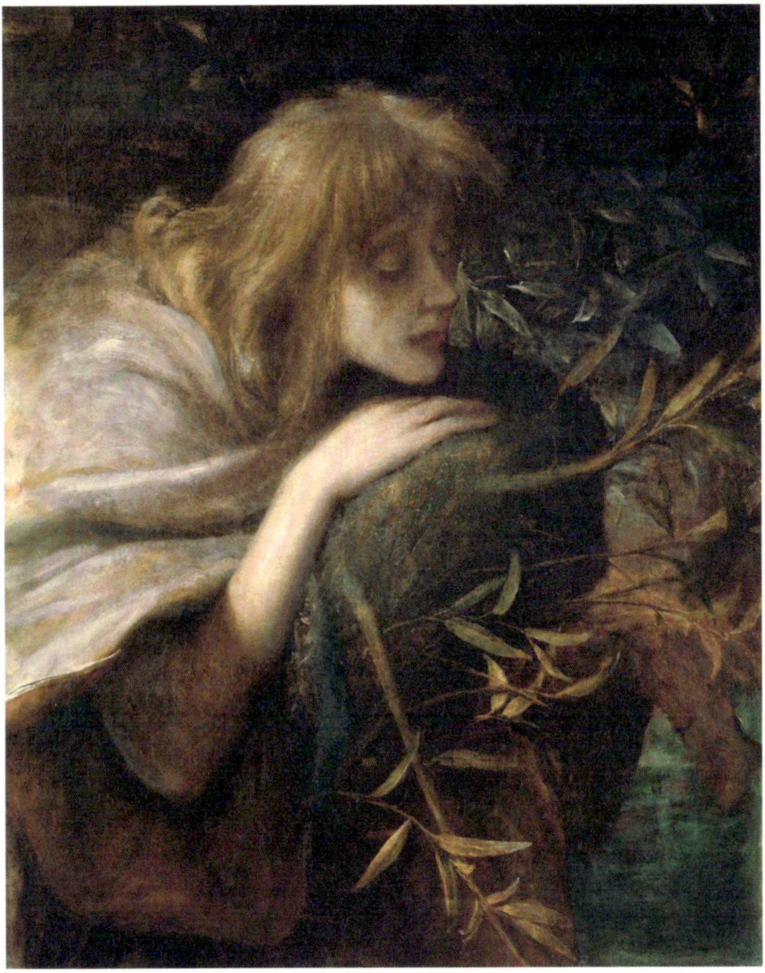

G.F. Watts, *c.* 1877–80, oil on canvas, Watts Gallery. Ellen Terry in the role of Ophelia in Henry Irving's production of *Hamlet*.

FRIDAY, AUGUST 4 I ran down to St Albans. My own Choons met me at the station. A lovely day, & I was in luck, for the Lady Chapel was just opened today to the public for the first time. We drove through lovely lanes to see Edward's dear little chapel, now nearly up to the roof, so pretty, of flint & brick, a cream brick, that looks extremely well. I am to plant my first bit of 'national work'[1] in the chancel there.

SUNDAY, AUGUST 6 Mr Richmond was our first visitor this afternoon. Signor had him alone, I am glad to say, for some time. The first visit for years & years. He says Gladstone was with him the other day, & got excited over an argument, & looked, he said, Satanic, eye turned outwards, & pale as death. He tells me that Gladstone had once said to him that no conversation was so delightful to him, as Signor's. He stayed all the afternoon, appreciated Signor's father's portrait, wh. I am glad to think he saw. I thought it the image of Signor. How different the temperaments are.

MONDAY, AUGUST 7 'I can't imagine Leighton married' Signor said. 'The only thing I could fancy for him would be a companionship, not tolerated by society, of some woman with a strong intellect, & very highly cultivated. It is possible he may yet marry as he feels himself old & alone, a lady who holds a great position of her own, & who would have a salon, live her own life. The ordinary wife, clinging round his neck, would not be tolerated by him. It would be a better position for him & so good for art. Now he is hampered by his loyalty to the Academy, & can do nothing to save it.'

A lovely day for Bank Holiday. S. worked at the hind leg of the horse which has so long puzzled him. We went over to see the crowd happy in the Holland Park. Signor delights in such a sight, the steam merry go round & the swings! The game of coconuts, all interests him. A happy orderly crowd on a fine day is pleasant to look upon.

WEDNESDAY, AUGUST 9 We went to the Gladstones.[2] Passing Mr Balfour on his way from the House, we knew we were late! But after all we did well & were at Downing Street before the Grand Old Man. A crowd

---

1. Edward Liddell had asked Mary to design and make a decorative cross for the chancel in this workhouse chapel. She worked on it through the following weeks. 2. Gladstone was into his fourth and last term in office as Prime Minister (1892–4).

outside waiting to see him arrive! Mrs Gladstone was in the garden, & received us kindly, looking well. It is rather a plunge to go out once in four of five years! Mr Gladstone soon joined us. I was duly presented, & his keen great eyes looked at me kindly. He & Signor were soon on two chairs, knees & heads together, chiefly about Homer, an old argument. Signor does not believe in the *Odyssey* being by Homer, & so they have their arguments! They talked too of young Mr Richmond's work, wh. they admire greatly in his studio, & we were able to tell them how far more beautiful the ceiling was.[1] Mrs Gladstone popped me into the central chair by the Great Old Man & we had some little talk together. He claims (she broke the ice) the right to an exquisite drawing of one of the Elgin Marbles (I fear the Theseus, now given to Sir Frederic). Signor has tried to recall the fact of having given Gladstone the drawing. His recollection is that he offered it, but somehow thought Gladstone did not care about the possession of it. He says he never had it actually. Years after, Sir F. Leighton liked it, & it is now his. Mrs Gladstone's story is that he gave it, & then asked for it back. I came away right glad we had been.

SATURDAY, AUGUST 12 *Limnerslease* Left London very early to avoid the heat. My sweet tired, but refreshed by his spin through country lanes, behind Dot. How happy to be here once more. Old Carpenter opened the gate for us, & I stopped to talk to him. The old man is much aged. Want of words & interest in life, & some pinching too thin in the last six months have told upon him, 55 years bailiff on the Stonycroft Farm, & now turned out. I had to only tell Signor, & talk it over with Andrews. We must make work for him here for the remaining days of his life.

I went to see his 'missus', who was 76 last Sunday, & it pleased & cheered the old dame to think he could get on here.

Our garden is more lovely than I ever saw it, a mass of flowers. The little house, too, sweet inside & out, a home indeed. My dear one very much exhausted. He went to bed at half past six. I sat out till it was dusk, stitching a little curtain for the niche.

SUNDAY, AUGUST 13 Sometimes my dear Signor near me, sometimes alone. Once when he came out I read him Mr Dressler's little paper proposing

---

1. See note 2, Saturday, July 9, 1887.

to work in Liverpool on outdoor decoration. The Liverpool merchants to grant them a small annuity sufficient to keep them from want for 3 years until their work is established. They are to have no machinery, they use their materials as they come fresh from mother earth & not manipulated by manufacture. Apprentices to be trained. How clearly I see now that one of the remedies for that foolish rush to become picture-makers lies in such work. 'All real learning is the construction of ideas peculiar to the individual.' Mr Dressler is so right in wanting to make a round man of his workman. He is to do hard work, thoughtful work, wh. he will love & be interested in from first to last. He will be creative. Our workmen are hungry for this.

MONDAY, AUGUST 14 I cannot manage to get up before six. Later to meet Shawcross the photographer,[1] who came & did the housie & my little man. This lovely summer has made me long to have some done another year.

TUESDAY, AUGUST 15 Old Carpenter with his bent back works away valiantly all day at our little paths. I went to talk to him & was telling him of Signor's early hours. 'Dear me!' he said at once. 'It's always harvest time wi Mr Watts.' What simple words they are, & like children's they have eternal truth in them.

I wrote to Mr Dressler about his scheme.

We rode after dinner & found May & Andrew in their kitchen garden. She looks worn, & he is worried. Things in the city are going so wrong. Certainly the life of a stockbroker is not to be envied. Andrew has had nothing but worry since 1890.

WEDNESDAY, AUGUST 16 I worked at my niche & did not feel the heat so much as yesterday. Signor feels it much, & is driven from room to room & cannot rest on work.

We did not ride, but drove to Monks,[2] & found them both alone. They must retrench, & are pulling down stables with no regrets. The brother has to sell his horse at Ascot! Andrew is in good spirits & he & Signor were talking it over, & he told him he did not feel depressed. As we came up he turned & said 'We have just been saying we are glad that tho. we have lost all our money, we can be quite cheerful, for nothing takes away the real enjoyment of life!'

---

1. William Shawcross, photographer in Guildford. 2. Monkshatch.

THURSDAY, AUGUST 17 A letter from Mr Dressler, who is just off to Liverpool to start his scheme, having had the money subscribed. 'We stand & mark.' Sometimes I feel our little enclosure of wood is the charmed circle I have to keep round my dear one that he may live & work. Beyond are the world's sufferings & groaning, even in little Compton.

Andrew offered Signor this little place for £1500. What if we could afford to buy it & Cook's Farm? So as to have room for a convalescent home & other things. How happy if we had done with London & could live here only.

Proposed to go to Coniston for a week, fresh air & sight of Ruskin, mountains, & such beauty of God's earth, as should make us well in mind & body. Signor agrees! to my astonishment.

FRIDAY, AUGUST 18 *Little Holland House* Up at four. Came down with Signor to see the dawn. The air hot though there is a little south breeze! He awakes with bad headache & feels giddy. I think the fresh mountain air will revive him. He said 'I feel 80 these last months.' Surely not. He forgets how well he has been. Talked a good deal about selling L.H.H. & living entirely here & buying Cook's Farm & the wood if A. will sell it.

Came back by 7.26 p.m. Not so bad then for travelling. I noticed what great bags Signor had under his eyes, & cannot tell if I want to attempt the long journey tomorrow night or not. So sad that he cannot control those travelling nerves of his. It deprives him of so much pleasure.

A letter from Kate Holiday[1] giving us the names of those who conspired to give the piano:

Lord Wemyss
Mr Ruskin
Mr Hipkins
Gerry
Kate & Henry Holiday
Lady Brownlow
Lady Lothian
Lady Pembroke
Lady de Vesci

Kate is the main conspirator.

---

1. Kate Holiday, wife of Henry Holiday; he was a painter, she a designer and embroiderer. John Ruskin, enormously admired by the Wattses, and Gerry Liddell, sister-in-law to Mary, were joined by friends and sitters in the 'piano conspiracy'.

SATURDAY, AUGUST 19 Awoke in the middle of the night by Signor complaining of dreadful headache & giddiness. Got up & gave him salvolatile. As the dawn began he asked me to shut the curtains as he could not bear the light. About four he had coffee & was on the whole better. I saw our Coniston was doomed.

I told him I would telegraph to Mrs Severne to give it up, & so I did, after getting her kind letter asking us to stay with them. Signor was well enough to work all day at the horse. I am grieved more than I thought, his ready acquiescence when I first proposed the plan deceived me, & I allowed myself to long for mountains more than I knew. Selfishly, I found it hard to give up.

SUNDAY, AUGUST 20 S. wrote to Lord Wemyss, Lady de Vesci, Ladies Brownlow & Pembroke & all the people who have entered into the conspiracy to give him the piano.

MONDAY, AUGUST 21 I went to the British Museum, & spent hours, first going upstairs where Buddhist ornament is to be seen. Beautiful patterns, far finer in stone than their coloured or carved wood ornament. I am searching for Buddhist religious symbols. I found myself presently with palaeolithic man, stone age, iron age, Celtic, & oh! such lovely bronze work there. How they understood curves. How innate the sense of beauty. I told Signor of the clear sharp edge of every splendid curve of their bronzes & how these early Celtic people felt the beauty of it as much as the Greeks.

TUESDAY, AUGUST 22 I went off to the Brit. Mus. & there by ten. The morning flew. It was a quarter to one when I thought it was 11.30! Back to find my sweet had had his luncheon. He is enormously interested in what I have to bring back to him, the struggle for light that has ever been going on since the world was peopled by thinking souls. And the earliest history of it greatly helps us to understand the heart of man in our own day.

WEDNESDAY, AUGUST 23 Signor down early. He had discovered that a candle helps him to see what his work wants in the sculpture studio. Fancy the little one there alone with his little candle in one hand, and his tool in the other, working out the great throat & breasts of his *Dawn*, her big form looming out of darkness over his head.

THURSDAY, AUGUST 24 Signor had a visit from Moore the Founder[1] who has presented a bill of £40 for my two bronzes. He had said they would be £10 or £12 each. It vexes me sorely! S. is so dear & patient, & tells me what is his is mine, but I worry over it. I am grieved & wish I had never tried to do the memorial at all. It was his suggestion, dear one, but it has led him into expense that ought never to have been his, I feel.

FRIDAY, 25 AUGUST Signor has begun little Agathonike Ionides.[2] He painted her great grandfather & great grandmother, her grandfather & grandmother, her aunts, & now is painting the fifth generation! Not many families can boast of that by the hand of one painter.

SUNDAY, AUGUST 27 My morning went too quickly, merely spacing out better for the bronze angel.

'In loving memory of Charles Edward dear child of Edward and Edith Fraser Tytler. died Oct 7 1886 aged three years'. This week I hope to get the bronzes off to Aldourie.

Mr Holman Hunt came in. He came at 4 & stayed till 7. Told us at great length all the story of their courtship & marriage.

MONDAY, AUGUST 28 Mr Conrad Dressler came. He had much to say about the condition of things. Would like to blow up all machinery. Asked me if we had a sewing machine in the house! He would begin with that. He seems much in earnest & I only trust he may be wise & carry it out sensibly, so as to convert & not discourage. Mr Dressler says the system is of doing work in parts. The man who makes the design by the yard never colours it, & he never sees it hung. Even in an 'art' trade he is turned into a machine. He believes there will be a revolt against it all, & men will not consent longer to be worse than slaves. He comes again on Thursday evening to read a paper to Signor too long to be gone into in day light.

WEDNESDAY, AUGUST 30 The Rider is set upon his horse,[3] & his head upon his neck once more. Signor is better pleased. I confess I do not see that he is more beautiful than he was a year ago. I wonder if he loses in

---

1. James Moore was the owner of Thames Ditton foundry at Long Ditton in 1882–97. He was casting the triptych in memory of Mary's nephew, father and brother. **2.** Agathonike Ionides, b.1887. She married George Demetriadi. The Greek Ionides family, living in London, were patrons of Watts from the 1840s onwards. **3.** *Physical Energy.*

his work, & has to regain. It seems like the turning of a wheel sometimes. The man has been so good for so long to my ignorant eye.

FRIDAY, SEPTEMBER 1 *Limnerslease* A fog very nearly prevented Signor from painting the little girl, but not quite. He got on well with it & Mrs Ionides was very pleased. I think she may well be! It is a little sparkling thing, all smiles & great vivacity. Signor allows that an expression on a child's face may be of the more transient kind than those he allows himself to paint on the face of a man or woman. He will finish this & make it very fine, I believe. I shall be glad if he does his best at 76.

SATURDAY, SEPTEMBER 2 How delicious! I went out after dark tonight. Signor had gone upstairs & I had turned out the lights in the drawing room.[1] The hall lamp only was burning, throwing a dim light across the little ceiling with its bosses & 'writing on the wall' of man & god.

SUNDAY, SEPTEMBER 3 Glorious! such a day. Dawdled, read, picked flowers, wrote no letters! How sweet the air.

We met Andrew in the bit of field we covet & walked all over it. Andrew is anxious to sell this place to Signor now. I do not want it very much. No one to leave it to, & I only feel it encourages my natural love (passion) for a home.

Andrew, Tyler & Signor worked out the boundary, & it was to be arranged with Cook. If my dear one has many years here the place will be a hallowed one to me. Its future when I & he are under the grass & flowers matters but little.

WEDNESDAY, SEPTEMBER 6 *Little Holland House* This never to be forgotten summer still goes on. We should have ridden to Ethel's but it was too hot so we went quietly in the Sandy Lane. How delicious our 'heavenly twins' Brenda & Rufus, stepping together so well & smoothly. I am enchanted with Rufus's paces, & Signor has consented to let me keep him. I am so pleased & have no fear of his ever giving me a fall. It has been difficult to persuade Signor that a woman's seat is a perfectly safe one for a tumble, but now he has consented.

Left at 6.30 & home to bed. London hot & stuffy.

1. The Red Room.

THURSDAY, SEPTEMBER 14 I look out & see my dear one, alert & well, in newspaper cap & smock, at 6 a.m. 'chiselling with free strokes the heads & limbs of plenteous supreme Gods' – & pray like the old Egyptian for the perfect length of life – 110 for him!

SUNDAY, SEPTEMBER 17 My dear one is kind to Alice Ogilvy,[1] who came with her drawings & seeking advice. It is so difficult for him to advise. He says too much to encourage, the words coming from him with such weight, this chiefly to people who have not been taught.

Then his own experience is an unusual one, & not one that can be very safely followed. He never remembers when he couldn't draw, & had a natural genius for taking pains that made anything like teaching unnecessary.

He worked at it just as a man would work at the language he intends to write his poems in. He meant to use his art to express his own imaginative thoughts. It was, too, his natural language. It was not a foreign one to be acquired, as it is to most.

Later in the day Mr Dressler came & sat some time talking over many things with Signor that bear upon this experiment at Liverpool. He seems much in earnest.

MONDAY, SEPTEMBER 18 My dear one telling me today how much he has tried & is trying to get his great *Energy* to look like man as he should be, a part of the great creation, Cosmos, in fact. His great limbs like rocks & roots, & like a sun. He has that already in his *Chaos* where the giants like huge mountain ranges lie immobilely about, but this he says should be his finest work.

WEDNESDAY, SEPTEMBER 20 'I am doing the most difficult part of my work now' Signor said this morning. 'Trying to give a sense of deliberate largeness to the lines.'

I was mastered physically & morally by a cup of strong tea, wh. having been sent for by Aunt solely for me, I felt bound to take. My morning more or less wasted by it, my temper vile, & it nearly cost me a day of life. What must this be for victims of opium & alcohol?

THURSDAY, SEPTEMBER 21 Mr Dressler dined & read a paper to Signor setting forth the principles upon wh. his brotherhood is to be founded.

---

1. Alice Ogilvy was Mary's cousin. She visited them in Constantinople on their honeymoon.

He says he had been reading the life of St. Francis of Assisi, & it had so influenced him that the society is the result. He wishes to bring about a revival of the feeling that the divine is in everything.

SUNDAY, SEPTEMBER 24 My dear one better, though condemned by wisdom, to stay in bed till Phoebe called him. The bright sun made it harder. 'I consider it irreligious to be in bed on such a morning' he said – 'Why are people not taught these things? They are not taught how to use money, they are not taught to use time – & that not to use them well is irreligious.'

Mr Harold Rathbone & Mr Dressler also here. They are full of their plans & of hope for their results.

SUNDAY, OCTOBER 1 My morning busy with church, flowers, & a mass of berries for Aunt Fanny's grave. I took it up, with the usual result of depression from the ugliness of the whole thing. What an opportunity wasted. The idea passed through my mind, could I do anything? Artists and friends who would design, use terra cotta & brick in our brick making counties, & stone in a stone country. No marble for out of doors. Teach the people to make their own.

Mr & Mrs Crane our only visitors.

MONDAY, OCTOBER 2 So the silver haired head of the Master of Balliol[1] is laid low. He made a great mark on the young men of England, & was loved by many. Large & liberal in religion, they say, 'he saw life as a whole & saw it sanely'. He was just Signor's age!

TUESDAY, OCTOBER 3 Signor put in the hands in the little Ionides portrait. The little mother is a happy woman. She says what few mothers would, that it is even flattering.

WEDNESDAY, OCTOBER 4 Sent Olive Schreiner[2] the photograph of Signor & the big horse. How much I love it.

THURSDAY, OCTOBER 5 Spent my day at the India Office Library, & enjoyed it much, though I cannot yet find the oldest symbols from Indian temples.

---

1. Professor Benjamin Jowett (1817–93), Master of Balliol College, Oxford scholar, translator. He sat for a portrait by Watts at Freshwater in 1877, and again in London in 1893, when he was staying with Florence Nightingale. **2.** The South African writer the Wattses admired so much.

The rock caves of Elephants seem of a late date, comparatively. Early Brahmanism had no temples. The prophets of it sat under the roof of Heaven only, touched earth, & believed that it was all one divine thing. How to symbolize, that is the question.

SATURDAY, OCTOBER 7 Mr Shields[1] dined with us. He came in the gloaming full of melancholy for the death of Madox Brown,[2] who had been as a father to him in early days. He is a gentle little soul, too sensitive & responsive for the busy world. I am wicked & tempted to laugh when with head on one side, sucking in breath in gasps, he listens, wrapt in ecstasy over Signor's benefit from mince beef, crying 'De-lightful!' at intervals. Madox Brown had told him that he learnt to love colour when his children began to use it! He saw how much more right they were than he was, in using dusky greys & browns as he was then doing.

SUNDAY, OCTOBER 8 The Rawnsleys[3] came to luncheon. As ill luck would have it Harry Prinsep[4] walked in, & stayed too. Signor had some time with him about pictures & drawings, *Alice*, *Lady Somers*, & *Arthur*, & that he must beg that he would see about their future, & undertake to carry out his wishes that they should remain as heirlooms in the Prinsep family. He promised this most readily & seemed to wish it as much as Signor! The Rawnsleys very nice. She tells me of an architect friend of hers who has given his mind much to design headstones, simple & beautiful for some churchyard in England.

TUESDAY, OCTOBER 10 I went to meet the Rawnsleys at Mr Petrie's.[5] Missed them but saw Mr Petrie, & saw old world things, or drawings

---

1. Frederic Shields (1833–1911), artist, illustrator and designer in stained glass. His work mingled biblical subjects with allegorical themes. He admired Watts, and was a good friend to Dante Gabriel Rossetti, whose mother commissioned him to design two windows in her son's memory. **2.** Ford Madox Brown (1821–93), historical painter. **3.** Hardwicke Rawnsley (1851–1920) built on Ruskin's idea for a National Trust, which he co-founded in 1895. He also founded the School of Industrial Art in Keswick, lasting until 1986, and Keswick High School, one of the first co-educational schools in the country. He had a lasting friendship with Beatrix Potter, and encouraged her to write her first book, *The Tale of Peter Rabbit*. **4.** Henry Prinsep (1844–1922), nephew to Sara and Thoby Prinsep. He was brought up in Little Holland House. **5.** Sir William Matthew Flinders Petrie (1853–1942), Egyptologist and eminent archaeologist. He raised interest in the pharaoh Akhenaten of the 18th Dynasty, who changed Egyptian worship from polytheism to monotheism, raising the status of the Aten (the sun) above that of mere gods.

from them, & heard that he had found a winged disc upon a 4th Dynasty stone. He marvels as we do at that wonderful symbol. Only late science has revealed truly the fact of the revivifying power of the radiating heat from the sun. Akhenaten knew it, & wished to bring about a reform, in the worship of that radiance, & in his symbol every ray terminates with a hand, crowning him with light, giving him food, & so on. The biography of Akhenaten is just coming out. Mr Petrie's face itself interests me. It is the type of an old Assyrian. 'Where do you come from?' was on my lips to say! If I see him again I will. 'Living in the Truth' is Akhenaten's motto – written everywhere. Had meant to bring back to my dear one.

THURSDAY, OCTOBER 12 Ran off to the India Museum, to meet Mr Maitland, who will kindly introduce me to Sir George Birdwood,[1] the greatest authority on Indian religious symbols, & had a good morning. Kindness itself, & helpful to the last degree. Came away, with books sent on in advance.

FRIDAY, OCTOBER 13 Getting up at 5 to try to master in the few remaining days more lore from India. At ten minutes to 8 Sir Andrew Clark was here for his final sitting. He tells me he is more full of uric acid than any patient that ever came to him. Strong little masterful man that he is, I enjoy my talks with him. He is illogical often, even I can perceive. He is making a library now, which is to be medical & theological.

Signor & I went to see Flinders Petrie – & enjoyed an hour in Egypt!

SUNDAY, OCTOBER 15 *South London Gallery* Never alone from 9 a.m. to six thirty when Georgie[2] came to drive me to Camberwell. The Stephen children came during the morning.

Then to Camberwell. Rooms full. Crowds great & orderly, so attentive to Mr Rossiter's creation.[3] Such lovely rooms. Came away with feeling of wonder that the little man had accomplished it all, & a feeling that they were permanent & the management was not.

TUESDAY, OCTOBER 17 Down to St Albans to see Edward's little chapel & say goodbye.[4]

---

1. Sir George Birdwood (1832–1917), Anglo-Indian official and writer. **2.** Georgiana Burne-Jones. **3.** William Rossiter, founder and Director of the South London Gallery. New galleries were being opened. **4.** The Wattses were going to Limnerslease, where they would spend most of the winter.

THURSDAY, OCTOBER 19 *To Limnerslease* Our great ark went off with all the luggage & big piano! A huge van filled to overflowing.

I went off early to return a book on hieroglyphics to Mr Flinders Petrie.

I have got some interesting history from these hieroglyphs, the symbol of sweetness – a bean – so pretty, & the heart vase-shaped, but with the arteries as handles, adoration prayer, the standing figure with arms upraised. Our old English expression 'it so fell out' is literally described by the figure of a man prostrate on the ground.

Mr Burne Jones came to say goodbye. He looks pasty-white, fat, altogether in a bad state of health. It grieves me to see him. Signor had Mr Rivière & his son, a nice looking young fellow.

FRIDAY, OCTOBER 20 *Limnerslease* We left at 2.37 – a lovely day, and as Guildford got near, I smelt that rare delicious sweetness I always meet at Guildford station!

Our little house still like summer, white clematis, violets, & still dahlias in quantities. How thankful we are to be here.

SATURDAY, OCTOBER 21 Such a sunny lovely morning. My cold bad, I had breakfast in bed! a wonderful event blessedly! How lovely! Violets in masses. Andrews brought in a bunch of enormous size, & the whole house is scented of it.

Signor soon at work. I unpacked a little, but even 13 hours sleep last night has not been enough, & I had to sleep again after luncheon.

SUNDAY, OCTOBER 22 Heard of Sir Andrew Clark's attack of serious illness on Thursday. We had missed yesterday's papers.

Oh, the peace of being alone together all this day. I feel sure that nature, that kind old nurse, wants us to come to her, & now & then, be alone in her lap, & she will rest & restore.

MONDAY, OCTOBER 23 Alas! for the flying feet of the year. The order leaf for a new 'Fatima' presents itself here! How soon it runs the circle. 'My life' shows little trace of change, & yet I know it must be going on.

Our evening cosy & for a while I read aloud from the *Wisdom of India*. Signor thinks that the conception of God in the Upanishads is the finest expressed in words. We came, too, across a passage where 2000 years before Copernicus, the fact that 'sun neither rises nor sets' but travels, lightening up the under world, flashed thro. the Hindu mind.

THURSDAY, OCTOBER 26 I looked out this morning about 7.30 & saw Monkshatch glowing in sunlight, flocks of doves about the chinks of chalk pit that I could see. We rode to Ethel's, Signor gaily trotting & inclined to do more than I could. Just seven weeks since our last ride in the Sandy Lane, one hot September day. The day lovely & our ride nice though I was uncomfortable in my old habit bodice, too thick, bad shape, horrid, can bear nothing that is not loose now.

Andrew here in the evening, only to be here for a few days though we are to enter into possession of our field at once, but the deed cannot be paid till March 16.

The field was lying idle for six months & all the cost of unnecessary brokerage etc.

FRIDAY, OCTOBER 27 The year cannot leave off being fine. We rode over Puttenham heath, & breathed in everything that was exquisite, almost too hot, as we turned our faces from the wind. Our little ponies so gentle & so dear. Signor very happy on Brenda, gallops about Andrew's stubble field.

May & Andrew came to luncheon, & we walked about afterwards planning the planting of our new acres!

Audrey has been at Monkshatch, sorry for Hallam's entire absorption,[1] feels that the moment when he might take up his life of public duties & others is passing while he is absorbed in watching by his mother's side. She herself accepting the sacrifice both from Hallam & Audrey without a misgiving. Indeed, her conduct to Audrey in giving her no place in her own home is wicked, it only shows one how cruel good & gentle souls can be. Signor fumes & calls her a wicked woman.

SATURDAY, OCTOBER 28 Took brush in hand to paint – a pleasure to use the colour again & I did not feel as if I had forgotten it all. I am grown dull somehow, & 'Fatima' dwindles – (I seem to know my dear one's mind so well now, there is nothing to note down.)

SUNDAY, OCTOBER 29 Letter from Mr Dressler, who wants to do, for Signor, a relief from my head. I told him it would be a relief to have it taken away, & he agreed!

---

1. Audrey Tennyson, née Boyle (1854–1916). She married Hallam in 1884 and encouraged him to accept the governorship of South Australia. She was a prolific letter-writer and founded Australia's first maternity hospital.

I walked across the heath to Puttenham, a radiant day again. Autumn breathed in & then to church where prayer & psalm soothed me with its spiritual hypnotic effect, & then had to listen to the good man's exposition on the 'Christian Church'. Home to find a far more religious teacher in Sir George Birdwood whose article on 'the Christmas tree' I took up, & read how he had his Hindu friends & dressed his Christmas tree with symbols sacred to all religions, to their great delight.

Signor wrote letters, one to Mr Dressler to help him with his scheme, & afterwards we read 'The Christmas Tree' & were comforted to meet with a kindred spirit.

MONDAY, OCTOBER 30 My 8th volume of 'Fatima' came today. Signor likes to see it & though he never reads a word of it fortunately, he is certain it is good for me to keep it. Today he said 'I wonder if you would find yourself much changed if you had kept your Fatima years ago.' I am changed, I think, but not in tendency. The cast of my mind is the same. I can remember the lines of Tennyson for instance that I leapt to, almost as a child. 'But since I have married you, I have lived.' 'Ah,' he said 'tendency is a good soil, but it needs cultivation. If left to itself it grows weeds.'

I wrote to Sir George Birdwood to tell him the pleasure his little article had been to us.

THURSDAY, NOVEMBER 2 Evelyn[1] tells me of a visit to Edinburgh when she went to see a Mrs Traquair[2] who has painted the choir house of St Mary's Cathedral. She climbed down a ladder to speak to her & told her what Signor's work had been to her. She had had a very lonely life, shut up with a Casaubon husband,[3] & suddenly had been lifted out of it, finding she could paint. Signor lighted the torch for her, & her life is one strenuous endeavour to work for love. She painted Signor, I know,

---

1. Evelyn de Vesci. **2.** Phoebe Anna Traquair née Moss (1852–1936) was born in Dublin. In her Song School murals, she painted the contemporaries she admired, including Rossetti, Holman Hunt and Watts. Writers have often compared her work as a muralist with Mary Watts' Cemetery Chapel, although their techniques and styles were quite different. She corresponded and stayed with the Wattses. **3.** Mary's phrase refers to Edward Casaubon, the fictional character in George Eliot's novel, *Middlemarch*. He was a pompous scholar and a poor match for the heroine, Dorothea.

among the *Powers* of the Benedicite, & so it was nice to hear of her. It comes like a voice answering suddenly which has cried long in the Desert. Evelyn promises to come here tomorrow or Sat. to bring some of Mrs Traquair's work.

FRIDAY, NOVEMBER 3 Andrew came down in the evening, knocking at the door & saying 'May I come in although I am a wretched Tory?' – & they kept clear of all difficult subjects. Signor talking of it afterwards says 'It is not his being a Tory I object to, it's more the different opinions. What I dislike & regret is that every man who does not agree is looked upon as an enemy.'

TUESDAY, NOVEMBER 7 Last night our vigorous strong indomitable friend, Sir Andrew Clark, handed up his sword in the great court of Death. The news seems difficult to believe. He seemed to have such a hearty grip on life, we feel it much. We had grown to know him well during these sittings & to like him so much, so right-hearted always, so large minded generally. He talked well & gave one much to think about. The low estimate he had of woman was the only thing I could have wished otherwise in his open & kindly & open mind. Was it forced on him by the class of rich & foolish women who went to him with their whims, or the rich & idle who had got into great mischief? It has been a good life, his compliance always on the side of the right & good, & I am glad my dear one has written his history with his brush. How pleased he was!

THURSDAY, NOVEMBER 9 The Lord Mayor's Show today.

Ethel came over, but before she did, Signor & I had a nice scamper round the field, warming us, & thoroughly enjoying it. It makes one see he is younger than one thought. The little ponies go deliciously. Ethel is sorry to have missed what she calls 'our wild west show'.

Andrew here later, ever drawn to Signor's side, though in chat upon books, politics etc. they differ at every word! Andrew sees nothing but 'Rot' in the *Heavenly Twins*. He sees nothing but exorbitance & unreasonableness on the part of the miners in their strike.[1]

1. This was the first coal miner's strike. The price of coal plummeted, and the owners of the collieries lowered miners' wages to a point where there was hunger and hardship. Riots followed, and the police and army were brought in to quell them. Eventually many men returned to work so as to survive.

MONDAY, NOVEMBER 13 Consulted about the planting of our new bit of field. Such a great addition to this little place. Our line of road marked out. Andrews will start digging at once.

TUESDAY, NOVEMBER 14 The day very foggy, & though all ready to go to London, when the cab came we thought it best to stay here safely. Kind little Emma telegraphed that it was foggy & it did not lift here all day.

WEDNESDAY, NOVEMBER 15 *Little Holland House* In spite of fog we got up to London, & went to the Arts & Crafts.[1] I enjoyed seeing it so much with Signor, who came away feeling 'as I never do from the Academy, that these are real artists, & that there is hope. That mantelpiece by the sculptor Mr Pomeroy is beautiful, & would be beautiful at any time.'[2]

THURSDAY, NOVEMBER 16 Signor had books from Mrs Traquair, & Mrs Barrington, Aglaia & others. He is much struck by the beauty of the drawings by Mrs Traquair. He says that probably the scientific drawings of sections she did for her husband has been very good training.

SATURDAY, NOVEMBER 18 We left early for Waterloo that we might leave Mrs Traquair's book at 78, Pall Mall.[3]

Our journey very cold – snow falling or driving along rather at Guildford. What a night for the poor cabman. The first one refused to take us.

But at last our cosy home received us, glowing fires, & slippers, warmed for Signor.

SUNDAY, NOVEMBER 19 Signor & I sat & looked at the Celtic cross on our fireplace & saw how in pre-Christian times it was the symbol of unity. God in all from point to point, east & west & north & south. Then in early Celtic times the symbol of love & self sacrifice, bound within the double hearts! Why did it ever in Christian hands lose its proportion, a change from cross to sword? The symbol of disseverance & disunion. Shall we end this parenthesis of darkness, misconception, a disunion in the name of Christ, some day not far off?

---

1. The annual exhibition of the Arts and Crafts Society at the New Gallery. **2.** Frederick W. Pomeroy (1856–1924), sculptor and architectural designer. He was taught by Jules Dalou, who also taught Mary Watts. One of the school of New Sculptors, he was a member of the Art Workers' Guild. His large sculptural works include the figure of Justice on the Old Bailey. **3.** The London home of Lord and Lady de Vesci.

MONDAY, NOVEMBER 20 *8th anniversary* My sweet with me, well, full of vigour. We bless each other, & feel blessed. Flowers & greetings from darling Choons.

May & Andrew came to stay, so good & dear of them, & Andrew toasted the day as one when Righteousness & Peace met together. It has been a blessed day to us.

WEDNESDAY, NOVEMBER 22 Signor in bed, strict Salisbury & rest, & I am thankful for we can now have turmoil & smell of paint downstairs (Andrews, Thompson & I) all day long, finishing the drawing room wall at night!

THURSDAY, NOVEMBER 23 Signor downstairs, grieved at the loss of his dear red muslin in the drawing room & I am filled with compunction! It was faded, & had a tawdry unsolid look to me. Its crooked stripes & all were dear to Signor! He is pleased otherwise with the colour in the hall & dining room, & we feel we have made a good step towards finishing the little house. The billiard room begun now.[1]

I read Miss Austen to him in the niche, always a help to recovery.

SATURDAY, NOVEMBER 25 Dear one got up but could do nothing, & lay on the sofa in the niche with two hot bottles & looking very ill. Pains all over him & especially in his hip.

Greetings from Choons, Nell[2] and mamma, for my natal day!

A delightful present (by co-incidence, today!) from Mr Hollyer[3] of two great volumes, all my dear one's work, portraits in one, pictures in the other. A really great gift, a sort of index! I must add the sizes, owners, etc.

MONDAY, NOVEMBER 27 *The Studio* quotes from an American critic who has been writing on art from Chicago. He singles out Sir F. Leighton, Signor & Orchardson as the three artists of England, & says Orchardson's[4] *Mother & Child* is the work of art of the exhibition. Signor, in spite of muddy colours & 'stringy effects' is the only one who can be called a 'genius'.

---

1. The billiard room was also Mary's studio. **2.** Mary's half-sister, Eleanor. **3.** Frederic Hollyer, photographer. **4.** Sir William Quiller Orchardson (1832–1910), Scottish portraitist and painter of historical subjects.

TUESDAY, NOVEMBER 28 The evening made lively by the arrival of the 'Ariston'.[1] Phoebe & Ellen coming in with it. Andrews called in to learn to open the case, then Emma, & all the tunes were tried, singing to them, Phoebe & Ellen kneeling at each side & working the organ. Emma & Andrews standing up beside them, a pretty group, so happy, & my dear one lying in his niche, looking out upon the pleasure he has given. A nice evening!

WEDNESDAY, NOVEMBER 29 Awoke at five, & after coffee had a little quiet talk. He says he is considering how he can paint *Love Triumphant*. 'These subjects of mine are not new. I don't try to be new, there is nothing new to be done in that way, but they are annotations, which, appealing as they do to a different sense, may call people's attention to a broader & higher level of thought than is common. Fairy tales keep their place very much because all the extravagant & impossible feats are woven about & also upon some really great truth of human nature. Their teaching is generally good.'

Ethel enjoys our big piano, & after Signor & I go to bed she has the household in to sing there. Such a pleasure for them.

FRIDAY, DECEMBER 1 A day of very hard work for us all, Ethel helping me as my panel gets on.[2] Signor has considered it, thought of my colour scheme, & has given me advice about it. All, I feel certain, is good. I had proposed too deep & rich a colouring to make a good background for the brass cross. He says the quality of the glittering, rather pale colour of the brass does not require rich colour behind it, & that it would only look hard. I see it clearly & have proposed a general silvery tone.

I trust that by this day week dear Edward will have it in his chapel.

SATURDAY, DECEMBER 2 My love woke this morning at four, & while I turned again on my hinges, hoping for sleep, pig as I am, I heard the candle being lighted & a little scribble of some thought put down, then the light blown out, & be lit again in a few minutes, & so on.

SUNDAY, DECEMBER 3 18 degrees of frost. I am troubled about the roses, for there has been so much to do this week, with the digging & planting

1. The Ariston Organette, a hand-cranked reed instrument producing music on cardboard discs, manufactured in Leipzig. **2.** This was the gesso decorative panel for the chapel at the workhouse in St Albans, that Mary was designing for Edward Liddell.

of the small orchard, but need not have been anxious. Andrews forgets nothing. He is a real friend to me.

My letters done, I posted them, & atoned at Compton Church thro. a long dreary service for having gone out before the sermon last Sunday.

My work is set up in the drawing room, & I made some very necessary & important changes. Tomorrow I may shellac & silver.

MONDAY, DECEMBER 4 'Fatima' grows thin, & is already threadbare, or she seems so these days of hard work & despair over my chapel panel. It leaves me little to say. Read a little & had a little lotus eating, in the niche, laying my head on Signor's shoulder & talking as if we were in the land of afternoons. 'How I should like it' I said, & then 'how one would rot!'

But oh! a few more hours of lotus eating would be good for us!

WEDNESDAY, DECEMBER 6 The event of our day was a visit from Mr Augustus Hare.[1] Lady Victoria Rowe brought him. He has been living with Lady Waterford for the last year, a beautiful companion! I hope he will make her live for all the world. The book comes out next week. He says her letters are not quite so interesting as Lady Canning's, living so much alone. Could it be so? I feel as if such a mind ought to have come to fullest flower & fruit in stillness.

Lady Vicky, always a great admirer of the work, finds her red letter day here. They were struck by the poetry of *And he went away sorrowful*, & by the drawing of Lady de Vesci, *My beautiful lady*. Mr Hare declared that it was the finest portrait Signor had ever done, & regrets so much that he did not make a drawing of Lady Waterford when she was older & had more history, &, yes, when <u>he</u> was older, & that power of analysing had ripened in him.

SATURDAY, DECEMBER 9 Saturday, so fine for Edward's chapel! The sun is pouring his benediction down on it & him, dear fellow! The altar has been worked by a lady at St Albans, & the lectern carved by a little picture framer in St A., the hangings worked by Christina, Signor gives the cross, & Christina the altar vases.

---

1. Augustus Hare (1834–1903), a prolific writer of biographies and historical topography. The biography he published in 1893 was of the two sisters, Louisa, Lady Waterford and Charlotte, Lady Canning.

TUESDAY, DECEMBER 12 My dear one asked me to go & look at his large *Rich Man*, & I was able to say I thought the drop of the head was much firmer. I see still that the small version is more reticent, & more poetic, but he will get his music right by & by.

WEDNESDAY, DECEMBER 20 A dear little letter from Mrs Traquair, looking forward to seeing Signor. She has set him on a pedestal that he dislikes. 'I feel I must be such an imposter' he says.

SATURDAY, DECEMBER 23 Worries because turkeys did not come! How small a thing may give one trouble & unquiet.

Mr Spielmann[1] came. He is much better for Switzerland, & finds the Swiss so simple, & life so easy & pleasant. My sweet bright & well & enjoyed his evening talking & being talked to.

SUNDAY, DECEMBER 24 Mr Spielmann gives us a nice account of Herkomer,[2] how a delightful friendship with North[3] has reawakened in him his old pure love of art, when, in the old days, he rushed to every exhibition to look only for the Walkers. Herkomer has done North good too. The fact that Herkomer's mind should thus be open to receive so much from North, is in itself a proof that he is not the conceited man people believe. He says more about himself than we are accustomed to hear, but he is a real simple Tyrolean peasant still. I heard Signor say to Mr Spielmann, as they looked out together on the fir trees lighted up by a beautiful sunlight 'I assure you I am never without a sense of awe & reverence, that is as a continual worship.'

MONDAY, DECEMBER 25 What a wonderful Xmas day. Mr Spielmann left early. Signor has enjoyed his visit. He is a very pleasant little man.

Our happy little household give us kindly greeting. The day is lovely.

---

1. Marion Spielmann (1858–1948), art critic and editor of the *Magazine of Art*. In the 1880s he wrote extensively on Watts's work, and asked permission to write the official biography, an idea that was vetoed by the Wattses. **2.** Sir Hubert von Herkomer (1849–1914), British artist of Bavarian extraction. After some years as one of the group of illustrators for *The Graphic* magazine he painted social realism subjects, and started and ran the Herkomer School of Art in Bushey, Hertfordshire. He was a pioneer filmmaker. He commissioned Henry Robinson, the American architect, to build him a Bavarian castle in Bushey. **3.** John William North (1842–1924), landscape painter and illustrator.

I ran to church, but the bells stopped half way! I turned aside, disliking to go in late & feeling that no communion would be like the one under sun & sky, upon a sheltered bank with nature all about me. Small thoughtfulness, even if not worries, are a great hindrance to contemplation. In church one has no time for it, & one must be alone. I have not enough of it.

Annie[1] who began the day at five, all the maids sitting on her bed while she opened Santa Claus parcels, is supremely happy. After tea they all danced, & enjoyed themselves in the billiard room, the little organ coming in well.

TUESDAY, DECEMBER 26 Neither plum pudding nor any other Christmas orgies has disorganized S. in the least. I called him to come & see a rainbow beautifully circling round the niche. He was pleased but wished it had come on Christmas day. I told him boxing day was the right one for spirits to promise favours.

WEDNESDAY, DECEMBER 27 I rolled my head in an orange silk turban, threw round me an old cloak with fur, & went to Signor, offering as a model for the *Rich man*. I feel sure he will not get the large one right without some suggestion from nature. He accepted the offer instantly & began to draw in pencil from my bowed head & back.

---

1. The young ward of Mary's sister, Ethel.

1896

In 1895 Mary had had the opportunity to start on her most ambitious work of art. Compton village needed a new cemetery, and bought land from the More-Molyneux family, the lords of the manor, for the purpose. As soon as she heard of the scheme, Mary put to Signor the idea that they could build a Cemetery Chapel on the site. She would design and decorate it, running a class for local people to take part in making the terracotta decorated tiles she envisaged for the exterior. They would be taking part in an initiative she and Watts were already supporting, and about which they were enthusiastic. This was the Home Arts and Industries Association (HAIA), and its aim was to teach classes in some of the fast-vanishing crafts to people in rural communities with no experience. If they worked in groups, they would, said Eglantyne Jebb, the founder of the movement, be able to achieve creative results, often saving ancient skills from disappearing. The Wattses were already on the committee of the HAIA, and Mary saw the opportunity to take an active part. Would they be able, Mary asked Watts, to offer the chapel to the village as a gift? He agreed, and said he would pay for it with fees from his portrait commissions.

The parish accepted their offer gratefully, and the building of one of the most interesting and unique small pieces of architecture of the era was initiated. Plans were drawn up in 1895, approved by a recently retired architect, George Redmayne, and the building was well under way in 1896. The exterior was finished two years later and decorated with terracotta tiles packed with symbols from many sources. Inside, the space was decorated quite differently, with Mary designing gesso reliefs painted with a dazzling array of angels, and the tree of life, in the four quarters of the circular interior. The chapel was almost completed before Signor's death in 1904. Throughout the project, Mary gives us a view of its progress in her 'Fatima' diary. After Signor's death, she wrote her book, *The Word in the Pattern* (1905), explaining her aim, in her chapel, of 'reviving in some degree that living quality which was in all decoration when patterns had meaning'.

The early part of the diary for 1896 is unfortunately missing.

FRIDAY, AUGUST 28 *Limnerslease* Every minute that I can spare must go to my 'path'[1] & to my 'garment'.[2] But having no temptation to write, I can the better see how hopeless it is to capture Signor's real 'views' upon the 'religions'. He has not put them into words himself, it is an air he breathes, & it can be only breathed out again from his pictures. Ten minutes in silence before one of them & his spirit will come & speak to the spirit, overwhelm it with a pure clear aim of aspiration, with the essence of the matter, which way to put it into words. Then it is as a dried petal by the living rose!

Down to our sweet haven – a lovely day.

WEDNESDAY, AUGUST 26 A dear letter from Mrs Josephine Butler:[3] 'Your expressions of affection are to me very precious. I have you & your husband often, together, in my mind's eye & my heart.'

'Ah' S. said 'she has, I think, taken very much to you. You are an accroche-coeur. Every one loves you.' I love that he should think so. It makes him smile, & that lights up my whole heart and soul.

---

1. Mary was designing a decoration for the exterior of the chapel, which she called 'the path of the just'. On each of the four sections of the circular path she designed a frieze illustrating different human attributes. The pattern is of angels flanking a central cross, with a bird each side of it. First is 'the path of truth', with the owl, bird of truth and wisdom. Angels carry roundels showing emblems of truth, for example, a set of scales, weighing true. Next is 'the path of hope', with the peacock, bird of hope, then 'the path of light', the eagle, and finally, 'the path of love', the pelican. **2.** Mary's design for what she described as 'the garment of praise' is based on the Judaic 'veil of the temple', separating the outside world from the sacred space within. **3.** Josephine Butler (1828–1906), active feminist and Christian. She worked tirelessly for the improvement of the lot of women, especially prostitutes. Watts painted her portrait in 1895, and she wrote to him: 'I thank you that you have not made that poor woman look severe or bitter, but only sad and purposeful' (M.S. Watts, 'Portrait cat.', p.25).

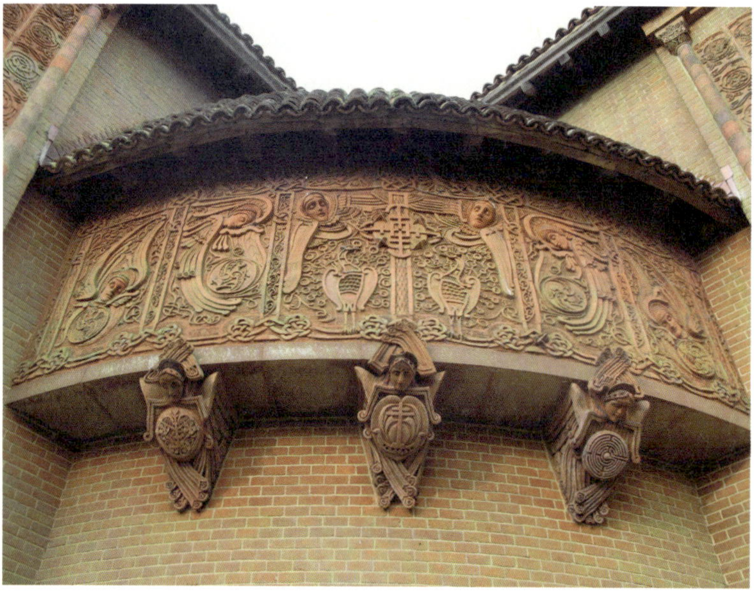

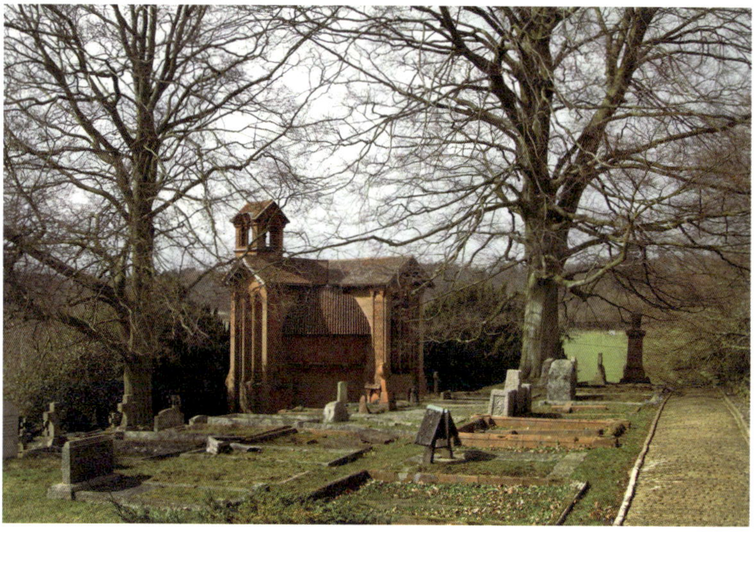

(TOP) Watts Cemetery Chapel, frieze with the peacock of 'Hope'

(ABOVE) Watts Cemetery Chapel, designed by Mary Watts

THURSDAY, AUGUST 27 Mrs Butler here at eleven, & we had a happy morning. She is so beautiful in her largeness! 'The kingdom of heaven is for all, even the downtrodden, mud besmirched.'

Signor & she had a little talk together by the fire, & he gave her his *Love Triumphant* telling her how he endeavours to speak to all peoples of whatever creed. 'I can't help their creeds' he said '& nobody can. They are necessary to humanity, but are allowed to become too all important.'

She tells us that after her long life & conflict, in the last ten years, feeble as she is & alone, her sense of hope is constantly growing.

SATURDAY, AUGUST 29 August dying! We realize we are in our sixth happy year in this darling little place. I tear my sweet away from his big pictures as often as I can, & we wander together looking down upon our sweet garden, & seeing how it is growing now to the sister wood, no longer looking the parvenu! A few more years if I am so happy, & we shall have shade & shelter on our lawn, & I shall venture on some bright parterres.

We went early to the chapel. It is growing well, & keeps a pleasant proportion if only the roof does not spoil it!

SUNDAY, AUGUST 30 My head is full of The Path of the Just, & I am making notes.

Since Egypt, my desire to say something in art has been a casting back, to send out a shoot from the root again, & I find myself, in this, in a sort of harmony with things generally, of this time. If this is so then my little effort is alive, at least.

MONDAY, AUGUST 31 *Limnerslease* Thompson greets us at the station with the news that the beautiful *Alps*[1] has come back with a hole burnt in it, a hole as if made by a red hot poker from behind, the paint blackened & charred ready to break away, & no word of explanation! Signor takes it perfectly calmly! I cannot.

TUESDAY, SEPTEMBER 1 He was telling me this morning of a beautiful symbol, human life being as a candle, the flame the soul, consuming the material & disappearing itself at last into the air. 'That is really the reason why I wish to be cremated, or one of them at least. The material being,

1. Watts's painting *Sunset on the Alps*, 1888, loaned to Toynbee Hall.

(by cremation,) compelled as it were to follow the spiritual. It proves how little of us is really material, we go into flame & air & what is left is just a handful of ashes – & the flame in the work <u>will</u> live as long as paint & canvas can last'.

WEDNESDAY, SEPTEMBER 2 Thirteen pictures from a Mr William Jarvis came today.

How should I your true love know (dated 1841, when Watts was 25) pleases Signor, & four pictures of horses, *Cavaliers & Roundheads*, & two Hawking pictures, about 1840 (one is dated) are charming. A beautiful little portrait of Mr William Jarvis (*père*) done, by the inscription, certainly by 1839. The canvas of *How should I yr true love know* – is addressed G.F. Watts 14 Roberts Road, Hampstead Road, his first studio. He remembers the Jarvises well, kind friends & pleasant people. Mr William Jarvis (*fils*) was a barrister. The widow, & owner of the pictures, promises to come to see us.

A good morning at ceiling panels.

SUNDAY, SEPTEMBER 6 Sweet this morning, speaking of the loss in pairs to art! Mason & Walker, & now Millais & Leighton.[1] 'Art in England practically without a head.'

A young man will come forward to take the lead, one may be sure.

WEDNESDAY, SEPTEMBER 9 I have a wonderful morning at the British Museum. I am shown first a marvellous drawing, a *Pietà* of Michael Angelo's.

Then to the ms. Room with the keeper Mr Warner, who showed me the first Celtic ms. I have ever seen. The Book of Durham. A wonderful work! It takes one's breath away to think that all-devouring love of beautifying & enriching the book as the holy man pored over it & wrought those marvellous lines, & coloured in that delicate tender way his beautiful devices. Under the magnifying glass only can one realize what the finish & perfection was. 'Edilwold' (a Saxon note says, made 200 years later) painted it, 'of men, none knew better how to do this'.

---

1. Leighton died on January 25, 1896; after his death Millais was elected as President of the Royal Academy but died on August 13 of the same year.

TUESDAY, SEPTEMBER 29 Mr Gilbert[1] came to sit. Signor just breathed upon it. It is a fine rendering, *résumé,* of him. We are glad to find him looking better, less nervous.

FRIDAY, OCTOBER 2 S. at my side, sitting up in his white flannel robe, his silver hair with the candle light shining thro' it. We talk of the burnt picture at Toynbee, & I said in my wrath, that he must not lend pictures for the drawing room wall there again. 'Well, not any thing important, I think' he replied & I still pressed for putting his foot down. He said 'Do not let us do or think anything ungenerous. The pictures are meant to be of service. We must not forget that'. Then he went on 'I am always so terribly afraid in case we should allow the best we have in us to lapse'.

Morris released from his sufferings.[2] Mrs Holiday told me yesterday that he had all his life had a great fear of death. In these last days he had allowed himself to think 'there might a place where I would wander about again'.

I kissed my Lamb tonight saying 'safe, safe with me?' – & he answered 'yes with all these strong men dropping around, it is wonderful to feel safe.'

SATURDAY, OCTOBER 3 Hollyer photographed the horse[3] many times.

SUNDAY, OCTOBER 4 We went out, after a fine interval, to the Grange.[4] We knew there were two sad hearts there, & we found them both in. They were touched at my darling's going to them. They know it is so seldom that he is moved to leave his work.

They are very good. Georgie is determined to be brave, but to both it is the cutting off of just such a friend as Leighton was to Signor, even perhaps a more unbroken intercourse, for every Sunday of the year he breakfasted with them.

She dwells upon the thought of his life, accomplishing so much, fulfilling so much, work she believes that has never been half recognised which will go on living. She says 'he is not dead', & that is true.

A wet afternoon – we are alone till Phil[5] came in, & stayed an hour. A good fellow & able to comfort his father again.

---

1. Sir Alfred Gilbert, sculptor. **2.** William Morris died on October 3, 1896. **3.** *Physical Energy.* **4.** Where Edward and Georgie Burne-Jones lived. They were close, almost lifelong friends to William Morris. **5.** Philip Burne-Jones, son of Edward and Georgiana Burne-Jones.

TUESDAY, OCTOBER 6 'A great art revival. Morris, Gilbert, & Burne Jones have shaped it, I suppose that is not too much to say.' Signor's verdict on the New Gallery exhibition, which we went to see. Closed, for the funeral at Kelmscott today.[1] We were fortunate in just walking in & finding ourselves there alone! A wonderful advance on a few years ago. The little leaven is working, & one was surprised after an hour there, to come out into hideous streets again & see the big ugliness still there for miles & miles on every side in mass & in detail. Yet I believe & have always said to Signor that a love of beauty sleeps somewhere in the soul of all men, though habit & circumstance have forgotten it. It is awakening now.

We were carrying the portrait of Gilbert to Maida Vale, to give it to him himself. It was a nice plan, though rather cumbersome company in the brougham! Then on to Regent Street. A wreath of laurel lay upon the case holding the splendid books,[2] & on it a sonnet in Walter Crane's writing. Touching, beautiful words, a life's monument to the great dead. Thro' a storm of wind and pelting rain he is being laid to rest at Kelmscott today.

We next find ourselves at Gilbert's, received by Mrs Gilbert, & the daughter. Mrs Gilbert has a feeble thin refined face – with a look of suffering & of struggle. He has ceased to look as young as he used. Work & worry tell. The wizard studio is more fascinating than ever. He is conjuring now a dragon from a shell! What exquisite fancy. Why do people ask him to do full length portraits of great big people!

We enquired for poor Du Maurier[3] on our way back.

WEDNESDAY, OCTOBER 7 Georgie Burne Jones here, who gave us a touching account of dear Morris's funeral. His coffin was met at the station by a waggoner & his wain, the cart just trimmed with vines & flowers by one of the young men in his works! All simple. He was laid to rest under the green sod. A wild wet day for it, the rain just stopping for those ten minutes by the grave side.

---

1. William Morris's funeral. **2.** Some volumes from the Kelmscott Press were on show at the New Gallery in honour of William Morris. **3.** George du Maurier (1834–96), artist and *Punch* cartoonist. He frequented Little Holland House in the 1860s, and wrote, of his first visit, 'Watts, who is a grand fellow, is their painter in ordinary; the best part of the house has been turned into his studio, & he lives there & is worshipped till his manliness hath almost departed, I should fancy.'

THURSDAY, OCTOBER 8 Signor walked out with me, stepping along so lightly to look at a Bicycle I thought would do for us, in the Kensington High Street. While I was out General Beadle came to see Signor & told him Du Maurier was dead! As we went down the Kensington High Street, sandwich men passed carrying the words 'Death of the Author of Trilby'. He dies the hero of his last bit of work!

In this 'Fatima' how many names from the company of English artists have been written down as drawn beyond the veil? Leighton, Millais, Morris, & Du Maurier – all at that fatal age of the sixties!

FRIDAY, OCTOBER 9 *Limnerslease* Here in our dear little home again. The sun shone & we drove out in the luxurious little brougham, laughing at our sharp limitations.

SATURDAY, OCTOBER 10 We hear Du Maurier is to be cremated at Woking today, & buried on Tuesday at Hampstead. Like Signor, he chooses 'to go away in a little flame'.

What a bunch of violets Andrews picked for us! Our garden is blown about but still gay with Michaelmas Daisies, white & lilac, & with Dahlias, & I have made our little room alive with them.

Signor is at home again in his niche, & I sit with my luxurious table, reading to him.

MONDAY, OCTOBER 12 We are getting back into our old ways, & feel as if we had never left this dear life. At breakfast we were talking over that book *The Children of the Ghetto*,[1] that so absorbs us now. I said to him 'every book of the kind that I read now makes me feel certain that we are moving on towards a universal creed'.

'Yes' he answered 'but that means an immense advance still in liberality. Religious people have not yet learnt to see how much more temperament & climate have to do with creed. If that had been understood, Dissent & Sectarianism would never have excited the horror it has. Depend upon it when people sacrifice for a principle you may differ from them as much as you like, but you must respect them.

TUESDAY, OCTOBER 13 He is working much upon his *Time, Death, & Judgment*. I regret *Time*'s face! but perhaps he will conquer in the end, & surpass the old fine dim-eyed one.

1. *The Children of the Ghetto* by Israel Zangwill (1892).

Love has spread a more sheltering wing round *Life* & I think that is made more beautiful by it. He is piling up the hideousness of *Mammon*,[1] beginning to feel afraid of it becoming an exaggeration.

WEDNESDAY, OCTOBER 14 A letter from Mr Alfred Gurney. He asks what Signor thought of the chapel.[2] He told me to say 'he was astonished by the excellence of the work, & delighted by the fullness & completeness of the idea'.

I ran to Monkshatch. The chalk pits full of radiant colour, the white cliff wonderful, such a grand Titian white & grey, rising above the filmy shades of tender greys & greens & reds, & here & there deep yew green! An atom of flesh & blood was on the grass below the cliff, a stoat or weasel at play, racing, running round & round, tossing himself in to the air, coming down breast upwards, breast downwards, the white vest on him gleaming as he twisted & flew in a glorious dance for joy in life. I stood hidden from him & watched for long. Those are wise creatures that choose their lodgings in that chalk pit.

FRIDAY, OCTOBER 16 I am giving finishing touches to the panels,[3] so that most of them may go up tomorrow. I have felt as if the ceiling would never be off my shoulders.

SUNDAY, OCTOBER 18 Our little grey Fluff[4] is very ill. At one time we thought him dying. His dear little mistresses all in tears & I with words of Signor's have a kind of feeling that footsteps were coming into the house heavy with the first message of death.

MONDAY, OCTOBER 19 Signor has a dear little simple note from Mrs Du Maurier. He had begged her not to answer his, but she said she must. What a wife she has been.

A beautiful letter from Mrs Butler too, filled with the joy of possessing those photographs of the pictures. She says they are speaking to many in her Geneva home.

---

1. Watts's painting *Mammon*, condemning greed and riches. **2.** This is one of the few recorded comments by Watts on Mary's chapel, but it leaves no doubt that he was very impressed not only by the work's appearance, but by the idea behind its decoration. Watts painted Rev. Alfred Gurney in 1895. **3.** This was Mary's second ceiling, again in white gesso, for the hall at Limnerslease. **4.** One of the long line of small dogs in the Limnerslease household.

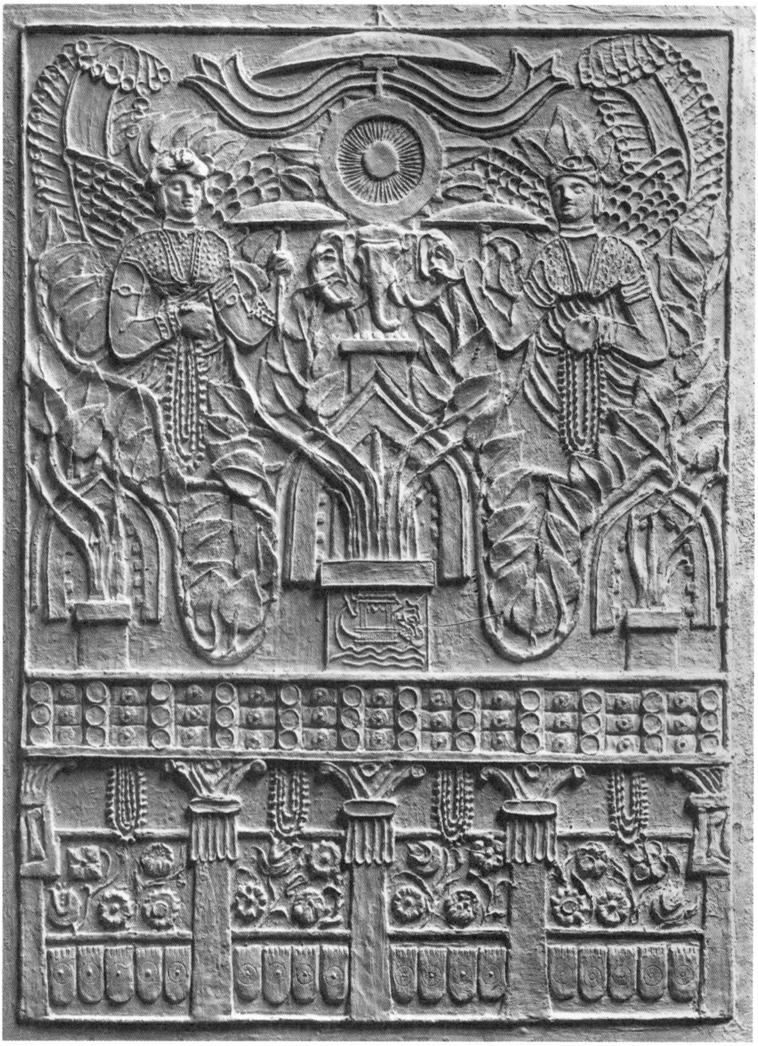

Chaldean panel from the hall ceiling at Limnerslease, gesso relief, designed by Mary Watts

Andrews & Steadman[1] have got 7 panels up today. What a lift! If I had had a peaceful morning I might have finished the last 4 but my head fails.

THURSDAY, OCTOBER 22 'I don't mind error on the road to truth' Signor said this morning, talking of what Mrs Wyndham had said about the bad ugly patterns that were being done all over the country now by the technical class pupils, & by our Home Arts too, sometimes. I do not know myself who is to decide about what is ugly or not. I think the roof of St Paul's is glorious, but seldom meet any one who even likes it, on the whole!

MONDAY, OCTOBER 26 A man from Warner's about the chapel bell. It is to ring 'C' as low as can be made for the size, 31 inches in diameter. The man was surprised by the unusual little chapel. We are to have an inscription.

TUESDAY, OCTOBER 27 I try to design. If I had only got all my designs done I should not fear. They will come, I hope. The garment seems coming.

TUESDAY, NOVEMBER 3 My dear one came in & asked me if I would like to put 'Be my voice neither feared, nor forgotten' on the chapel bell. His own dear words thought out for me! Make his voice ring in the bell he gives, so long as it lasts.

Inscription

'This bell is given with the Chapel
to Compton, by George Frederic Watts
& his wife Mary – 1896 –
Be my voice neither feared, nor forgotten.'

My love very happy this morning because I had my 1st turn on my bicycle, Andrews kindly holding me up. He ran about, & finally I got upon it. I daresay as a plaything it may be good for me. I feel sure it will give me new power.

---

1. John Thomas Steadman (sometimes Stedman) (1858–1942). He was one of the four craftsmen Mary employed to help in the chapel and pottery. He was a wheelwright and carpenter. A Compton man, he studied at Guildford School of Art for an unknown period, and was responsible for the low-relief carving on the chapel door.

THURSDAY, NOVEMBER 5 Poynter is the new president.[1] Signor thinks him a good man but dry. It seems a good appointment to me, as Richmond was out of the running, apparently.

SATURDAY, NOVEMBER 7 A good day upon my veil. I hope the weight of it is lifting. I must expect to go through the usual processes of feeling, hopes before beginning, & then an ever increasing certainty that they won't be realized. Then something very like despair, when utter failure seems inevitable, & then one more struggle & it comes, fought out, & no one knows when it is done that it has not run from one's finger ends.

TUESDAY, NOVEMBER 10 What a day! May & Andrew's 23rd wedding day. We were just going up to luncheon when Hallam walked in.[2] We have not seen him since that May time when we went to the Briary. Father and mother both gone. He talks of reading to his boys, so one hopes he is taking up life with the new generation. He walked with us to Monkshatch, & the dear people were pleased. Signor had the little Sonnets & *Love Triumphant* for May. We had a lovely little luncheon in their green drawing room, & oh what a lovely day.

WEDNESDAY, NOVEMBER 11 Mr Deuchars started class work, enlarging & drawing out the Veil from my design. He can help me much.

Wobbled on my bicycle, & felt very angry.

THURSDAY, NOVEMBER 19 The day of our party.[3] I had planned everything, & with Andrews & Steadman to carry it out all was arranged. I have sent about 110 invitations, & how to seat them is the trouble. Unluckily I was quite knocked up by sickness & pain. I shut my eyes & thought of the All Pervading Good, & said Spirit must overcome Matter. I got up, & went to see about everything, always aware of great pain, but going as Aunt Amy would have done, saying to myself 'Spirit can't be overcome by matter.' I came back when things seemed ready & rested till 6.30, dressed & went down feeling well, & that all would go well. Our guests arrived, & after taking off hats & cloaks in the housekeeper's room, came through the hall where Signor & I greeted them, &

---

1. Sir Edward Poynter became the President of the Royal Academy following the deaths of Leighton and his replacement, Millais, in 1896. William Blake Richmond had initially been in contention for the position. **2.** Hallam Tennyson, son of the poet. **3.** An evening for friends and neighbours to see Watts's paintings.

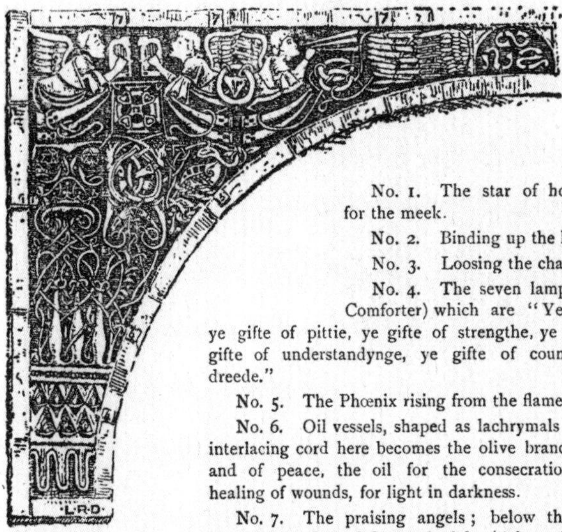

No. 1. The star of hope, and the crown for the meek.

No. 2. Binding up the heart.

No. 3. Loosing the chains.

No. 4. The seven lamps of the Spirit (the Comforter) which are "Ye gifte of wisdome, ye gifte of pittie, ye gifte of strengthe, ye gifte of comfait, ye gifte of understandynge, ye gifte of counyinge, ye gifte of dreede."

No. 5. The Phœnix rising from the flames.

No. 6. Oil vessels, shaped as lachrymals or tear bottles; the interlacing cord here becomes the olive branch in sign of victory and of peace, the oil for the consecration of mourning, for healing of wounds, for light in darkness.

No. 7. The praising angels; below them trumpets which bear the symbol of day and night ("the red day and the black day"—Rig Veda), very often found on the Celtic crosses, and carried down to this day, over the doors of wayside inns, where, in the name of "The Chequers," this sign of the hospitality of the old hostel still lingers.

8. A Celtic monogram for the Sanctus or Holy, Holy, Holy! with the wings of the Spirit on either side.

Drawing by Louis Deuchars of the terracotta 'wall veil' above the chapel door, designed by Mary Watts, illustration taken from Mary's book *The Word in the Pattern* (1905)

they took their places on the benches & chairs & in the end we had a few spare seats!

A moonlight walk & my love's work! I hope the evening is never to be forgotten.

FRIDAY, NOVEMBER 20 'Ten years together, I hope you remember this is our wedding day' my love awoke saying to me. Ten years of holding his hand completed. I think of the spirit companion I have had these full ten years.

What I have had can surely never again be lost by me. Rich & sweet my days have been. They are a little more full now perhaps. He has made me a little unhappy by saying 'The 1st years we were more together than now. We are seldom alone now' he says.

SUNDAY, NOVEMBER 22 Sweet May. I say to Signor she is like the Lady Ride o'cock horse, only she makes music wherever she goes. Signor says 'she is so well balanced' & perhaps that is true. It is balance & tact we all need.

TUESDAY, NOVEMBER 24 A new 'Fatima', & 'Fatima 10th' is fading away. What a poor creature she has been.

Thompson here, & my day was spent grinding at getting plates out in plaster, to make moulds for the class to model upon.

Thompson's report of the health of London is 'that they are all dying like flies up there'.[1] This north east wind means yellow fog.

WEDNESDAY, NOVEMBER 25 Incessant work for the class, but I did not find it hard somehow.

My birthday – 48.

THURSDAY, NOVEMBER 26 Work!! If I could but have thought out all my patterns for the class this summer how glad I should have been. By & by I hope to have so big a bunch to draw upon I shall not have this rush for each day. As it is we got things ready for those who did not come. Mr Deuchars has done decoration for plates to encourage the weak members to work neatly.

FRIDAY, NOVEMBER 27 Went to see the chapel belfry to settle about height.

It does not look too high now we think.

SATURDAY, NOVEMBER 28 My dear one & I had a little argument upon genius, or rather more particularly upon his own imagination, which refuses to see anything but a sincere painstaking endeavour when looking at his own work. Sees in all the imperfect.

Speaking of genius S. said 'Millais had it (it was shackled by circumstances later) but I can hardly say that any other man in the Academy had it.'

WEDNESDAY, DECEMBER 23 Paying off today the frame bill, £109, without a fear! Giving me £50 in my bank for small cheques, & I can send my little ones without fear of overdrawing, & the chapel well nigh paid for.

---

1. Thompson's joke about the effect of winter fogs on the health of Londoners.

THURSDAY, DECEMBER 24 Amongst other letters today is one bringing Signor the 1st quarterly payment of a pension from the Royal Academy. It was some time before he could realize it was not something he had to pay. When he did he told me that he had hoped the Academicians had agreed to do away with this pension. He tried to get this done years ago.

A Xmas Eve, with a ripple on the face of the waters! My love so angry with me for not having the brougham to go down the village with my little gifts.

When he was soothed again, in the evening, I having walked at the tail of the pony cart, as if I was going to Tyburn to appease him, I told him he had gone near to breaking our marriage contract, that when we were angry we were not to say things that could not be forgotten.

FRIDAY, DECEMBER 25 Awake on another Xmas day to be blessed by him.

Signor & I walked up to Monkshatch & stayed till it was dark. I walked home carrying a row of Trollopes for Signor, Andrew & sweet May's present, while he carried a lantern. A mild evening. It was something to have him walking up & down so vigorously! Are we to have another ten happy years?

SUNDAY, DECEMBER 27 We awoke this morning to talk about the Leighton pictures, I have an occasional fear that the two exhibitions may a little compete. A thought that does not enter Signor's mind, but I feel it will into the critics'.[1]

Signor says he expects the exhibition to surpass expectations in so far as beauty of drawing, noble composition, & sentiment are in question. They may (the later work especially) disappoint by a certain similarity.

We read Trollope this evening! Signor likes it & says it is like an 'afternoon call'. I tell him he shall make all mine for me! I confess I am rather weary of being amused by Trollope's people.

MONDAY, DECEMBER 28 I have put off the class again so that we have 3 weeks holiday. Mr Deuchars being laid up with inflamed eyes frees me.

---

1. Watts's exhibition at the New Gallery had just opened. The retrospective exhibition of Leighton's work at the Royal Academy opened in January, 1897, a year after his death.

We read the 3rd volume of Hare[1] tonight. The March Hares seem to survive in the family traits & he is one of them. It is impossible to read without feeling how much is highly coloured, & how very undesirable it is that any one should turn out their family behaviour in that way for the public amusement.

TUESDAY, DECEMBER 29 My dear one tells me if the day is not fine I am to send Mr Deuchars in the brougham. (He has to go to London about his eyes.) 'If it is a bad day he might take cold. We must have nothing on our conscience, at least as little as possible.'

The newspapers. *Times*, *Telegraph*, & *Daily Graphic* speak well of Signor's show. They accept the challenge he has given that the symbol (the moral almost) is more important than anything else. They say the Leighton pictures will be an example also of another painter who has approached his work with a noble purpose, if with a different aim. A devotion to the melodious, in idea, colour, line, a passion for completeness, are the qualities we may expect to see in the Academy show.

I feel of the two painters the star that led each was different, but they belonged to the same constellation.

WEDNESDAY, DECEMBER 30 The post brings us cuttings from newspapers. I handed them to Signor, who found the *Chronicle* (probably, we think, George Moore[2]) has determined to demolish him. I don't think he will, & all through the article one feels somehow that he found it difficult to say all the nasty things he does, in the face of my gentle lamb's spirit.

Andrew here. We made him spurt smoke and flame by extracts from the *Chronicle*. He would hang George Moore!

THURSDAY, DECEMBER 31 The last day!

How much loss of dear friends. How much blessed quiet work.

The Chapel risen. The New Gallery filled, all thro' my love's sweet flame of aspiration burning steadily at my side. Just, tolerant, appreciative, generous, noble. I think of all the happy days I have had these ten years, & how he has gained in health & vigour.

I drive to see Ethel. Home to end the year in the niche, the last waking hour of it, & to wake at 5.30 to be blest by my love on a New Year's morning.

---

1. Augustus Hare's autobiography. **2.** George Moore (1852–1933), Irish novelist and critic.

1898

This was the year when a young girl in her teens named Lily Mackintosh came to live with Watts and Mary as their ward. She was an orphan, and had lived for some time with Mary's sister, Christina, nicknamed Choons, and her husband, Edward Liddell. Lily had often been to stay with the Wattses in London and Compton, and, despite Signor's misgivings, she settled quickly and easily, and was enjoying her time as a pupil at Roedean School. Watts had been involved with its foundation, and knew the Lawrence sisters who had started it, from the time when he had a studio in Brighton in the 1880s.

The year 1898 was momentous for Mary on another count. Her Cemetery Chapel was consecrated and opened, with its external decorations completed. In the autumn, after a holiday in the north of Scotland with her sister Ethel, staying for part of the time at Aldourie Castle, she came back with her energy renewed, and began on the quite different decorations of the interior of her chapel. They were to take six years to complete.

Mary had trained a workforce in terracotta, and wanted to provide work for many of those who had become skilled modellers in their own right; she could also add pot-throwing and painting to their skills. She put to Watts the idea that, now the exterior decorations were done, she might start a pottery. He was extremely worried at first that she was taking on more than she could cope with, but he was finally convinced by her determination, and her willingness to give the project up after a year if it did not prove successful. Mary re-employed the kiln burner who had worked on the chapel, and there were members of her pottery class, some extremely skilled, who could adapt to the new challenges of

G.F. Watts, *Portrait of John Everett Millais*, 1871, oil on canvas, reproduced by kind permission of the National Portrait Gallery

modelling the sundials, gravestones, and garden pots and ornaments the Compton Pottery was to make. Ernest George was asked to design four cottages for pottery workers.

Watts was commissioned to produce a sculpture of his old friend, Alfred Lord Tennyson, to stand outside Lincoln Cathedral, in memory of this outstanding son of Lincolnshire. He was delighted, but wanted a suitable space to work on it near to Limnerslease. The figure of the poet was to be twice life-size. The Wattses were able to buy a high-roofed barn that adjoined their property, and there was the possibility of making a short railway track, so that the sculpture could be drawn in and out. Watts would be able to stand back from it and see it from a distance, and work on it outside in fine weather. Known as the Barn Studio, it was ready on December 13. Mary wrote 'when I went up at sunset a great prism of white lay thrown against the dark background of the barn. The Laureate is to have birth upon nothing less than the Goddess of Dawn. He is to grow out of her, a son of the Morning.'

SATURDAY, JANUARY 1 *Limnerslease* This evening I was able to be in the niche beside him, & read him the *Times* article on J. Millais' pictures gathered now at Burlington House.[1]

MONDAY, JANUARY 3 Gerry came bringing her wine of life with her, to stir our hearts & souls & minds. She is going to follow the sun & is off to Cannes on the 14th.

I read her Mrs Alfred Waterhouse's[2] 'verses', a sweet little volume just come to me from her, in a garden dress, & with poems straight from the heart, through the beautiful house of her beautiful mind. Gerry springs to them, & doubles my pleasure in reading them.

TUESDAY, JANUARY 4 A delightful day having long hours with Gerry & in the evening, our little concert[3] quite a success.

---

1. Sir John Everett Millais's retrospective exhibition at the Royal Academy, a year and a half after his death. **2.** Mrs Alfred Waterhouse, sister-in law to George Redmayne, the architect who helped Mary with the plans and structure of her chapel. **3.** There were frequent concerts at Limnerslease, and later in the Hostel at the Gallery, organised by Mary. Professional musicians, potters and locals took part, and were all required to perform.

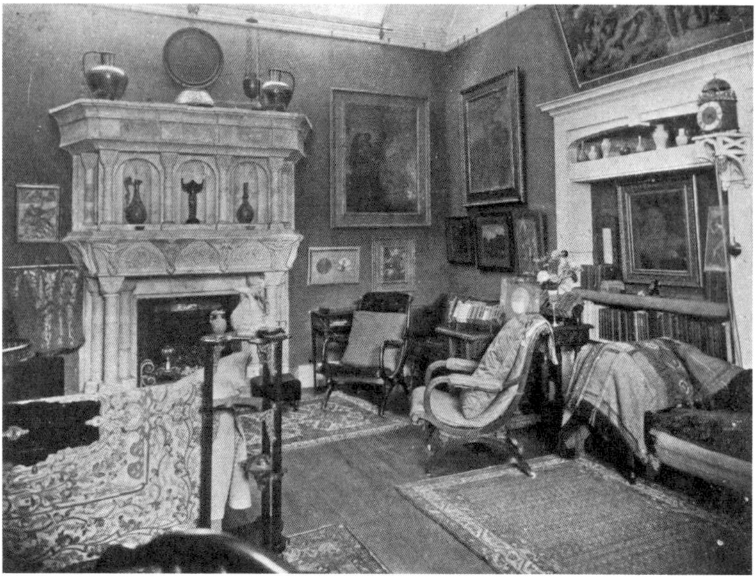

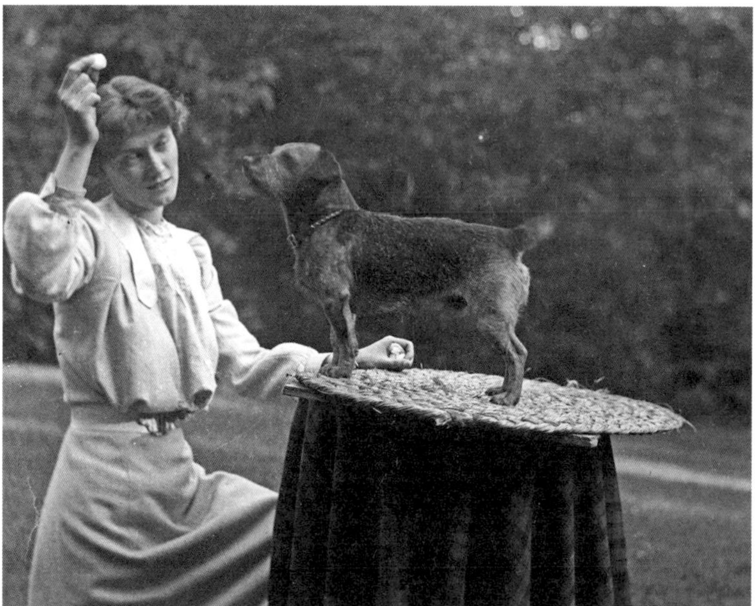

(TOP) Mary Watts's studio at Limnerslease, with the fireplace designed by her

(ABOVE) Lily Mackintosh in the garden at Limnerslease

FRIDAY, JANUARY 7 A letter from Andrew Hichens this morning telling me that Signor had apparently refused the offer of the government to cast & erect the statue![1] I was disturbed & vexed not because the casting will be thrown upon him. I was averse from the first to the plan & wondered that Signor accepted it, but because I think it must seem so ungracious to many people who have taken such trouble to bring it about.

Andrew is very distressed & vexed – but Signor was firm, tho' May & I & Andrew said what we could.

SATURDAY, JANUARY 8 Our children's party today. We christened the new room. Tea spread there for something like 60 & for us, in the north studio.[2] All went merrily.

After tea the north studio was cleared, & Lily & Vi,[3] from a chain, had a fishing rod with a bag of bon-bons on it for which the children jumped. When each had had its bag, Lily was ready as a dwarf to give away crackers to each child. To some she seemed too awful & they wept.

Then musical chairs followed & shrieks of laughter, Lily playing well & cheerily. It was extremely bright. They went away cheering, near & far.

WEDNESDAY, JANUARY 12 Today S. compared past & present.

'The world is worse than it was when Christ came. The peasants he spoke to did not kill their children for a little money. They did not drink as we do.'

I said 'they had not the difficulties we have to contend with'.

'No' he answered. 'Civilization & increased population bring increased complications. Blind faith has been preached & it has been more than useless. Without Science & reason on either side faith is useless, supporters of doctrine & dogma being not leaders of progress but eventually opposed to it.'

Dear Edward Liddell came. He read us *Three Men in a Boat* later.

THURSDAY, JANUARY 13 I had about nine hours sleep last night. Taking Bromide crystals every other night. They suit me, I think. What a boon to get back my sleep & lose the tension.

---

1. *Physical Energy.* **2.** Parties were often held in Mary's 'north studio', also sometimes referred to as 'the billiard room'. **3.** Lily Mackintosh and a friend.

Lily has written quite a pretty little accompaniment to Signor's song 'Little brown brother',[1] the little seed song in Mrs Earle's book that charms him so.

FRIDAY, JANUARY 14 Signor said this morning 'When I look at that little bird's wing (a little dead tit we had brought in) & see the exquisite adaptation of every bit of it to its purpose, I know that that same care about everything should be the religion of our life. That is what I call the Love of God.'

I went over to fetch Choons. Brenda & Rufus[2] out for the first time for weeks. Poor little souls. They look sorry for themselves.

SATURDAY, JANUARY 15 My dear one took a gloomy view of our being in touch with our child,[3] telling me he saw we must give her up as she was rooted there with Choons and Ed, only a cut flower here. It depressed me very much as I do know the life is old for her child-like spirits, here with us. I let her young spirits have their full vent, even if it costs us something of her company (I don't feel that it does). I think Choons must have suggested this to him yesterday & it has fallen into his mind on a grey day, & turned everything into gloom. He came to bed early, leaving the field to 'Cled'[4] who is of course their boon companion in their games, & telling them stories.

TUESDAY, JANUARY 18 Choons reminded me of a story of Tennyson which I had forgotten. Colonel Graham telling us in '68 when he was a young subaltern in the artillery that on one of his first visits to Farringford and the poet and his family, he had, in talking, said 'Mr Tennyson, when you shoot your rooks ...' but a look had stayed the sentence & Mr Tennyson said in a voice of thunder 'Shoot my rooks?!!' Colonel Graham added he had never said any words that he so regretted.

THURSDAY, JANUARY 20 Lily writes long letters, happy at school[5] again with just enough regret for home.

---

1. A popular song written by Edith Nesbit about two seeds, one growing to be a tall plant, the other a very small one! Quoted in *Pot-Pourri from a Surrey Garden* (1897) by Mrs C.W. Earle (1836–1925). **2.** Two riding horses. **3.** Mary was already referring to Lily as their child. **4.** A nickname for Edward Liddell. **5.** Lily was at school at Roedean, outside Brighton.

FRIDAY, JANUARY 21 Choons & Ed left.[1]

Andrew Hichens came down. He & I had a little talk about Signor's refusal of the government offer. We are both so sorry to be at odds with him. However, he will not, I think, budge from his point. Andrew did not open the discussion again.

S. was reminded in talking of the Millais pictures again that he had met Millais at the door at the old show at the Grosvenor Gallery, & he had said 'Oh, such vulgarity, there!! – but some devilish fine things too, I can tell you, & you'll say so too.'

SUNDAY, JANUARY 23 A school magazine of Lily's amused Signor when I read it to him. Our child writes a good little account of the Excelsior club (Dramatic). The plays sound excellent.

WEDNESDAY, JANUARY 26 A letter from Gerry at Hotel Californie, Cannes, happy in the blues & greens & oranges & lemon & golden white all about her. Her latest office, to soothe Gladstone, suffering much from pains in his head. She says she sat down to play, not knowing in the least what he would care for. Being told that he liked soft soothing music, she began in fear, & he with his head back & feet on a chair sat without speaking & finally went to sleep. He said to her 'You understand the right music to play to a tired brain, better than anyone.' Mrs Gladstone says he 'has joined the Pupseys', her graphic description, meaning what doctors call 'senile decay'. It is very sad now.[2]

SATURDAY, JANUARY 29 I woke to find my sweet sitting up, the white folds of his dressing gown like some apostle's robe about him, his silver hair like a halo, for his head is in between me & the candle. Then we talk a little, & at length he says 'What happens to poor little Fatima now?' & I say 'she is mum'.

'Ah' he answered 'you will be sorry if you give her up, even the trifling things put down lightly just as they happen from day to day, become valuable after years.'

I know it, & hope the Spirit will say 'write' to me now, if I can sleep!

---

1. Christina and Edward had been looking after Lily before she came to Limnerslease. They had stayed at Limnerslease for Lily's first few days of living there to help her feel at home. **2.** This was a few months before Gladstone's death in May 1898.

SUNDAY, JANUARY 30 Conscious of a light burning, my darling writing busily soon after four, I keep sluggardly still. Later I tread over the cold sheets, his empty place in our bed, to the side of his little bed, where my bad night has sent him, & he talks. He tells me the character of his thoughts have not changed all his life long. In these later days he thinks he has formulated them, & perhaps certain subjects that had seemed difficult to him before, here seem clearer, but he knows his incapacity to put the thoughts into words. I don't.

Talking of the different motives for work, he regrets Burne Jones has somehow not allowed himself to take the higher range of thoughts & imagination, & leave the world of fancy.

MONDAY, JANUARY 31 Mr Redmayne[1] came over, most friendly, to see our door hinges. Alas, he does not quite think them well done. The work is too heavy, he says.

Signor began a beautiful drawing of him to give Mrs Redmayne, as a thanksgiving for all he has done for us.

TUESDAY, FEBRUARY 1 Mr Deuchars began to work again for us, preparing the patterns.[2]

FRIDAY, FEBRUARY 4 A nice letter from Emily Loch,[3] so pleased because in the Winter Palace at St Petersburg she hears Signor's name on everybody's lips! The Grand Duchess Elizabeth has got up an English art exhibition & Signor's *Burne Jones* is there & Signor's *Walter Crane* & *Lady Granby*. She sends on his name cut from the Russian catalogue.

'How nice to be alone' my darling said to me tonight, while I am grieving at being so dull a companion to him.

---

1. George Tunstal Redmayne (1840–1912), architect, advised Mary Watts on the structure of her Cemetery Chapel, and approved her plans in 1895. He also helped with advice on the building materials (he advocated the small bricks, which help to give the chapel its Byzantine dimensions). He was married to Alfred Waterhouse's sister, and built several substantial houses during his retirement in Surrey. **2.** Louis Deuchars was preparing the patterns from Mary's designs for the remaining terracotta tiles needed for the decoration of the chapel walls. It was to be consecrated and opened in July. **3.** Emily Loch (1867–1925), Lady-in-Waiting to Princess Christian, Queen Victoria's fifth child. She was a friend of the Czarina Alexandra of Russia, and visited the Czar and Czarina during 1898 with Princess Christian's daughter, Thora.

FRIDAY, FEBRUARY 11 Began my pot for Signor's birthday.

I have got him *Holland House*[1] & another copy, alas badly bound, of the illustrated Tennyson, of which he is so fond. He is very pleased. He had two, but they were both taken from him.

Miss Ellice[2] came over. Looking at Fluff she said 'I always believe that our power of calling out love in animals is investing them with a higher power in their lives, which afterwards will lead them to another life, just as our love of God calls out our spiritual & immortal side.' I thank her for that thought.

MONDAY, FEBRUARY 14 My little love tells me as he is stepping up gladly to his bath that he thinks Ruskin had perhaps the most original mind of all the great men of his day, & adds 'you see that the ordinary mind is almost always interested by the facts that are close at hand, while Ruskin is far more deeply interested by the ideas behind the facts'. He went on 'Perhaps painting may be said to represent ideas, words to suggest ideas, & music to create ideas.' These I know he believes to be the general characteristics of each, but they do not belong exclusively to each. I fancy in his own art he attempts all three.

'I think my idea of the law of conflict is best illustrated by the shuttle which has to go backwards & forwards to create the web.'

I like that. It is hopeful.

TUESDAY, FEBRUARY 15 Preparing for class next Thursday.[3]

THURSDAY, FEBRUARY 17 My class! We were prepared for 40, but 48 swarmed in, & nearly overwhelmed us, all good & well mannered. So happy to be at work again.

FRIDAY, FEBRUARY 18 Something made me speak of the Queen, & her curious apparent dislike of Signor, for it was evident that she refused to allow him the honour of Privy Councillor. Of course I am told I ought not to think of such a thing, & then he added 'possibly she may remember

---

1. *Holland House* (1874) by Princess Marie Liechtenstein, a detailed illustrated history of the house, seat of the Hollands, in Holland Park. **2.** The daughter of the owner of Eastbury Manor, Compton, 'was a frequent & welcome visitor to Limnerslease. Mr Watts admired her mother much, and asked her to sit for her portrait' (M.S. Watts, 'Portrait cat.', p.51). **3.** Mary was restarting her terracotta classes for adults on a Thursday evening, and for children on a Saturday morning.

that when I was asked to meet her & Prince Albert, when they went to see the Lincoln's Inn fresco, that I did not go. I couldn't make up my mind & didn't go, & also to Osborne once when they wanted Redgrave to go, I refused, & she may think it is because I am socialistic or something of that sort. One never knows.'[1]

SATURDAY, FEBRUARY 19 S. spoke of how small things mattered, the want of good feeling, the disregard of others that makes those complaints against large hats at the theatre so common. Selfish race to be bred from such selfish women & disaster & downfall from loss of national character.

My class of children came. Very good and attentive.

The excitement in Paris over this Zola trial is astonishing.[2]

L'armée has its mailed heel upon justice & fairness just now & France wild for change is ready to rush after any new leader who will talk of *gloire* & flourish his sword before their foolish eyes, hungry for change.

MONDAY, FEBRUARY 21 Very cold, & snow showers! I am afraid because of our promise to Brighton[3] & their disappointment.

TUESDAY, FEBRUARY 22 From Gerry, Lady Earle, Miss Ellice, Miss Jackson, Arthur & Phoebe flowers come greeting his birthday, & kind words, & I get some thanked from the day before.

There is a wickedly cold wind from the north east but he thinks it better to walk a bit on the sheltered side of the wood, & so we go. He says he would like to finish his *Love Triumphant* tomorrow & thinks he will![4] It will be practically finished, but many 'a pair of touches' will be irresistible for months & months, I know. It was glowing & glorious

---

1. Watts twice refused a baronetcy, but accepted the Order of Merit from Edward VII in 1902. **2.** Emile Zola (1840–1902), the French writer, was tried for libel when he wrote an open letter in *L'Aurore*, which he headed 'J'Accuse', indicting the President of France of anti-Semitism in his conviction of Alfred Dreyfus, a Jewish army officer. Dreyfus was wrongly convicted of giving away intelligence secrets to the Germans, and sent to Devil's Island. In February 1898, Zola was convicted for libel and fled to England to escape a prison sentence. The Wattses were very sympathetic to him, as was much of Europe. **3.** They were going to see Lily at Roedean. **4.** *Love Triumphant* was started in 1895–6, and was shown at the New Gallery, unfinished, in 1896–7. It was finished in the winter and spring 1899–1900 (M.S. Watts, 'Subject cat.', pp 95–6).

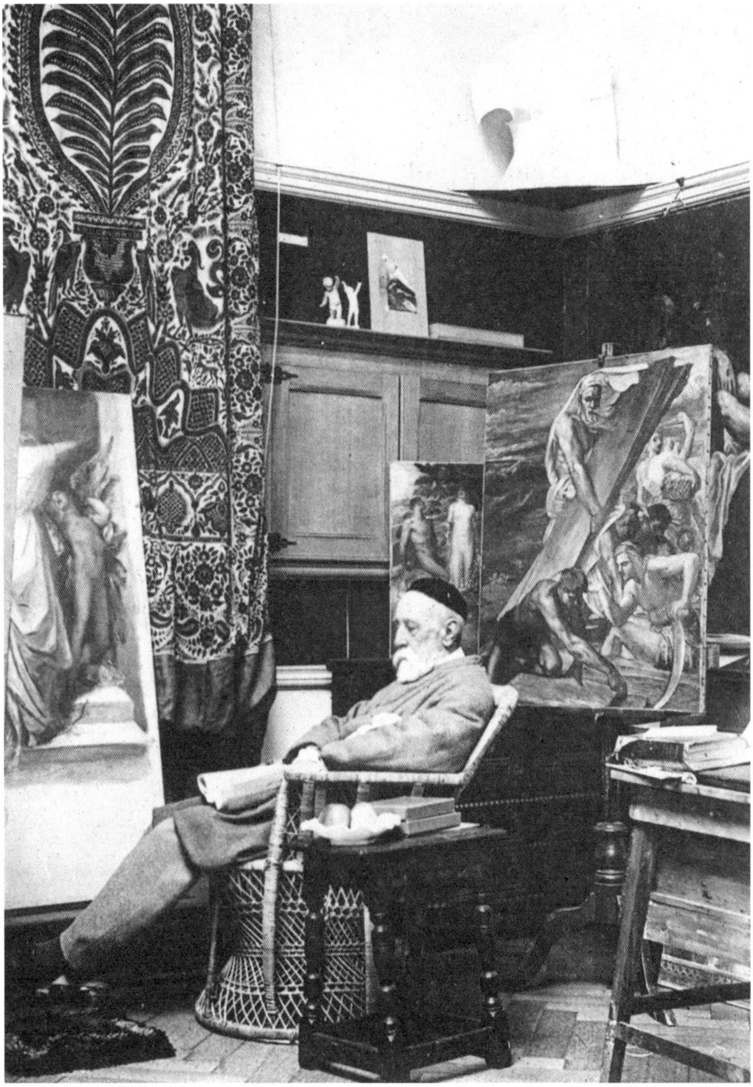

Watts in the Great Studio, Limnerslease

when he called me in today to look at it. He has done much to the right arm of *Love* which gives it a great refinement & exaltation. Every breath tells now. What a life of work consecrated to the highest. How terribly happy am I!

We are interested in the summing up to the jury in the Zola trial.

WEDNESDAY, FEBRUARY 23 *St George's Day. Birthday.* I woke at one o'clock, just as it struck, & knowing my darling was awake, I went & kissed him, beloved & beautiful & peaceful. Why has he all those wonderfully soothing essences?

Oh my beloved, too fast the birthdays come!

81 past since 'into this dangerous world he leapt'.

'I wish I had made more use of them' he says simply.

This morning at six, I, having greeted him at the first hour, lay still, & Phoebe gave him the next greeting, but he soon held out his hand.

'Well, I suppose you remember you gave me my birthday greeting at one o'clock?'

I loved & he asked for more & we knew it. My beloved, how great my love seems to me in these hours, & little fears grow great, too. I was miserable because our night-light went out. I knew it would, somehow, & dreaded it being the life candle. That was the thought in my mind, but I got up & relit it at one o'clock. So I take it as a symbol of the year only.

The sun shone & flowers & love streamed in in all sorts of shapes & forms. Dear Andrew & May came down & brought such glorious flowers, pure white camellias, pure orchids. Ethel here in the afternoon. A happy day.

The class in the evening.

Light & shade by turns, but love always.

THURSDAY, FEBRUARY 24 Before the curtains were drawn my sweet had made up his mind to give up Brighton. Glad for him. Sorry, very sorry, we had ever promised, & feel I must not allow anyone to be sure of our plans. 'Never promise again' I write here. The day very sunny but mercifully I am relieved by hearing from Miss Lawrence that there are cases of measles & that the play got up had been put off. This makes me rejoice, for indeed I never wanted to move, & the weather is cold for it & risky.

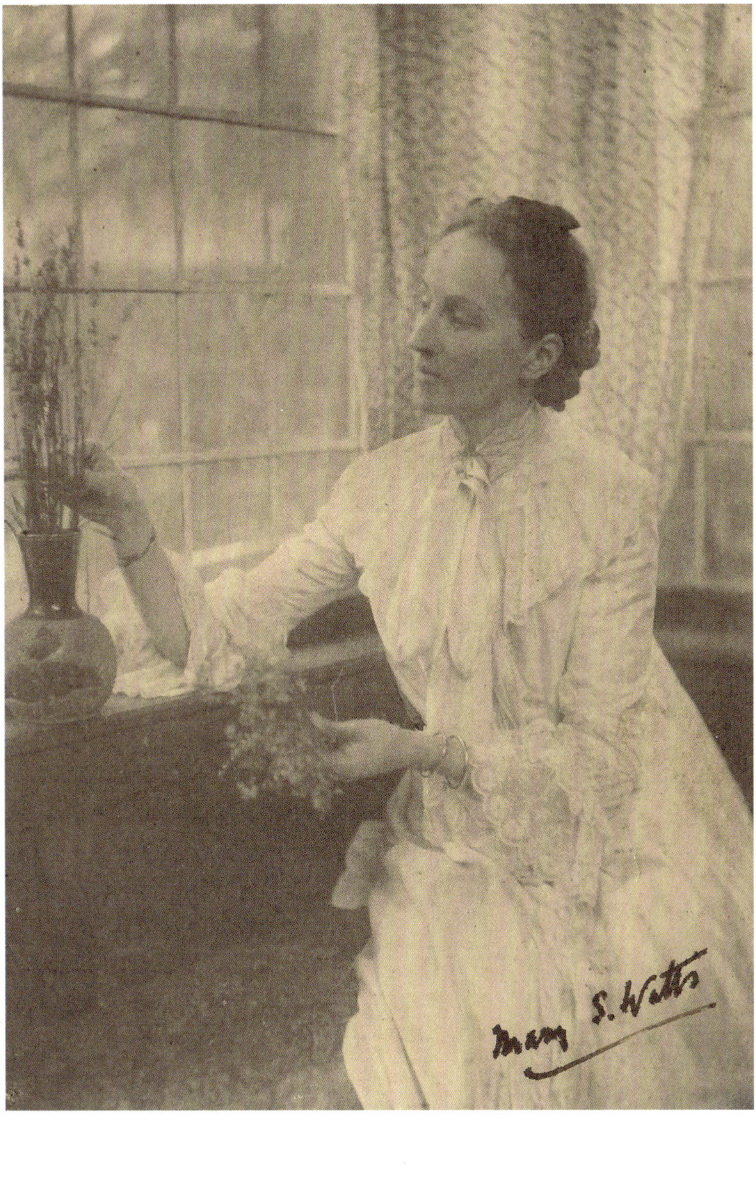

Mary Watts sitting by a window, photograph by Frederic Hollyer

FRIDAY, FEBRUARY 25 Walked to Sex's[1] to borrow broken tools for the *Dry Bone* picture.[2] Very cold wind.

SATURDAY, FEBRUARY 26 A little walk in the sun I had, & brought in a handful of neapolitana.[3] How sweet.

My class of children, & a visit from W. Mitchell, the builder who built our little home.

Reading in an article that said his *Ophelia* was painted from Miss Siddall, Signor told me he had never seen her.

'I wish I had, & I wrote to Rossetti that I would like to know his wife, & he said "Oh, come & dine. I will write to you" & afterwards he wrote "I did write, but as you did not come, I thought the letter had miscarried & was partly confirmed in that impression by finding it in my pocket.'"

Sir Martin A Shee's[4] verdict on the young Millais' work reminded us of his on Signor's. I said 'I think it was very wonderful of your father to let you go on with art in the face of that.'

'Yes', Signor said, 'my father thought he had an unusual perception. He neglected his own work, some sort of Clerk's work, to dabble in inventions. He had, I remember, a fine appreciation & read a great deal. Of course I was always so sickly that it was difficult for me to do anything that required constant application, but no doubt he allowed me to have my own way & go on drawing, when I ought to have been supporting him. I did this later.'

MONDAY, FEBRUARY 28 *Little Holland House* Came up to London & went to the New Gallery, where there are great gems, but such a mixture that

---

1. Five members of the Sex family worked on the chapel, including Clarence Sex, the village blacksmith, who made the decorative hinges for the door, and the gates to the cloister. 2. *Can these Bones Live?* (1897–8): Watts' enigmatic painting shows a fallen oak tree, representing England, weighed down by the golden pall draped over it. It illustrates Watts' pessimism at the state of the country, and a small piece of writing on the tree reads 'Aefred mee plantode'. The message is that King Alfred had created the country, but that it now lay in moral ruins, with broken hand tools giving way to industry, and greed and love of wealth undermining society. It is one of Watts' most heartfelt symbolist paintings. 3. *Cyclamen neapolitana*. 4. Watts's father showed some of his son's work to Sir Martin Shee, then President of the Royal Academy, who made the comment 'I see no reason why your son should take up the profession of art.' For Watts's early drawings, see Chloe Ward, *The Drawings of G.F. Watts*, Philip Wilson, London, 2015.

it is evidently a mistake & failure. The public do not care for a Potpourri of pictures. One room given up to Rossetti is very fine & very interesting.

We went from there to greet virile, joyous, strong-armed, true-eyed Millais, rejoicing in his boy-like natural powers, a great child to the end, & we were delighted.

TUESDAY, MARCH 1 We went to Millais again. A great pleasure this bright March morning, to find ourselves in such vigorous company.

S. said 'The Sir Isumbras! it needs no words. That landscape always made me urge Millais to paint landscape long before he had done anything.'

WEDNESDAY, MARCH 2 Out early by myself. I find Edith & chicks[1] at 61 Cadogan Square, a nice little flat, for dancing lessons. Neil with his funny little mouth screwed up over the announcement 'I hate dancing.' I fancy it is not manly enough for him. London will be more to his mind.

THURSDAY, MARCH 3 *Limnerslease* I hear there is a case of scarlet fever at Lily's school, developed last Saturday. I am glad we did not go.

My class. It was a good one, in spite of snow. Certainly more earnest workers, & I am pleased that the one dirty boy, Mike, now comes clean & washed with a new coat & takes pains tonight, after a year of hopelessness, when I often wished he would not come.

MONDAY, MARCH 7 S. still talks of the Millais work with pleasure, today wishing that the Academy would learn to hang pictures as they were hung in the Grosvenor.

'I never saw pictures look as well as they did there,' Signor said.

He agrees with me that the early Millais should have been hung together with space round each, & the portraits & large single figures kept more together. 'I would have hung the big room with the greatest of his subject pictures only. Millais was wonderful in giving the aspect. Even the Tennyson, which I do not consider very like, at some distance is astonishingly like – the aspect is so right.'

FRIDAY, MARCH 11 Thompson here for the day, & took up Mr Deuchars' *Robert Burns*[2] on the chance of getting it into the New Gallery.

---

1. Hester, Neil and their mother, Edith Fraser-Tytler. **2.** The New Gallery accepted Louis Deuchars's painting of Robert Burns.

SUNDAY, MARCH 13 Looking at the *Love Triumphant* S. said to me today 'You see, I want to plant his feet distinctly on the ground. All that is spiritual must get its impetus from the ground beneath our feet. That must be recognized, tho' many people would think it wrong.'

TUESDAY, MARCH 22 Into Guildford to see a cook who did not come, & to see Mitchell & he did not turn up. Went to see our sweet cottages in the sun, now painting is going on.[1] Mr Yeates has promised to help me about an asbestos material for doing the interior of the chapel. Asbestos, light, fibrous, & flexible.

THURSDAY, MARCH 24 A hard day of work for me. Class, a garden plan to make to quote for the cottages & send to Mr George. Dear Mary[2] at six. Bright & beautiful still, so strong looking.

She came into my class & spoke to them so charmingly. I fear they did not rise as the Irish would have done. 'As a rule she is a child, & will always be a child' Signor said, holding her hand.

FRIDAY, MARCH 25 Dear Mary! So earnest & so happy, drawing out Signor's thoughts. Mr Anderson, Mary's own brother, came down to fetch her. She had never travelled alone in her life till yesterday!

SATURDAY, MARCH 26 In the evening Andrews came to tell me Mitchell[3] had come to see me. I had written him two letters & had no answer. A shivering little figure all covered with mud was sitting by the modelling room stove, his mob of curly hair all wet, like a raven he croaked that we could never make our work pay. Nothing that I said seemed to him to be possible. I told him I did not want to make the work pay, but to pay for his expenses, & told him to think of it. His sister is dying of

---

1. Ernest George, the architect, had been commissioned to build a group of cottages for workers on the chapel project and in Mary's new pottery, where she was employing the workforce by now well trained in all aspects of terracotta work. It was in its infancy in 1898, but was to last over 50 years and to become famous for its large garden pots, sold to Liberty of London, and for its terracotta gravestones. **2.** Mary Anderson, the American actress. See note for October 21, 1887, page 46. **3.** This was Frank Mitchell, the kiln burner who had worked for Mary on the chapel project. She wanted him to do the same for the new pottery. The Compton Mitchells, builders, were an extended local family, who worked on the construction of the house.

cancer & the outlook is not bright for him. I felt so glad to see him again. He croaked me into some despair too. I have offered him our next cottage.

SUNDAY, MARCH 27 At 3 a.m. I was awake. I heard a sigh from my dear one's pillow. I drew myself across the empty bed space, for we are still divided, & glad I was that that little sigh had reached me. He was lying awake a prey to the demon thoughts that so often haunt 3 o clock & such early dark hours. My having used the expression 'make a little success' of our work was on his mind. He told me he foresaw nothing but misery. I had no head for business, no nerve for extra work, writing, & worry. I would probably go mad, or he would go mad & die, knowing that he would leave me to a miserable impoverished old age. I confess I had had a few of the demons about my pillow, but on talking it over together again, we got the matter down to its right proportions.

I have proposed to take Mitchell for a year,[1] the expense of this & sundries will probably come with Mr Deuchars to £150. If I can sell tombstones, sundials, & one other thing to fill time & the kiln when artistic work does not fill it, I think we should get back our money or some of it. That is all. If I find we cannot make any thing I must at the end of the year stop the whole thing.

But given the class, the kiln burner is a very necessary supplement. No 'roots' without him as we have long seen & often agreed together, Signor suggesting that our pottery shed should be by the gate near Cook's Farm. I think I am not very rash if only I am well & able to carry out a sufficient number of designs.

MONDAY, MARCH 28 Steadman came to make a mould for my first tombstone.

I was feeling well & bright & able for work.

S. has begun to write his AEFRED mee plantode, or 'wyrtmalode',[2] rooted, which is better. (To root, to fix roots)

Measuring the chapel for some material to cover the wall.

---

1. Mary is here outlining her detailed intentions for the new pottery. In spite of Watts's anxieties, she had, as we see, realistic plans of her own. They developed into the Compton Pottery, and then the Potters' Arts Guild, which she designed for and ran as a business until her death in 1938. 2. 'AEFRED mee plantode, or wyrtmalode' – inscription on Watts's painting *Can these Bones Live?*.

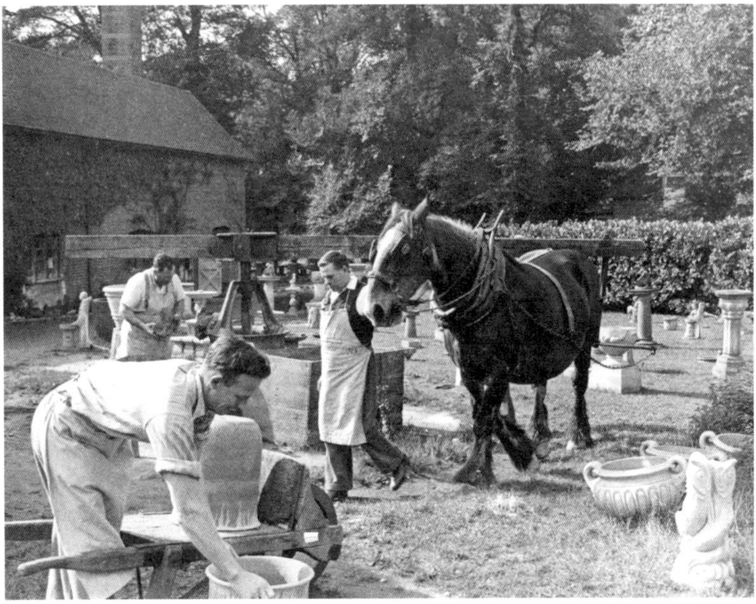

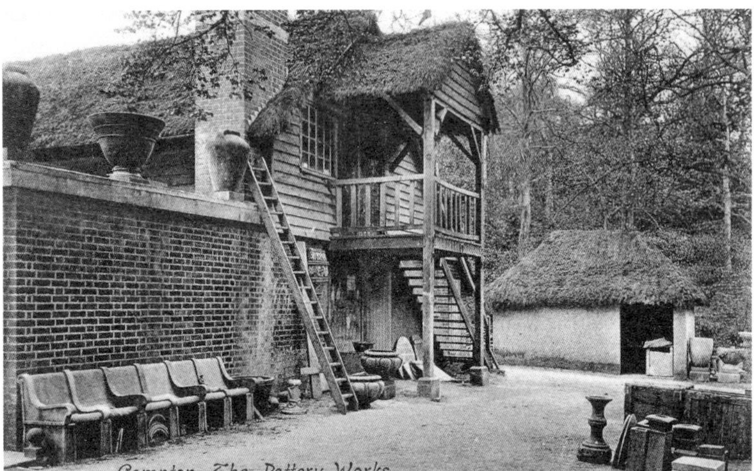

(TOP) Mixing the clay with horse power at Compton Pottery

(ABOVE) Compton Pottery, with terracotta seats ready to be placed outside Watts Cemetery Chapel, postcard by Lee Tate

WEDNESDAY, MARCH 30 Mr Deuchars has carried out the capital of our first sundial, east, west, north, & south as suggested, with their little frown & smile. It gives it a touch of the human.

THURSDAY, MARCH 31 'The most sweet Failure on the road to Success', Signor's little aphorism to comfort himself for the difficulty he has had today over the head of *Death* in his large *Time, Death, & Judgement.* 'I had it rather nice once' he said 'but the quality of the texture seems poor to me, & now I cannot get what I want at all.'

My class. I wrote to one of them asking him to give some words for his pot. 'Home sweet Home' is what he chose to put on it! He does not like to put his name or his wife's. I wonder why.

FRIDAY, APRIL 1 We hear today from Choons that Gladstone's 'murmur' is that fatal one, cancer.

A lovely bright day. Our Lily came back to us, & young Mr Tovey[1] here for luncheon. After luncheon he played a glorious sonata of Beethoven's, the grieving voice strong & recurring, after the triumphant & the glorious. The thread of sorrow & yet a noble holy sorrow underlying all.

SATURDAY, APRIL 2 A lovely morning. We walked to see the cottages.

In the afternoon we went up to see Miss Jekyll in her new house.[2] It is wonderfully simple & gives one a good, conventual feeling. These new grey tender-coloured oak beams are my envy.

Mr Lutyens explains that it is 'English oak' that is honeyed. 'Wash it with lime & leave it lying about,' he says. That might explain it better! I wonder if it keeps that velvety grey.

MONDAY, APRIL 4 Mitchell began to work here. Shall I be able to cope with it all? I ask myself.

---

1. Donald Tovey (1875–1940), a musicologist, composer, conductor and pianist, who was a close friend of Joseph Joachim. Mary had asked him to give guidance over Lily's musical abilities. They were not convinced that the tuition at Roedean was good enough.
2. Munstead Wood, near Godalming, was designed by Edwin Lutyens (1869–1944) for Gertrude Jekyll, the horticulturalist. She wrote a detailed description of it in her book *Wood and Garden* (1899). She and Lutyens, many years her junior, worked together on many houses and gardens throughout their lives.

Signor saying today of the work generally, that I do not get my patterns strong enough. He wants me to design a pedestal for his *Clytie* to be put outside somewhere.

TUESDAY, APRIL 5 I have a letter from Mr Spielmann asking (for Cassell) if this book of his may be the Biography.[1] Too absurd. I wonder at his asking.

Emily Loch came without Gerry. It is just as well for us as Emily has so much to tell us about Russia. Four months there, the first part in their country palace, really in Finland, & she found it dull rather, some disease of the nature of smallpox being about, & she could go nowhere for fear of bringing infection to the Czar's children. The Czarina very simple & happy, too much so, she does not care enough to go about among her people, & sees nothing of her own household even, very shy. He enjoying his autocracy & full of life, a sportsman, & caring for many things. He hates our form of government, but would like to be friends with England, & likes the people.

They travel with soldiers, each man within sight of the other, lining the whole way from the time the train enters Russian territory. The people cross themselves when the Royal carriages pass, & 'Little father' is shouted by the soldiers with one voice after the Czar has passed.[2]

SATURDAY, APRIL 9 Our beloved Gerry goes, having taken Lily's good first tutor in her two hands, & inserted Mr Williams, who had telegraphed before she left to say he would come to us today. What a gift she has been in my life, what a gift to my darling.

Mr Williams came to luncheon & was giving Lily, from his delightful standpoint, such an intelligent glimpse into the heart of the art of music, & I was grieved only to hear snatches of it. I had my class for the first hour & a half, for he talks, plays, & gives no set lesson of an hour, but spreads it over five, sometimes, & keeps his pupils' attention by his brightness.

He played delightfully all the evening, a wide range of great masters, & simple masters, who wrote our ballads. Of the *Men of Harlech* he

---

1. Marion Spielmann wrote extensively on Watts's work, particularly in the *Pall Mall Gazette* and intended to publish, as this diary entry infers, a critical biography of Watts.
2. Tsar Nicholas II and his German wife Alexandra, granddaughter of Queen Victoria. The Tsarina encouraged her husband to maintain an autocratic leadership, words she used frequently to Emily Loch.

said 'all the true principles are in it & that is always so when an air is fine. They would not live without it.'

SUNDAY, APRIL 10 A showery Easter – Signor & Mr Williams have long talks.

Talking of the 'bangners'[1] as some people call them, Signor said he was sure it was wrong as it left one with the idea that the sound of the piano had been strained to its uttermost, while he believes that all pleasure in art depends upon the feeling that there is still a reserve of quality where strength or tone or brilliancy is left behind which could be used if necessary. Mr Williams quite agrees with him. They took their parallel from a wave. 'One knows' Signor says, 'however huge a wave may be, there is probably a bigger one behind.'

Lily listens & enjoys, & is getting to be quite at home with Mr Williams. She is growing in our midst very delightfully. I do so want her love & confidence. Tonight she took my hand unasked & stroked it. It means that she feels we desire her best good, & also that she is happy. That is much, that she should be happy, because her life is opening up to her. It is what we have hoped.

WEDNESDAY, APRIL 13 Lily & I went to the Rectory & round the village a little on our bicycles.

TUESDAY, APRIL 19 My morning quietly in the clay studio, working out my capital. 3 steps of the sun. It ought to be pretty & interesting, the cock for morning, peacock for noon, & owl for the evening.

Mr Gillett came about the furnishing of the chapel & the consecrating. In the afternoon his girls came to play with Lily.[2]

Lady Betty Balfour later also.[3]

WEDNESDAY, APRIL 20 'The morning breaks.'

'The morning breaks' answers my little sweet. 'Let's take care of the pieces – What do you think of that?'

---

1. This seems to be a contemporary way of describing music when it was played as loudly as possible by pianists who 'banged' the piano. **2.** The rector of Compton. **3.** Lady Elizabeth 'Betty' Balfour (1867–1942), who was married to Gerald Balfour, younger brother of Arthur (Prime Minister in 1902–5). She joined the social group 'the Souls', and became a society hostess in her house in Addison Road. Watts painted her husband's portrait in 1898.

'Not so bad' I answered. 'Not so bad for me! as dear Leighton used to say' & added 'There are things I never get used to. Why did he die?'[1]

FRIDAY, APRIL 22 *Little Holland House* Out with Signor early. Academy, & then home for luncheon.

A photogravure arrived from Hampstead of *The Happy Warrior*,[2] a real reproduction of Signor's work. One feels sorry, but the machine can sometimes give what none but the hand of the most experienced engraver can give better, & with what ease.

Our next interruption was a visit from Madame Antoinette Sterling.[3]

MONDAY, APRIL 24 *Limnerslease* My last class this evening. Mr Deuchars ill, so I had it to myself.

TUESDAY, APRIL 26 Edith[4] came – very nice to have her.

WEDNESDAY, APRIL 27 Ethel & Edith making plans for us to go to Dalcrombie[5] for a few weeks. Signor wants me to go. I will see my darling hills again & rest, smelling the bog myrtle, & the heather, & hearing the curlew whistle & the black cocks crow. There is still in me, perhaps something my nature drew in as a child, that now my more restrained nature wants to feed on. I feel sure it is what would do me good. Ethel feels much the same, & fancies Choons will, but I doubt it.

Drove Edith round by Ethel's & they made their plans for June!

THURSDAY, APRIL 28 Lady Henry Somerset[6] came to luncheon. She was kind & nice about the work. May joined us & we went to the chapel.

---

1. 'Half my life is gone with Leighton', Signor said in grief following his friend's death in January 1896. 2. This may have been the first of many photogravures by Emery Walker (1851–1933) of Watts's work. He was an engraver, photographer and printer with premises in Hampstead. 3. Antoinette Sterling was an American contralto who, after an adventurous life and concert career in the United States, settled in England. She shared many values with the Wattses; she was a strong anti-corset woman, and became a Christian Scientist after experimenting with several different approaches to spirituality. 4. Wife of Mary's half-brother, Ted. 5. Dalcrombie is close to Aldourie Castle, where the Fraser-Tytler girls spent some of their childhood. 6. Lady Henry Somerset was the daughter of Charles Somers-Cocks, 3rd Earl Somers and Virginia née Pattle. She separated from her husband, a politician, after he became infatuated with a 17-year-old boy, and was involved with the temperance and women's suffrage movements.

SATURDAY, APRIL 30 My last class of little people.

MONDAY, MAY 2 Arthur & Verena[1] came this evening from Worcester.

TUESDAY, MAY 3 Children ride in the morning, Signor being riding master. Alas, our last ride together has been years ago. I am sure to never ride together again. He does not like to ride with the little hurts he now has, & wh. often trouble him.

WEDNESDAY, MAY 4 We have our sweet Dorothy[2] with the blossoms, & she is still like them.

They are very dear, Arthur particularly careful of Signor.

'Doesn't Signor want the little screen?' Arthur asked, when I was giving them a lamp, to throw light upon their Halma board[3] in the drawing room. The lamp was opposite to Signor's niche.

FRIDAY, MAY 6 Such a glorious day, & made happier by the voices of the children. All 'such fun' to them.

Just before luncheon Verena, going on an errand for me to get water for a vase, saw Arthur & Dorothy starting the mowing machine.

'Oh, do wait for me' she cried in a despairing imploring voice, as if the gate of paradise was just being shut upon her. She had two minutes to go & then luncheon, & they were all just as happy to scamper in to that.

Piladex[4] in the evening, Signor sitting beside us & laughing at the shouts & screams & stamps. Afterwards a game of old maid & he played too, to the children's great delight.

SATURDAY, MAY 7 Our kiln packed. My patterns alone seem to fail. Steadman making a model of the little chairs[5] for outside the chapel.

Children happy as the birds. Dear Dorothy has them in hand & keeps them going.

---

1. The children of Watts's ward, Blanche, and her husband, Herbert, both deceased. Arthur became the 6th Baron Somers, and Verena became Countess of Clarendon. The children were looked after by their father's family in Worcestershire after their parents' deaths. **2.** Dorothy Kellie-MacCallum (b.1885), daughter of Nell (Mary's half-sister) and James Dalgleish Kellie-MacCallum. **3.** Halma, a board game, was invented in 1883 by an American surgeon. **4.** A 1895 game in which an inflated bag was lobbed across a table using the hands, a little like table tennis. **5.** The chairs, in decorated terracotta, were a large item for Mary's kiln, but their successful firing underlined the fact that bigger items, such as gravestones, sundials and large garden pots, could be made in her new pottery.

Arthur has a sense of fun, & wild spirits, & a tender love for Signor, & cannot bear that he should be 'old maid'. I sat next to Signor & found he took the uppermost card, so suffered it, dear sweet. 'Oh don't offer him the old maid' Arthur implored, & still afraid I might not be tender hearted enough, he said 'Signor, don't take the card she puts uppermost. Take the card she puts last.' In the end Signor was old maid & they both exclaimed that the deal had not been a fair one. He would not have been 'old maid' but for that. So Signor was made happy again.

SUNDAY, MAY 8 I need Dalcrombie to get back to my real life again!

Church with the chicks. Signor made anxious by the rain, but how much less anxious he is now than he used to be! He has a nice letter from Miss Gladstone today. A kind, dear message of thanks. It is a wonderful end, if the fiery trial is laid upon the poor body the soul at least is at peace, & the mind delivered from all the strife & dust of battle; surrounded by love, & at peace with all the outer world at last.[1]

Designed outside chairs for chapel. Sir Algernon West[2] here later with Andrew.

Signor played Piladex with chicks! & we had fairy stories afterwards.

WEDNESDAY, MAY 11 May & I drove over to Farnham & had luncheon with Mr Davidson the chaplain & Mr & Mrs Hogle. The Chaplain took us afterwards into their sitting room to talk over various things about the Chapel.[3] There seems a doubt about whether it may be consecrated or not, but they hope that as it is a private gift this may be got over.

THURSDAY, MAY 12 Letter from Cecil Rhodes,[4] proposing to sit.

MONDAY, MAY 16 Andrews left with the Home Arts things,[5] carrying the gates with him.

1. Gladstone was near to death. Watts wrote to him and to the family during his illness. **2.** Sir Algernon West was Principal Private Secretary to Gladstone in 1861–94. **3.** The new cemetery at Compton and the chapel were due to be officially opened on July 1. **4.** Cecil Rhodes (1853–1902), imperialist and politician in Southern Africa. Watts's bronze sculpture, *Physical Energy*, was accepted by the government and given to South Africa in his memory after his death in 1902. It stands on the steps of the Rhodes Memorial outside Cape Town. Two other casts are in Kensington Gardens and in Harare, Zimbabwe. **5.** Mary's class was contributing to the annual exhibition of the Home Arts and Industries Association at the Albert Hall. Andrews took designs from the chapel terracotta decorations and iron work, including the gates to the side recesses inside the chapel.

TUESDAY, MAY 17 *Little Holland House* We came up by an early train. Dorothy & Signor went to the Academy together, & I went to the Albert Hall, where I luckily met Mr Ricardo,[1] & had a delightful talk with him about our clay. In an instant he told me that the white clay was too brittle for very large pieces of work. He says we are working on the right lines, using terra cotta with freedom, as a grand material for strong, good work, not for the delicate artistic work, not copying stone, but using it as freely as we please, limited only by the material. He does not think the white clay or the red will bear glazing.

WEDNESDAY, MAY 18 Mr Rhodes came to sit. He & Lord Grey[2] were shown into the drawing room & I had the first words with them there. Then they went up & when Signor sent for me I found Mr Rhodes standing with his back to the screen near the door, the place Signor likes best now for portraits. The light is the most diffused there, in the whole room. Lady Granby[3] came at 10 o'clock with her pencil & paper to make a drawing, with her fine point. Signor had a short sitting, just blocking in.

THURSDAY, MAY 19 Mr Rhodes came again & for the first half hour they were alone, & Signor was explaining to him that his series of portraits was of the men who form, who make England. 'The prominent, who perhaps may be said to make, <u>or</u> mar, her. I don't know which you are doing'!

He told me this afterwards, adding that he was not sure of the means Rhodes was using, & that to him, the words 'extension of Empire' were not the highest ideal.

FRIDAY, MAY 20 'Don't go away, Mrs Watts, I should like to talk to you' Mr Rhodes said this morning, when I went in & found him in the study behind the green chair, & I did stay, to talk & <u>stand</u> from nine till eleven, & learnt to know the spell of a man who can lead. Never have I known

---

1. Halsey Ricardo (1854–1928), architect and designer. He worked with glazed tiles in many of his decorative designs. He was in partnership with William de Morgan for ten years, and designed tiles for him. **2.** Albert Grey (1851–1917), 4th Lord Grey, Governor-General of Canada, 1904–11. **3.** Violet Manners (1856–1937) was a talented amateur portrait artist who showed at the Grosvenor and New Galleries. She was a prominent member of 'the Souls'. Her husband, Henry Manners, Marquess of Granby, later became Duke of Rutland.

such a sudden conversion from all my former ideas of a man. I went in thinking I should not have anything in common. I stood there finding the minutes too short for all we had to talk about. I expected a man of the world, with a head full of enterprise, I found a man with simplicity of manner & language. He thinks swiftly, & says what he thinks rather concisely sometimes, always very simply.

SUNDAY, MAY 22 My white lilies' scent, round the portrait of Gladstone,[1] makes the air heavy.

Signor wrote 'Whatever record leap to light, He never shall be shamed.' Words I had quoted in speaking of him, & I begged him to write them for me.

MONDAY, MAY 23 Lord Brownlow came to see Signor about the statue of Tennyson in Lincoln.[2]

Signor out at work on the horse. I bring him indoors.

Later to the Home Arts Exhibition, where Signor came. So hot I could wear my white clothes, & Signor was pleased & found me 'smart'! Funny little one. He gave great pleasure, going round to all the class holders.

FRIDAY, MAY 27 *Limnerslease* I came down rather late. A cool May evening, & all beautiful. Such a mass of white blossom! We are happy to be here.

Signor returned the funeral ticket[3] & was able to say he would not be in London.

SATURDAY, MAY 28 A day at letters & clay, & then to Monkshatch to see Andrew who is quite laid up.

Mr & Mrs Kemp Welch here. They had tea & saw what Signor has to show.

Then to the chapel on their way home. Very much pleased with it, somehow. I did not think they would have been, but they were quite enthusiastic. It did look rather sweet. It is growing every day less red, & the green enfolds it all so beautifully now. The trees are in leaf, it looks a sweet resting place.

---

1. Gladstone died on May 19. **2.** Watts had been commissioned to produce a twice life-size statue of his friend, the poet Alfred, Lord Tennyson, to be placed outside Lincoln Cathedral. The poet had died in 1892, and Lincolnshire was his home county. **3.** The ticket for Gladstone's funeral, an enormous event at Westminster Abbey.

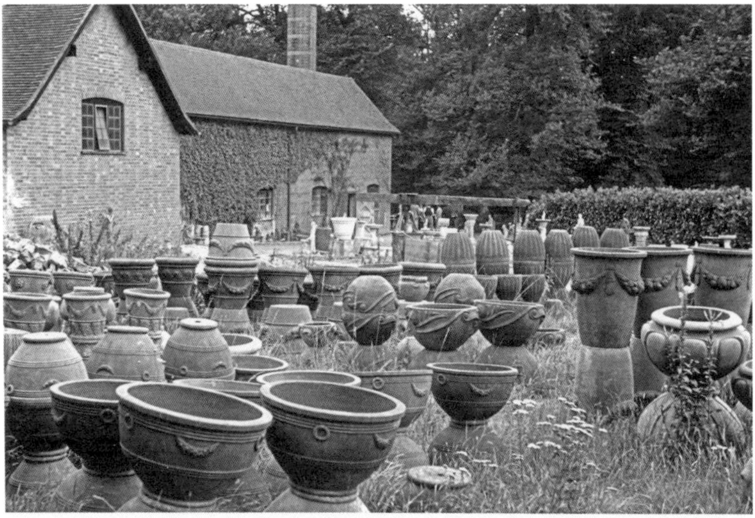

Compton pots outside the pottery

SUNDAY, MAY 29 What do I see before me? The whole of the interior of the chapel. The whole of my terra cotta to be kept going summer & winter, never letting the standard of design drop. Raising it, raising it, using the material to its utmost.

TUESDAY, MAY 31 My love in bed, & deploring the evil arrangements that bring him this waste of time.

'I suppose I must sleep now like a hog,' he said.

'Yes,' I said. 'Sleep sound with your mind at ease, your big banking account, your big achievements, your big reputation & your gigantic ingratitude.'

'No, no,' he answers. 'It is as if I was sewn into clothes that are too small for me. I feel I ought to be more free, but I can't break the bands.'

'Ah,' I said, 'they will crack some day like the dragonfly chrysalis, & you will fly away with a flash on dragonfly wings from me, & then you will be happy!!'

'No, not that' he said 'for you will come too. If, like the parable of my daisy, we grow like the sun from looking at it, you will come too, it may be a little later, but you will come, & then it won't matter if you have had to wait a little.'

WEDNESDAY, JUNE 1 Signor slept through the whole day, almost! I was able to be much in 'the pots' & got one handle[1] out that pleased me immensely. Told Signor so. It is a curly ear that seems to suit so well, in form, & in the beauty of fitness.

FRIDAY, JUNE 3 Sir Edward Poynter came with Andrew from Monkshatch to see S. He so much liked 'the old Horse'[2] which has had some background added to it, also the landscape from the window which I like so much. It is a treat always when we have breakfast in the studio, & there is time to sit amongst the pictures. The worst part of my busy life is, that I have too little time now for being quiet with pictures or books.

SUNDAY, JUNE 5 I had a nice letter from Lord Grey sending me one from Cecil Rhodes written from Madeira, simple & straight with deep feeling lying underneath.

'Your home is quite different to anything I have come across in my rough life' he says.

I was going to Puttenham but Signor wanted to sit out, & seemed to need me, so we stayed & met Andrew & May on our way back at the chapel to decide upon raising the altar.

The little place was cool & sanctified today as I knelt there for the first time. The hassocks & the lectern are there now! I am glad they had first footing before the bier!

Darling May full of making a beautiful altar cloth. I went back with them after they had had luncheon with us, to look at work & chairs for outside the chapel.

MONDAY, JUNE 6 *Little Holland House* Left early, busy to the last. I don't leave Limnerslease with the same quiet & deliberation as Mr Rhodes leaves for Africa.

Came back by Waterloo, & the New Gallery.

SUNDAY, JUNE 12 Mrs Barrington broke her self imposed silence of the years, & wrote in, quite as usual, to ask for the little Leighton picture!! Signor had waited, feeling the fate of the house is still uncertain but now he sent it & a drawing, saying that if no permanent arrangement was

---

1. It was always known as 'The Round Handle'. 2. Watts's painting, *Patient Life of Unrequited Toil* (1890–91, Watts Gallery).

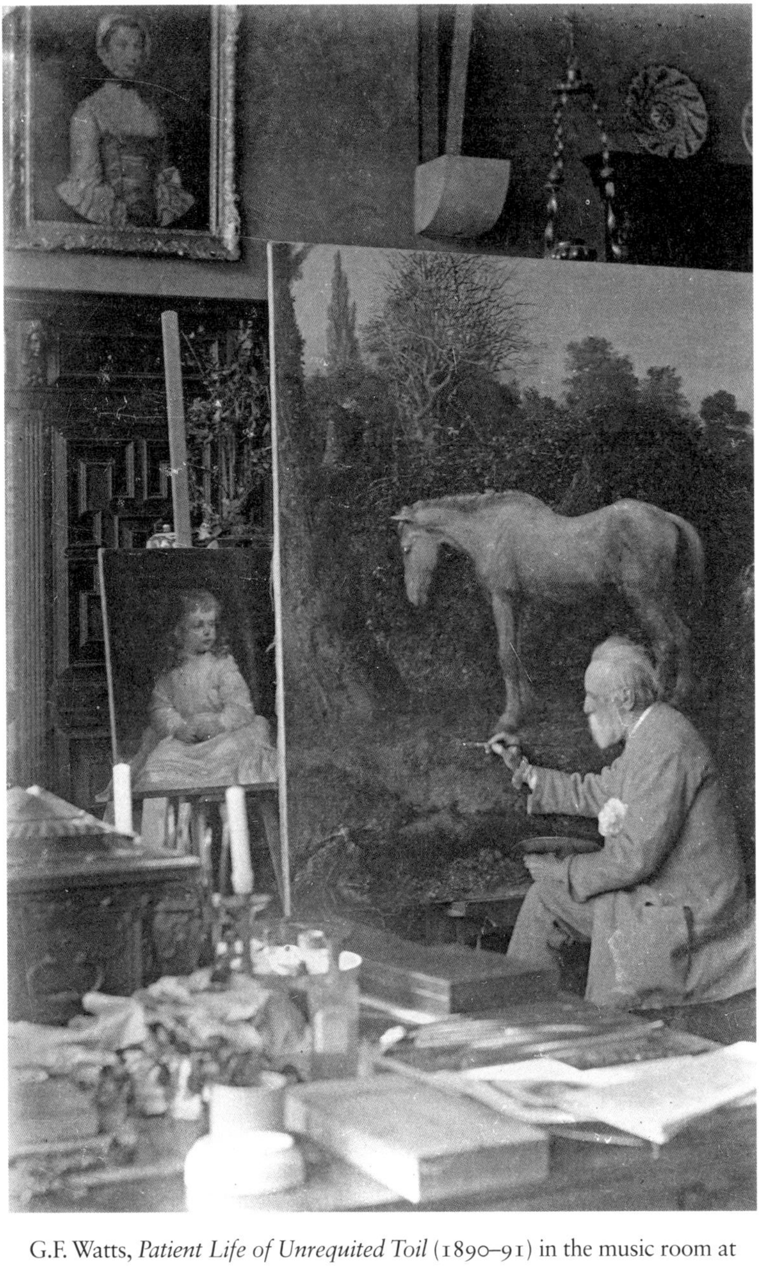

G.F. Watts, *Patient Life of Unrequited Toil* (1890–91) in the music room at Monkshatch, with a portrait of Hester Fraser-Tytler in the background

made he should wish to have them back.[1] She replies again inviting him to go to the Leighton house. He has refused. I think he knows too well what peace we have had, to allow the old ways to be resumed, & he tells me his answer made that clear. I shall never take up my foot! I know we should bitterly regret it if we did. She is impossible.

WEDNESDAY, JUNE 15 *138 Marine Parade Brighton* Miller brought Lily down to meet us at the station,[2] & we were glad to find ourselves at Mrs Bass's comfortable rooms. It was nice to have the great sea sound to go to sleep by.

There has been a bad bicycle accident at the school, a Miss Cornell run into by one of the younger girls & she has concussion of the brain, & possibly a slight fracture.

THURSDAY, JUNE 16 Lily & some of her friends ran in early.

The afternoon with them at the school. New front to the school, where the architect met us, a slim tall man called Simpson[3] & the school seems well arranged with every comfort thought out, a fine design in a good position with the grand downs rolling about it.

Annie Ritchie[4] is to give a bell for work not for prayer, & one that 'can be heard by the sailors at sea'. We must give some pots, I think!

We went back for tea & saw the girls drill, a very pretty sight & the master, Mr Harvey, talks to them all the while explaining the uses of such movement, 'beautiful strength' as the saying is.

SATURDAY, JUNE 18 Came back from Brighton bringing Lily with us to see an oculist. As I came away from the ticket office Signor, who had gone on with Lily, came towards me & said 'I have got to tell you something very sad, & that will shock you very much indeed', & then he told me that Sir Edward Burne Jones was dead!!

The news was being called in the streets. He had died yesterday!

What a journey we had home! My poor darling Signor!

---

1. Watts was very interested in the preservation of Leighton's work. Mrs Barrington (see note 2 Sunday, March 12, 1893, page 122) worked, from 1898 onwards, to collect as many paintings and drawings as possible to make a collection in Leighton's house. (See Mrs Russell Barrington, *G.F. Watts Reminiscences*, Macmillan, London, 1905, pp 201–2.) 2. Watts and Mary were visiting Lily at Roedean. 3. Sir John William Simpson (1858–1933), architect. The new buildings at Roedean were among his most noted commissions. 4. See note 1, Wednesday, July 20, 1887, page 36.

TUESDAY, JUNE 21 I went down to Rottingdean with the Holidays.[1] Little Kate talked all her mind out as we went. Sometimes I wanted a little silence, but if she leant back he leant forward & began all his schemes for socialism. All his arguments & the arguments against were brought out & hammered down, to the rhythm of railway wheels.

At last came the drive through misty & cool greyness on the great green downs, till we reached the little valley & turned up to the church. Margaret[2] in her white dress carrying flowers. Phil & Rudyard Kipling.[3] We went up to the little church & saw the little grave, lined with roses & roses. A perfect hedge of valerian making a bright pink border was planted by the church wall like a little ribbon round the grave. The silence in the little church where we had an hour to wait was very beautiful. The oak box laid before the altar covered with roses, white ribbons at each end, candles burning at either side, & behind all his 3 archangels, the marriage window, he had given them in memory of Margaret's wedding. The whole place lighted through his living & abiding thoughts while the little handful of ashes was all that was left of that vivid, wonderful personality! It is a wonderful spot, a village green, the houses round it & then the little flint church built on rising ground, with 3 levels, the nave, the outer chancel & the inner. The service over, without music, Margaret & Phil came down the church carrying the casket, & followed by Georgie & the Mackails.

Then to the grave. All over. Georgie dropped her little 'heartsease' into the grave, & passed down the path like a creature turned to marble, her eyes shut, & that look of suffering, that I have never seen before on any face with such speechless tearless sorrow.

Dear Mrs Holman Hunt came & kissed me, & I walked down, the gentle kind men about me. They guessed my thoughts, perhaps, to be of my own separation.

WEDNESDAY, JUNE 22 *Limnerslease* I went to our darling little home. Before I left for the chapel my sweet came in to my dressing room, holding

---

1. Henry and Kate Holiday, the painter and his wife, the designer. **2.** Margaret, Edward Burne-Jones' daughter, married John W. Mackail, Professor of Poetry at Oxford, friend and biographer of William Morris. **3.** Philip Burne-Jones and Rudyard Kipling. The latter's mother was Georgiana Burne-Jones' sister, Alice. They were two of the four remarkable Macdonald sisters. Their sister Agnes married Edward Poynter, President of the Royal Academy, and the fourth sister, Louisa, was mother to Stanley Baldwin, Prime Minister. (See Judith Flanders, *A Circle of Sisters*, Norton, London, 2002.)

me in his arms for long & long. 'The night cometh' was in both our minds! Went to Monkshatch where darling little May has been working at the beautiful altar cloth for our chapel for the day of consecration.

Then after luncheon May & I met Mr Gillett at the chapel. So home rather late. Signor in his niche. He tells me Lord Wemyss came. In the drawing room he pointed out the niche. 'There he lives in a niche, with the most charming woman in the world worshipping him'! The little love! How nice it was to come back to him.

THURSDAY, JUNE 23 We were in the drawing room after luncheon when Margaret & Phil came in, poor grey things running about together as if Margaret were still the unmarried girl again, & she looks it in her smart little white frock. Poor things. They are so good & brave & yet one can see they are like withered leaves just now, driven about, & like to be kissed & befriended.

His friends come here, liking to come & talk of him. Lord Carlyle came later, & said he only cared just now to go to see those who cared for him too.

FRIDAY, JULY 1 I got up when Signor did 'on such a morning'.[1] The sun had not got over the ridge of the down when I went down to the garden to look for flowers for the altar vases which May had brought to make all so beautiful for today.

I found a bunch of beautiful white poppies standing with their grey green metallic leaves one gemlike mass of dew, & thought 'the emblem of sleep. These will do'. I have a forget-me-not & the first rose from dear Sir Frederic. The rose was then dried to keep as a sign that I did have that wonderful daybreak alone with my thoughts & the world fresh from the beauty of sleep. What a dawn for a day of blessing on the little sanctuary we have built in love.

Andrew & I went up at six with poppies & water, our vases were beautiful. I stood for a moment alone under the domed roof, where colours & life & thought must climb some day & where the last sacred dust of us all here may some time come for its great amen, & felt that the blessing of the place had begun to fall that hour.

The day was glorious & so many came.

---

1. This was the day of the opening and consecration of Mary's chapel – to be known as Watts Cemetery Chapel.

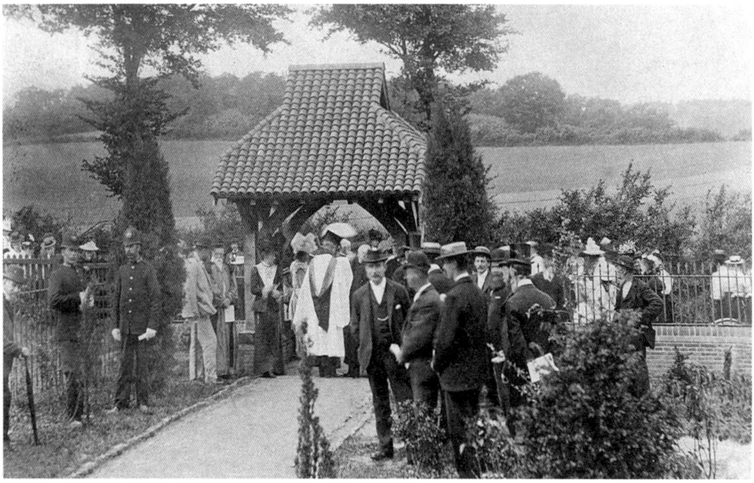

Watts and Mary at the lynch gate with others at the opening of the chapel on July 1, 1898

MONDAY, JULY 4 *Little Holland House* I kissed my dear one, looking at him to draw in a draught of his dear blessed looks to carry like a camel across a desert. He said 'why are you looking at me?'

I said 'because I shall be so far away. I wonder how I can go'.[1]

'How can you be far away?' he said. 'I shall feel that you are very near, thinking the same thoughts & desiring the same things. People can be close to each other & yet be very far away. Distance makes no difference to us.'

WEDNESDAY, AUGUST 10 *Limnerslease* We prepare for our party. The afternoon nice, & in the shelter of the garden we had a tea for 30, 'The Guildford Natural History & Microscopical Society'. 39 came, but we managed all well, & it was very sweet in the garden. Then came the studio to be seen, & the chapel building, which I did guide for.

---

1. The plan by Edith and Ethel for Mary to have a holiday in her native Scotland came to fruition. She and Ethel went north for four weeks, staying for some of the time with Ted and Edith at Aldourie Castle, and some in houses on the estate. It was a very successful and restful holiday. The two were accepted by everyone they met as homecoming Highlanders. They returned to the south on August 1, first to Little Holland House and then, after a few days, to Limnerslease. Mary picked up her everyday life again easily, and was quickly plunged back into chapel and pottery work.

FRIDAY, AUGUST 12 A lovely hot day, our kiln out, satisfactory except that the tombstone is broken.

We get the 2 sundials up in our garden. They want more base I feel, so does Andrew who came with May. Signor & I paid a visit to the new cottages. All nice, & grateful, except the first, Mrs Mitchell.[1]

TUESDAY, AUGUST 16 Strange to read that Mr Spielmann wrote in 1885 of the big horse 'Now very nearly completed.' It must have been then that Millais saw it, & said 'Now leave it alone. Don't put another touch upon it. It is a d----d good thing, I tell you, & I know one when I see it.'

THURSDAY, AUGUST 18 I went down at ten for the last hour of Mr Balfour.[2] I think he has one of the most charming faces & expressions I ever knew. His beauty & the kindling look that lights up a rather lined face at times is quite delightful. I fancy he must have a beautiful nature, far more sympathetic than 'Prince Arthur's'.

FRIDAY, AUGUST 19 Signor works out of doors till it is too hot. Hollyer came to photograph the G. Balfour picture.

THURSDAY, AUGUST 25 Signor's hammer click begins by candle light today at four. 'It was very useful to me' he said afterwards. He watches his big work now under every sort of condition of light & I am sure 'with the eye of an enemy'.

SATURDAY, AUGUST 27 I went to see dear little Georgie, that noble little soul who has girded herself for the rest of her lonely way, & 'has the sense of a wonderful pleasure of life burning within her'. It was all so beautiful, even the end. She said she was reminded only of the words of a Methodist hymn. 'The Lord shall come in love & carry away the souls of his servants in a flame' was the sense of it. She is going to live in his memory doing all that she can as a sort of expression of thankfulness for such a life as his. Opening the studio at the Grange, though the house itself is to be given up by them in December.

---

1. This was the first cottage to be completed, promised to Frank Mitchell, the kiln burner. Mrs Mitchell found fault with it for not having enough storage space. **2.** Watts was painting a portrait of Gerald Balfour, younger brother to Arthur, the future Prime Minister ('Prince Arthur').

'He used to think it would break our hearts to leave the Grange, but it is not the Grange any more' Phil said to her. She feels it is wicked to have anything of his turned with its face to the wall.

TUESDAY, AUGUST 30 Sent for Steadman & began to draw out the design or rather to space out the actual size in which I may design behind the altar.[1]

WEDNESDAY, AUGUST 31 I stay behind feeling that I must have a few hours alone with shut doors to think out the first bits of the internal decoration.

How strange the silent house, how terrible the silent night. I think of the little light step that slips off so lightly & so gladly before dawn each day. Our room is the 'Salle des pas perdues'.

TUESDAY, SEPTEMBER 13 *Limnerslease* My sweet flower, my Lotus lily! May she be rooted & grounded in love, that so she may pass over the troublesome waves of this life. I have said nothing in her past can possibly be proportionate to the great fact that life has been given, life to live, to be, to work in, to fill with all that is good & bounteous & high goaled.

I have said that she is to have her roots here in love, her room, her home.

SATURDAY, SEPTEMBER 17 Gerry came early & went to luncheon at Monkshatch. She nearly wept when she heard the old 'Take claret or hock, Miss?' behind her. He is comfortable, to nurture May so.[2]

MONDAY, SEPTEMBER 19 The De Morgans here.[3] All this cut up my time, & my work lies undone.

TUESDAY, SEPTEMBER 27 May brought her Princesses,[4] down to see us and all we have to show. They walked to the chapel.

---

1. See illustration page 225. **2.** Andrew and May Hichens were, from all accounts, popular with their staff. Geraldine Mary Liddell had stayed often at Monkshatch, and was well known to Alfred, their butler. **3.** William and Evelyn De Morgan, a couple well known to both Wattses for many years. William was one of the finest ceramicists of the period and advised Mary on the building and use of her kiln. Later he turned to writing novels. Evelyn was a subject painter, admired by both Watts and Mary. **4.** Princesses Christian and Victoria (Toria), daughters of Queen Victoria. Emily Loch was Lady-in-Waiting to Princess Christian.

WEDNESDAY, SEPTEMBER 28 Trying to photograph the friezes.[1] Infinitely difficult. Wind & rain, uneven ground & the width of the panels! A high dangerous scaffold built of trestles, planks & ladders, upon rather frail wooden boxes of various sizes to get over the difficulties of the uneven ground. The patient Andrews & Thompson at work yesterday & today. I have overcome some of the difficulty, leaving 2 holding the black cloth, getting the camera clamped to a board which is fixed to the top of the steps, as no tripod can stand our erection. I felt quite ill after a morning there. Only half a frieze done successfully. The 1st one was experimental, & without my small helps, & therefore useless, tho' it cost all the trouble of the scaffold.

TUESDAY, OCTOBER 4 *Little Holland House* Mr Gerald Balfour came to sit. Mr John Burns[2] came to luncheon. Went with Signor to see St Botolph's, Aldersgate.[3]

MONDAY, OCTOBER 17 *Limnerslease for the rest of the year* I rambled down by 12.26. A lovely day! Off at once to Shackleford with the loan things & arranged them.[4]

TUESDAY, OCTOBER 18 A busy day at Shackleford. Lord Middleton made a grand opening speech, so carefully thought out, digesting all the reasons for our work & putting them so clearly. Andrews did a good trade in pots.

WEDNESDAY, OCTOBER 19 I was startled this morning by Laura's[5] coming to tell me that Andrews had had an accident last night. I hurried on my things & went down before breakfast without telling Signor, to find

---

1. The four friezes, illustrating different human attributes following what Mary named 'the path of the just', round the walls of the chapel. The pattern has angels flanking a central cross, with a bird each side of it. 'The path of truth' shows the owl, bird of truth and wisdom. Angels carry roundels showing emblems of truth, for example, a set of scales, weighing true. Next is 'the path of hope', with the peacock, bird of hope, then 'the path of light', the eagle, and finally, 'the path of love', the pelican. **2.** John Elliott Burns MP (1858–1943), trade unionist, politician and Privy Counsellor. Watts painted him in 1897, saying he wanted the portrait to be given to the nation as representative of the growing prominence of labour in politics. **3.** St Botolph's churchyard and surrounding Postman's Park was of interest for Watts's idea of a memorial to forgotten heroes who had given their lives to help others. This appears to be the first visit made by the Wattses to St Botolph's. **4.** Examples of Compton Pottery at a local exhibition. **5.** A housemaid at Limnerslease.

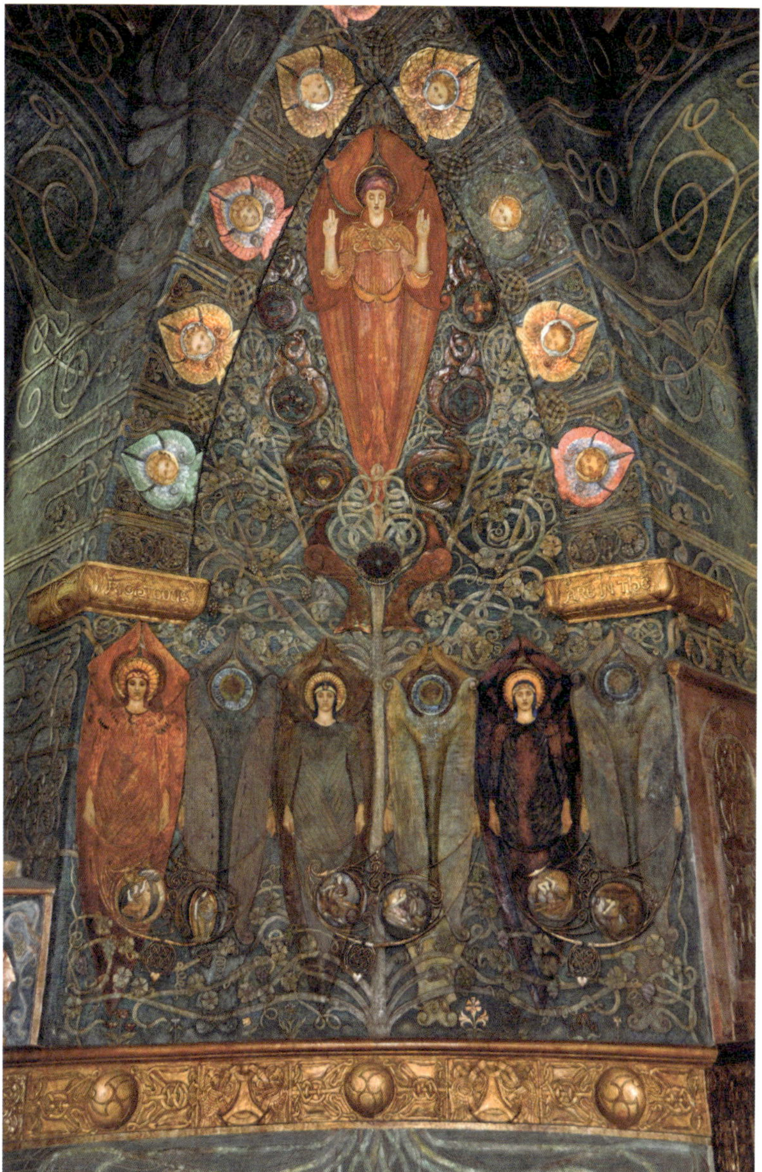

The interior of Watts Cemetery Chapel, with angels and the Tree of Life

him in bed in great pain from a dislocated elbow! A miracle only that prevented his neck being broken, for, going home in the great darkness last night by an unknown way to him by Farncombe, he found himself carried away on his tricycle full pace down that tremendous hill, & was upset in the ditch.

Mitchell was behind & followed up & went on to the doctor, his arm being numb, & waving round the wrong way. The doctor got the elbow back into place before an hour had passed, & before the swelling had become excessive. He was brought home.

Mrs Andrews says she 'had seen it all', & only asked when they came if he was much hurt. 'I saw him in the ditch at eight o'clock when I was sitting working here' she said, but I think, dear soul, she has seen the ditch & the accident every night when he is late. A serious matter for all. Signor misses his right arm!

SATURDAY, OCTOBER 22 Andrews goes on well. Stores & books to unpack & try to get in order.

My darling showed me a new picture, his thought of *Humanity & her Children.*[1] Naughty children, he says they are.

In the evening we read a really fine story called 'The Bridge Builders' in Rudyard Kipling's *The Day's Work*. Full of imagination, vivid, original as it is, it was a delight to read it, & under all you feel the kind manly heart that lets no sacrifice or toil go by, without its due praise, a kindly eye that sees & feels with all the work-a-day world, the sweat & tears that made the sound of a torrent in Whitman's eyes.

How good to be alone, & with my sweet in his niche.

MONDAY, OCTOBER 24 My sweet is not very well, but he urges himself to work. 'I felt very much inclined to stay in bed this morning' he said to me 'but I know if I had I should have been vexed with myself all day' – My little St. Francis!

WEDNESDAY, OCTOBER 26 A new 'Fatima' comes as a reproach to me. So few days do I feel up to writing now.

Signor drove with me to see Mr Molyneux. Quite a matter to record.

So hot I was glad of my muslin tea gown in the evening. Signor felt a little giddy & went to bed in the evening before dinner.

---

1. The final title of this painting was *Evolution* (1898, Watts Gallery Collection).

My hands full of Martha cares, autumn bulbs, boxes of jams from a new fruit farm, new coffee roaster.

FRIDAY, OCTOBER 28 I drove to Mr Molyneux to do a photograph Signor wanted of an acacia. Back by Loseley to see the sweet old place.

SATURDAY, OCTOBER 29 Andrew brought a long letter from Lord Meath.[1] He & his 'open spaces' are opposing violently Signor's little sheltering nook where his plaques to Heroes are proposed to be inserted. Andrew has to go to London about it. It seems quite ridiculous that such a harmless proposal should be met with such a storm of opposition. Andrew heard big words about it & went along in the rain to interview Lord Meath.

WEDNESDAY, NOVEMBER 23 Florence Bligh[2] & I journeyed to London to see *Pelléas & Mélisande*.[3] Mrs Pat Campbell had sent me a box. It was difficult at first to forget oneself & the people, & be lifted right away, specially with a bright healthy-minded woman at my side to whom the breaking waves & sound appealed more than the acting. I felt the stage too big & the footlights jarred, but afterwards when I looked upon it all I felt I had been wonderfully soothed by the strangely unreal & yet real little play.

FRIDAY, NOVEMBER 25 A happy quiet birthday, forgotten till the post came to remind me.

SATURDAY, DECEMBER 3 I lie awake 2 hours, & think out the weak points in the chapel book.[4] I see that it fails most in the illustrations of the text. Deuchars' drawings are maps, not sketches of the detail, & therefore

---

1. Reginald Brabazon, 12th Earl of Meath, Anglo-Irish politician and philanthropist. After he inherited the earldom from his father, he became involved in many philanthropic enterprises, including, having become a member of London County Council, protecting 'open spaces' in the capital. He misunderstood Watts's intention, thinking that the whole of Postman's Park would become a private, enclosed space. **2.** Florence Bligh (1860–1944) was born in Victoria, Australia, and married Ivo Bligh, 4th Earl of Darnley, English cricketer. According to the *Hobart Mercury*, 4 June, 1908, she was the leader of a group of Melbourne ladies who presented Ivo Bligh with 'a tiny urn, containing the ashes of Australian cricket'. **3.** The 1898 production of Maurice Maeterlinck's play with music by Gabriel Fauré, in which Mrs Patrick Campbell and Johnston Forbes-Robertson played the leads. The tragic love story was also turned also into an opera by Claude Debussy in 1902. **4.** Louis Deuchars' initials, 'LRD', appear on a number of drawings in the book, *The Word in the Pattern* (1905, first edition), and his large drawing of the altar was published in *The Studio*, vol.17, 1899, p.103.

thoroughly uninteresting. Signor says he has got to learn that however much form you may use, it will be nothing unless it provokes the impression of form. Mere strength of line does not give this. 'What you want is not form but the impression of form.'

What I want is the flexibility of the terra cotta work to suggest beauty. Signor went on to tell me that while you require flexibility in drawings from architecture you have also to get the grist & weight of the works. Two laws always in action, form propelling & gravitation steadying.

WEDNESDAY, DECEMBER 7 Our first class. A fine night & fairly well attended.

SATURDAY, DECEMBER 10 Did not expect my little class. 2 came. They came scampering up & were sent off by Deuchars. Andrews, I fear, scattered them with the policeman's instinct. I heard the sound of vanishing feet & merry voices & ran out too late!

Our kiln filled today. Alas, a big break in the chapel works.[1]

TUESDAY, DECEMBER 13 Signor had Thompson down today & the Great Barn Studio[2] was opened! A fine day. They were out from 10 till 4 & when I went up at sunset a great prism of white lay thrown against the dark background of the barn.

The Laureate is to have birth upon nothing less than the Goddess of Dawn. He is to grow out of her, a son of the Morning!

We telegraphed to May & Andrew, 'Opening of the Great Barn Studio. Sculptor at work from 10 until four, delighted with Studio'. & they answered 'Bless the work & the worker'.

THURSDAY, DECEMBER 15 Thompson came down, & they are there labouring along at the building of the poet all day. The weather delightful. I go to Godalming to see the School of Art, & to Ethel's cottage to see to things & so home.

---

1. More than one kiln was built before satisfactory results were achieved in firing the big terracotta pieces. The first chairs outside the chapel, some gravestones and very large pots were among items that had to be jettisoned. 2. The barn adjoining the Limnerslease property that had been bought so that Watts could work on the large statue of Tennyson for Lincoln Cathedral. A railway track was built so that the sculpture could be drawn outside to give him space to see it from a distance.

SATURDAY, DECEMBER 17 Andrew came. He tells me the village want to present Signor with the thanks of the Parish! May illuminating the parchment. It is a lovely book, but oh![1]

THURSDAY, DECEMBER 22 Lily comes, I don't think her looking quite so well as she did last summer. The cold & drying rain have nipped her.

The great poet looms out huge now, like the white ghost of him!

SATURDAY, DECEMBER 24 I awake with anxiety about our afternoon at Monkshatch. I had not told Signor that the object of it is to thank him for his gift of the chapel.

In the brougham on the way up, I said 'One thing that is to happen today is that some of the village people want to thank you for giving them the Chapel.' 'Oh, dear' he said laughing 'I should not have come if I had known that.'

I knew very little about it all, Andrew having asked me whether this presentation of names was to be at Monkshatch or at Eastbury or here! When we arrived we were shown the beautiful book, all their thoughts & work of darling May & who with such care & colour have made the book beautiful within & without.[2] Chapel patterns illuminated on the pages of the address, & round the photographs & other things. Mr Gillett gave the book with a very kind speech, saying all he felt about our work in Compton & the good results it was having. Signor answered shortly thanking them, but it was so great a surprise to him that he who never had any words at his command had none. He had been going to say the building & carrying out of the chapel had been a work of love.

SATURDAY, DECEMBER 31 Today, 80 children. Monday, I am afraid to think how many may come!

---

1. Mary knew how much Watts would not enjoy the presentation. 2. The illuminated album is in the Archive at the Watts Gallery.

1902

Both Watts and Mary were working hard. Mary was continuing the decorating of the chapel interior, with only a small group of helpers. The painting and relief work was very skilled, and she did a great deal of the painting of hands and all the faces of angels and cherubs herself.

Good orders came in for the pottery, and Mary lured down from Ayrshire a new manager, James Nicol, who had worked at the Cumnock Pottery for 20 years. A house, which he named Helmstead, was built for him and his family near Limnerslease, and Watts was godfather to his son, George. A new kiln was built, said by Mary to be 'the first thoroughly good one'.

Life was a little quieter, although Lily was now living at home and nearly grown up. She and Mary were very close, and rode round the village on their bicycles performing errands. A newly discovered neighbour was Christopher Hatton Turnor, an architect who had studied with Edwin Lutyens. He was living with his parents. Mary and Lily visited the Turnors in February, and found the parents and son 'a rather unique 3, the son so clever, & sweet, & good'.

Mary had a new idea to commission a gallery to be built, so that Watts's studio collection of his own work could be shown in perpetuity. She soon had it in mind that the young Turnor might be exactly the right man to undertake it.

The Court of Death had been in the Limnerslease studio for 11 years, and Watts considered it finished. It was intended for the recently named Tate Gallery, and in March it left Compton for London. Mary asked Watts the next day whether seeing it go made him sad and he replied,

'I forget all about it, to tell the truth. I want my work to be of some use, and when it is done and gone I don't think any more about it.'

In March, also, Cecil Rhodes died, and his friend Lord Grey made the request to Watts that the first cast of his great sculpture on which he had been working so long, *Physical Energy*, should be sent to South Africa as a memorial to Rhodes. Eventually, three bronzes were cast, but not until after Watts's death two years later. One is in Cape Town, one in Harare and one in Kensington Gardens, London. The model is at Watts Gallery, where you can still see Watts's thumbprints in the plaster.

TUESDAY, FEBRUARY 4 Big post, & a wretched article written on our pottery by Mrs Erskine.[1] Blowing of trumpets to do us so much harm. Somehow everything she touches upon seems spoilt in the handling.

An order for 32 pots from Somerset! Unluckily yellow clay, not red, & Nicol[2] is afraid of not doing them well. We don't know our pale clays yet.

My sweet well & hard at work, tho' really stopped now & then by darkness. Heard him playing Mendelssohn to himself & later Mozart.

TUESDAY, FEBRUARY 11 18 degrees of frost. Bright sun.

I am drawing a little Dandy Dinmont, for Sligo's grave,[3] from a photograph.

Signor, Lily & I walked to the Turnors,[4] & had the most interesting visit, seeing drawings, photographs, furniture, house. In general, a rather unique 3, the son so clever & sweet & good, & the old father kindly & good, the mother so clever, & the old puritan so alive in both the parents.

My sweet has become anxious & on our return. I find him really agitated because we are out at sunset, & he is afraid of influenza!

---

1. Mrs Stewart Erskine (1860–1948), journalist. **2.** James Nicol, manager of the pottery from 1901 to 1931. Mary lured him down from Cumnock Pottery in Scotland. He married and brought up his family in Compton. His son George married Kathleen Titcomb, a colourist at the pottery. **3.** Sligo, one of the black and tan terriers at Limnerslease. **4.** Christopher Hatton Turnor (1873– 1940), whose parents lived in Compton, was the architect who designed Watts Gallery. It was opened to the public in 1904. In 1907 he married Sarah Carpenter, daughter of Admiral Carpenter of Kiplin Hall, where five of Watts's paintings of the Talbot (Carpenter) family hang.

WEDNESDAY, FEBRUARY 12 My sweet Lily & I had a walk through the copse to the village & back, talking heart to heart. She grows ever dearer, ever tenderer. Sweet, pure, blessed stream of young life. I do not think that we quite reverence youth enough.

SUNDAY, FEBRUARY 23 *St George's Day* Here in my bed,[1] but so much better, & my beloved goes in & out & even comes to lie upon his bed, & be at my side. But even raising my voice is an exertion.

FRIDAY, FEBRUARY 28 Got down-stairs after a fortnight.

Have had some time for thinking out the outlines of my work, its aims, objects, & reasonableness. Also my own shortcomings in it.

SATURDAY, MARCH 1 I get out & see our kiln. The first thoroughly good one.

MONDAY, MARCH 3 Kept our birthday, put off one week.

Andrew, May, Mrs Ellice[2] have luncheon here. There are the sweet children too who come afterwards to dance & see the cake.

FRIDAY, MARCH 14 An article in *Country Life* on our pots gives us all pleasure.

WEDNESDAY, MARCH 19 I never believed that Signor would see the great *Court of Death*[3] leave his studio, but it has gone today, a glorious March morning. I had gone out to see our work & just came back at the moment when the ropes were being loosened to drop it forward gradually upon its face on the floor. One saw it better than it has been seen, just tipped forward for the final move. Mr Holroyd came a few minutes later & by luncheon time the great picture was a roll of canvas, in the van. Begun at old Little Holland House, it must be now more than 30 years ago, the 1st picture.

THURSDAY, MARCH 20 I asked Signor this morning what he thought of his studio this morning & he said 'One might think after working so long upon a picture of some importance that one would feel the loss of it, but I really did not. I forget all about it, to tell the truth. I want my work to be of some use, & when it is done & gone I don't think any more about it.'

---

1. Mary had been in bed with influenza for ten days. **2.** The owner of Eastbury Manor, Compton. **3.** *The Court of Death* (Tate Collection). In 2016, the painting was loaned to Watts Gallery Artists' Village Studios to be hung, as before, in Watts's studio.

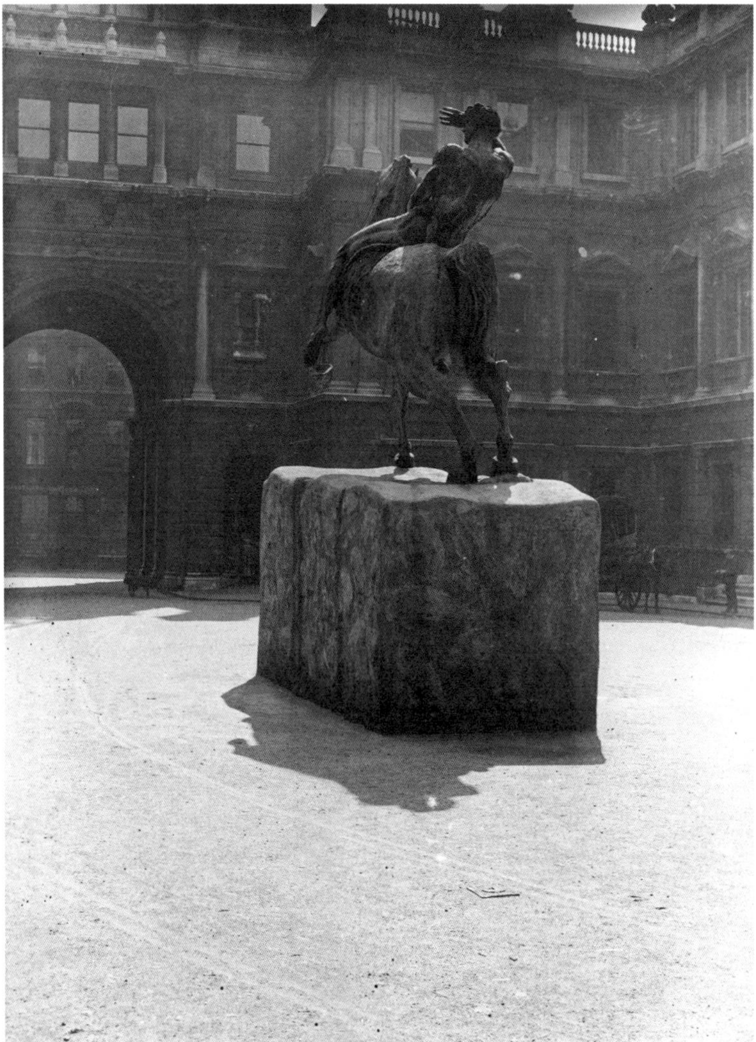

Physical Energy (1883–1904) in the forecourt of Burlington House, Piccadilly, 1904

SATURDAY, MARCH 22 *Little Holland House* We met Lord Grey, just back from America & a visit to Roosevelt. Charmed with him. He was as usual, delightful to see & meet. 'Funny my running across two of the nicest people in London, in this way' he said.

Alas, he says Rhodes is dying! Dr Jameson had cabled last night that the rally was quite temporary, & that there was no possible hope of recovery.

WEDNESDAY, MARCH 26 At his cottage at Muizenberg, Cape Colony at 4.30. On this day Cecil Rhodes died & South Africa lost a great leader.

SATURDAY, MARCH 29 *Limnerslease* Pot room cleared & made quite tidy I have storage now beyond, under a new lean-to roof.

The editor of *Country Life* came. He had intended giving an order for our pots but driving via Munstead,[1] I think he had been made to think we were not doing the right sort. Possibly Miss Jekyll has an Italian protégé, to whom we are rivals.

SUNDAY, MARCH 30 *Easter Day* I walk alone across the sweet brown common to Puttenham. Am soothed by the service, flowers of the earth, spring, the little candle flames, all recalling the old day when those seekers after God sent up the saddest aspiration of the human heart. How wise those old Christian teachers were to link them all together.

SUNDAY, APRIL 13 Our dear Lord Grey came, whom we love, full of the schemes for casting the great statue.[2] He brought a will made by Rhodes in '77 when he had come back to go to Oxford. The same aims, the same boylike simplicity!

MONDAY, APRIL 14 I write, & then work a little in my hut at models for Alice & Shem's graves.[3] The cuckoo singing & all the promise of life after death about me. The hut is a great joy.

---

1. Munstead Wood was Gertrude Jekyll's house. She used Compton garden pots in some of her garden designs, and a large pot was named after her. **2.** The sculpture *Physical Energy*. **3.** Mary's hut was built as an extension to the 'pot room'. She was designing one of the finest memorials in the chapel cemetery for her cousin Alice Hansen née Ogilvy, and a dog's grave for the garden at Limnerslease.

TUESDAY, APRIL 15 Letter from Emma saying the *Energy* is going away today![1]

Signor had hoped to have seen & looked it over, but there is no halt when Lord Grey takes the command. In the afternoon a telegram, '*Energy* just started, Thompson going with it'. In the evening a telegram '*Energy* arrived all right at the Foundry'.

'I confess I feel ashamed of having let it go' Signor said with a sad, depressed look. 'It seems like presumption.'

FRIDAY, JULY 25 Signor went to dine at the Athenaeum. How young & slim & well he looked.

FRIDAY, NOVEMBER 14 The Akouphone[2] came late tonight.

WEDNESDAY, NOVEMBER 19 Tonight we used the wonderful Akouphone with the greatest comfort. I reading in a low voice, he hearing every sound.

THURSDAY, NOVEMBER 20 Our wedding day. So quiet & alone we two.

My crowned fulfilled life. My blessed one given to me all these 16 years. It seems unbelievable, & he so well! My work going on by his side.

Our festa was a bowl of Roses, spared by frost & east wind, & some champagne, this evening! We felt like Roman emperors, Roses & a Libation!

FRIDAY, NOVEMBER 21 *Joy & Sorrow*, *Spirit & Flesh*, *Real & Ideal* panels, ready to go to the chapel.[3]

THURSDAY, NOVEMBER 27 *Little Holland House* Picked flowers for Gerry & Ethel & did 1000 letters & other things at the Pottery, then off to London with Lily & Signor, and straight to the Portrait Painters' show.

Found the Lovat casket.[4] Looking like lead, worn like an old odigi lamp stand. I fear it may disappoint. Ethel came, & ran off with Lily to Stoke's, & got him to re-silver it.

---

1. Emma, housekeeper at Little Holland House, was reporting that *Physical Energy* was being taken to be cast at the Parlanti Bronze Foundry in Fulham. Alessandro Parlanti's foundry was the first in England to use the 'lost-wax' casting process. **2.** The first electric hearing aid, designed by an American electrical engineer, Miller Reese Hutchison, in 1898. **3.** The panels, raised plaster roundels illustrating opposites, are held by angels. **4.** The Lovat casket was designed by Louis Deuchars for the Lovat Scouts. This was a Scottish Highland Regiment of the British Army, founded in 1900 during the Second Boer War. Ted Fraser-Tytler was a founder member. In the First World War, the Lovat Scouts formed a sniper unit named the Sharpshooters.

I fear it is a monument to my love of trying to do more than I can. Deuchars's hands are not what I can work with.

SUNDAY, NOVEMBER 30 *Little Holland House* Journey to London, reaching Duke St. about 3.30.

Found Ted & Bill. Had to promise Signor that I would stay the night at L.H.H.

Saw all the dear Scouts party, Lord Lovat, Sir J. Campbell Ord, 'The Best Adjutant', Kenny Macdonald, Capt. Ellice, Mr Hart, Ted & Bill.[1] Lord Lovat gave them the casket. They thought it interesting & unique & were pleased.

MONDAY, DECEMBER 1 *Limnerslease* Darling Signor said to Lily yesterday – 'I do hope Mary is safely at her journey's end.'

I came back to him & my child & my work, by a workman's train!

TUESDAY, DECEMBER 2 Sun for a wonder, so saw our panels in the chapel for the first time.

THURSDAY, DECEMBER 4 I am happy looking at my roses snatched from frost yesterday by happy chance. Fringe of sweet & beloved Summer's skirt.

SUNDAY, DECEMBER 7 A friend & I went to the Chapel. He was so kind, his criticism is that the colour of the angels is not quite monotonous enough. I feel the same. It is astonishing that in the chapel light my green central angel has disappeared into the background, while the red & blue angel is bluer & redder than those in the studio.[2] Of course the day was very dark. He wants to speak more about principles of line, & through line, to say what he has to say, more than through symbols. He is a delightful companion, so gentle & self respecting, with a kind of quiet reserve of strength.

THURSDAY, DECEMBER 25 Signor not very bright.

We all went to Monkshatch, but Choons & I hurried back to be with him.

Christmas is nearly over, & the shortest day gone too.

---

1. Mary's two half-brothers. Edward Fraser-Tytler and William Fraser-Tytler. **2.** It is difficult to know if the colours of Mary's decoration inside the chapel have faded or not. From what she says here, it seems that she may have softened the colour of the angels herself.

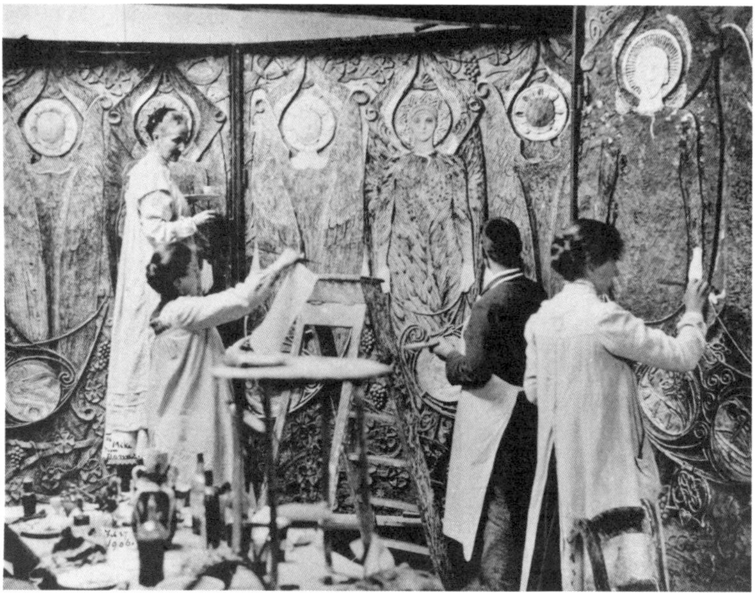

Mary Watts, Alice Jacobs and two other helpers (on the right) working on the decorations of the interior of the Cemetery Chapel

TUESDAY, DECEMBER 30 Signor in his room, being hoarse. We had the chore of preparing all the downstairs rooms for our children. Upwards of 80 came!

Tea spread in hall. Drawing room, dining room, north studio, cleared for games. They were very happy from 3.30 till 7 p.m.

WEDNESDAY, DECEMBER 31 The year dies, & I have so many undones. I am going to try for better things next year. The house has gone back to tidiness. I had an hour alone, & dreamed thro' 32 years of my life.

It has been a very happy one. All these last years since, with my beloved, I have loved, served, & I would not unlive any of my sorrows. We are richer for them.

May I dare to hope the garment of the chapel[1] will all be finished next year?

1. The decorations. They were finished in spring 1904.

1904

In the early part of the year Mary was near to finishing the decorations of the interior of the Cemetery Chapel. Watts was completing a small version of his painting *The All-Pervading* to place above the altar. It shows the Creator, an enigmatic, seated figure, with a globe in his or her lap. The painting was put in its place in April. In May Watts went to the Home Arts and Industries Association annual exhibition, and came home very tired. By mid-June he was worryingly ill.

Mary chronicles his illness in great detail in the diary, and hardly leaves his side. His death comes on July 1. 'The End', she writes.

The next part of her diary, written in extreme grief, reads as if this daily writing was to some extent a comfort to her. She was surrounded by her 'beloveds', all fully aware of what she was going through, and giving her all the help they could, and Watts's position as a celebrity did mean that there was plenty to organise. First, the coffin was placed in the chapel, and a vigil was arranged so that it was never left alone there. The next day there was what she describes as a consecrating service in his studio, with a choir and the archbishop reading. Then, her two half-brothers and George Andrews took the coffin to Woking to the new crematorium, the first one to be built. They brought back the casket and on July 7 there was the full-scale service at St Paul's Cathedral, about which Mary alerted all his friends with 500 letters. The terracotta casket, decorated by the finest modeller from the pottery, Tom Wren, was finally brought back to Compton, to the Cemetery Chapel, where the actual funeral service took place, and Watts's ashes were buried in the grave, which had been prepared at the top of the hill in the cemetery.

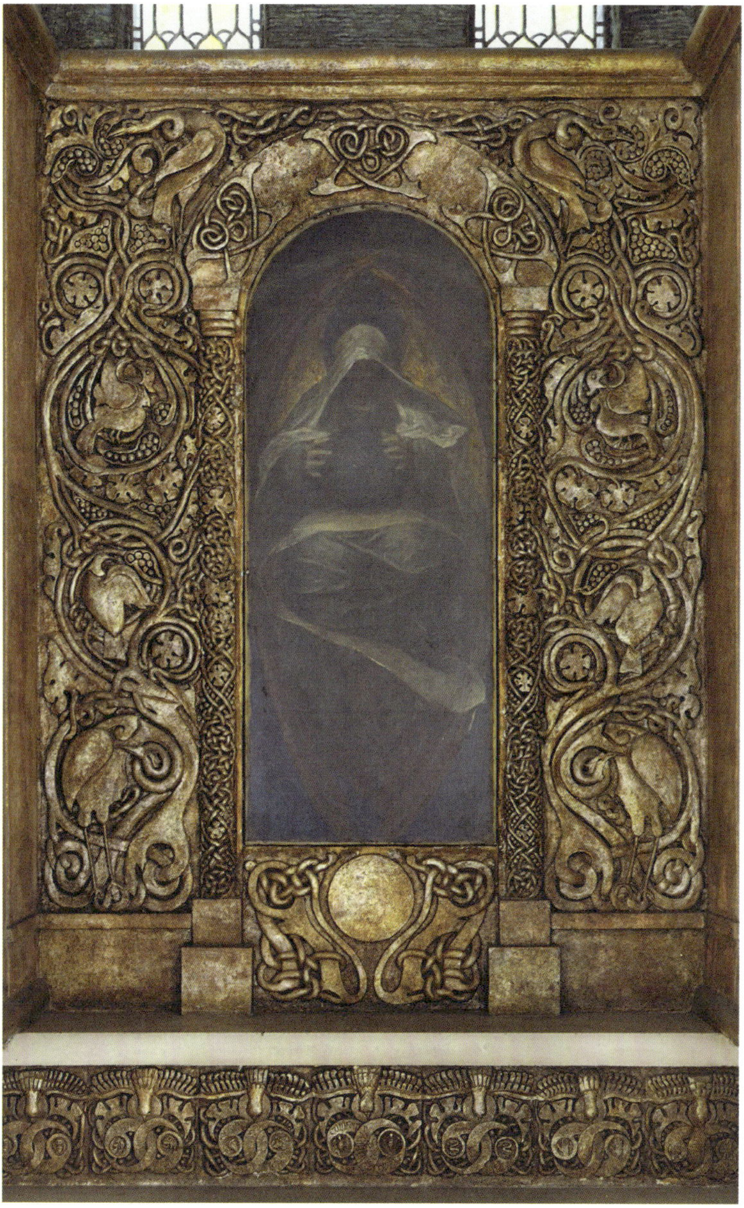

G.F. Watts, *The All-Pervading*, 1904, in situ over the altar in the Cemetery Chapel

After this week Mary decided to go away to somewhere she was not known, and so she and Lily spent some days at Aldeburgh, Suffolk. When they returned, Mary was ready and determined to start work again; she felt sure that was what Watts would have wanted her to do.

Over the next weeks and months she worked extremely hard. She painted angels' faces in the chapel interior, saw to the completing of the first Compton sundial, and worked with Sir Edward Poynter on planning the retrospective exhibition of Watts's work, set for December/January. She supervised the casting of *Physical Energy*, and arranged for the removal to Compton from Little Holland House of much of the furniture, the books and many of the paintings, so that the house could be let as soon as possible.

A happy note in the last months of that year was the engagement of Lily to a young man Mary thoroughly liked, Michael Chapman, who was staying temporarily with his parents a few miles away.

Mary's grief is best read in her own words.

FRIDAY, APRIL 15 The picture[1] is placed in the chapel. Beloved has worked since Easter to finish it.

THURSDAY, MAY 12 My dear one at the Home Arts[2] in the afternoon. Very, very tired.

THURSDAY, JUNE 16 *Little Holland House* I awake to find Signor in pain & this is a very solemn moment! An hour & a half of great prostration, the pulse intermittent, the whole face truly seeing the borderland between life & eternal life.

Little nurse resourceful & calm & helpful. I hardly knew what we did, but he rallied by nine. Even then the Dr thought he had been round a bad corner.

The blackbirds sang & the woodpigeons cooed & somehow the intense <u>strength</u> of the soul <u>alone</u> in the supremest anguish came down upon me. If my beloved & I were parting, I somehow knew of a strength

---

1. *The All-Pervading* in which the Creator sits, in the act of creating the universe, holding a globe. This is a smaller version of the painting in Tate Britain, and was painted by Watts for the space over the altar in Mary's Cemetery Chapel. **2.** The Home Arts and Industries annual exhibition. This was the last time Watts attended an exhibition.

stronger than myself, or a sense of the absence of the human, the absence of the need of the human, & the sense of the strength of the divine.

SUNDAY, JUNE 19 My beloved one told me he wanted to tell Gerry & me something. 'Come to me' he said, 'when you & she can.' So we came & knelt at his bedside. He wanted us to know what he had been seeing & yet knew he could not put his thoughts into words.

He said 'It was not a dream, it was not an illusion, it was not an hallucination, it was a reality, a glorious state', & when he spoke of it & of its being 'no place' & having 'no people, myself the only blot' he had to cover his dear face with his beautiful thin hands.

Can we ever forget his face, when he said those words, so spiritual, enraptured?

'It is not that I have no beliefs, but I believe nothing is true that is not simple. If there is a power that asks belief of its creatures it cannot ask them to believe that which they have not been given the power to comprehend. If my idea is crude, at least it is simple. There is no use in saying "There are no laws of nature", or that there are, & that we understand them, for we cannot understand, though we are in them.'

SUNDAY, JUNE 26 My darling Choons came up. She came to comfort me. Before she left he was less well & I hurried to his room, & ran out to kiss her on the stairs & cry & say nothing could ever take from me those seventeen years & seven months of blessed life with him.

He suddenly asked for a peach, & Lily ran to Val's to ask for one & Gerry to four shops, which opened for her, & Mr Shannon, kind man, hearing Lily's mission, ran off & brought him seven.

MONDAY, JUNE 27 My Darling beloved was rather wandering this morning. I had not told him Choons had been yesterday, & yet he opened his eyes & said 'Christine has come now to take me away.' I said 'no, darling, she is not here'. 'How strange' he said 'I thought she said she had come to take me away.'

TUESDAY, JUNE 28 This is our most hopeful day. 'In 48 hours we shall know' the doctor had said confidently, & this day he seemed almost round the corner, he was so much better.

'Oh, Mary, I have so craved for you,' he said to me when I came back from dinner.

WEDNESDAY, JUNE 29 A bad day after a better night, with hours of comfortable sleep. Nurse took his temperature. It was 104. Then all hope died within me.

Dr Knightly will not give up hope. He has unbounded faith in his reserve strength.

THURSDAY, JUNE 30 Today someone left a little bunch of white flowers on his doorstep.

As Bill came here this evening, over London passed slowly a lonely Heron! He felt it was an omen of the soul 'migrating to the unseen'. I lay down on my bed about midnight, Nurse Hart being busy making S. comfortable, moving his pillows, so that my restful communion in silence with my beloved was interrupted but I had not been there many minutes when quite strongly he called 'Mary, Mary, Mary, come to me.' I sprang up & was quickly holding his beloved hand once more.

FRIDAY, JULY 1 I had my bed (now nearly a month away from his side), pushed up once more & lay beside him. At 6.30 he said quite suddenly, 'Read to me.' I had no book, but said the verses of the opening of *In Memoriam* 'Strong Son of God Immortal Love'.[1] I could not remember them all, but he must have heard & liked it for he said 'Say it again.' I ran out & Lily, hearing I wanted *In Memoriam*, ran to the Holman Hunts & brought his precious copy, his since 1850, & I read again 8 verses of 'The Strong Son of God' & also the 'Charity' sermon from Corinthians he so loves.

'I want you to be happy' he said.

'Why, why don't they come?' he cried often, meaning the great messengers he had so implored to come.

The End.

SATURDAY, JULY 2 I have my beloveds all about me & yet I have gone through much today, at first finding tears & sweet sad thoughts, & heaven near, but later struck down to earth again.

A business letter & some talk with my dear tender-hearted Bill.[2]

May & Gerry & Lily have made all beautiful & fair. Cantoni did the cast of the beloved features & the hands, & now under the exquisite

1. In Memoriam by Alfred, Lord Tennyson. **2.** Bill Fraser-Tytler was Watts's executor.

pall, with flowers & light, he lies in his empty studio. One month since he stood there & laid by his work.

SUNDAY, JULY 3 It was this day 18 years ago that he said to me 'I want you.'

I awoke at 4 a.m. Went to the studio. All quiet. The silence terrible. I could not stay. No comfort. I went to church at 8 a.m.

These words were some comfort. 'God is not unrighteous, that he will forget your works & labour that proceedeth of love.'

I asked to be alone. My beloveds understood. I am a spirit as it were outcast from a high heaven. I feel as if never again would I attune my life to that sweet high pitch that for 18 years (so nearly) I have had daily in my ears, making such music in my heart.

Alone till six with my sorrow. Then came peace.

My Ted came & brought me Aldourie ferns & flowers from the dell at half past five.

A beautiful consecrating service in his studio, all made so fair by May & Gerry & my Lily. The beloved Archbishop reading. The choir from Holy Trinity singing 'Oh strength & stay!' 'Oh God our help in ages past'. Angel voices choiring in that high vaulted room, just once before he leaves it forever. It was very solemn & beautiful with the consecrating kiss, as much as the prayers.

MONDAY, JULY 4 I went down at six this morning to the studio, a great shaft of light poured straight through the east window down upon his own portrait so that he was bathed in light, & was there himself in a mist of light. I found myself making the only shadow, so I moved, & then I knew the light fell also like his blessing on my head. I remember the shaft of light in *Progress*. My beloved one is now all spirit.

Bill & Ted & Andrews take him to Woking[1] under the beautiful pall. Andrews dropped in a flower from me, from May, from Lily, Gerry (her thought), before the casket closed.

The terrible list of names to be gone through, that all who care for him must have the chance of a ticket for the Abbey.[2] In the evening we left for Limnerslease.

---

1. Watts and Mary had both decided they wanted to be cremated. The first crematorium in the country was at Woking. The casket for Watts's ashes was designed at Compton Pottery by Thomas Wren, pottery apprentice. **2.** Mary was assuming that the memorial service would be in Westminster Abbey. However, it was in St Paul's Cathedral.

How strange the station & the people passing are all the same, & yet to me all changed.

Over my heart his watch. The little helmet cap he wore. That is all I take back to the little earthly paradise.

18 years since we knew we were to be a strength & stay to each other. Now we are divided.

What living beloveds I have. Andrew & May came in thru the little doors, & there we kissed each other, & I tried to say all we owe to them.

Oh, sweet, sweet home, where I have known such peace, such joy, such high communion with a noble soul.

TUESDAY, JULY 5 One second of delicious forgetfulness, I turned, when I awoke, to see if he had gone to work!

I went up at 6 o'clock to the chapel to find dear little nurse already watching. She & I with our own hands took the casket from the altar steps & laid it on the central pedestal.

Later the candelabra were placed, & flowers in masses.

I cut & make the wreath of poet's laurel, the victor's laurel!

The bell tolls these days from 3.15 till 3.30. His words, saying 'Be my voice neither feared nor forgotten.'

May & I walked in the beautiful calm dusk. The garden is a wonder of roses & colour. Shrined in the little casket made two years ago, with little thought of its destiny. It lay for a year forgotten in London, till this year I brought it back here, to try my wax colour upon it.

'Till the dawn breaks & the shadows flee away.' White lilies stand about it, & masses of flowers, great bay wreaths from many, to small bunches of cottage flowers.

WEDNESDAY, JULY 6 No blessed forgetfulness this morning when I woke!

I got up quickly & went again to pray in the chapel. Andrews watching there. This beautiful thought of May's has given infinite comfort to all about. Each offers to take his two hours! Of all my letters no word has quite so much gone home as a line in Mr Spielmann's today, 'and I hope your sorrow will strengthen you'.

Choons telegraphs that they will come to St Paul's tomorrow.

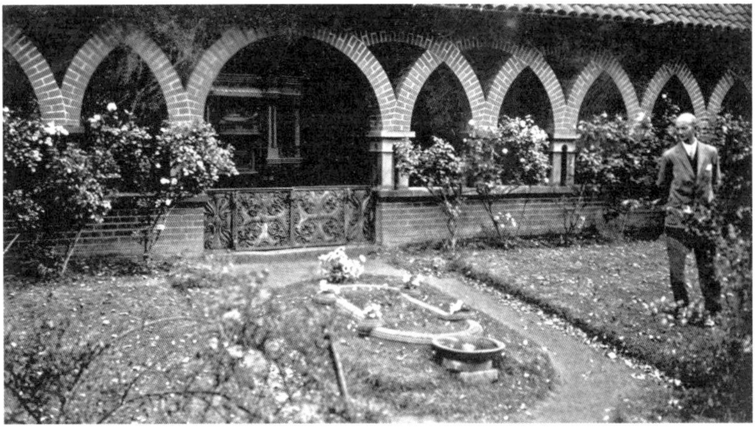

James Nicol standing by Watts's grave

THURSDAY, JULY 7 Am awake by six o'clock to go to pray in the chapel.

We go to hear the nation say the last Amen for my beloved. We meet at Canon Scott Holland's[1] little house in Amen Court. I had hastily telegraphed to him for leave to do so, that Edward & Choons might have this place to meet in.

Then to St Paul's. All overwhelming, but I was strong. The glorious music. The voice of his beloved friend saying 'Peace. Come away.'

We are back, as I much wished, in time to hear the last toll at the hour of his passing, 3.15. Upon my knees I pray that my life may be ever one with him.

FRIDAY, JULY 8 An absolutely perfect day, calm, radiant. I am at the chapel at 6 o'clock, to find Andrews there. How beautiful. The sun through the east window strikes against my own red angel just by the door.

My beloved, all that is he now on earth, shrined in the little casket designed two years ago, little dreaming it would be so sacred. Modelled

1. Henry Scott Holland (1847–1918), Canon of St Paul's Cathedral. Watts gave his painting, *Time, Death, and Judgement*, to the Dean and Chapter of St Paul's, at Scott Holland's request, in 1897. It was hung in the nave as an inspiration to the many people who slept rough there, said Scott Holland, and it was joined ten years later by *Peace and Goodwill*. Both paintings have been on loan to Watts Gallery since 1977.

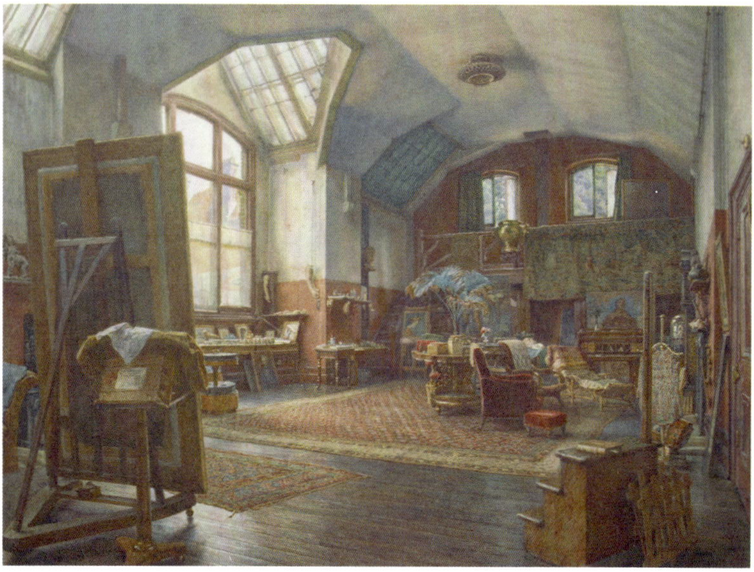

Thomas Rooke, *G.F. Watts's studio at Little Holland House*, 1904, watercolour painted a few days after Watts's death, Watts Gallery

by Tom so carefully. Burnt in our own little kiln. 'Till the day breaks & the shadows flee away.'

From eleven till twelve I have my watch alone. The flowers are gone, the candles burning low. Then the service & the end. Living beloveds all about me.

SATURDAY, JULY 9 My day has been to write a little, a letter to Mr Nicol & our works, to Ted & Bill to say that I for the moment must go to some strange place with no associations, & no friends. Darling Aldourie is too full of things for me to love, to remember, & to do. I must be alone somewhere. Only my now nearly 500 letters to answer.

Gerry lies beside me on his bed, & I have my dear Tennyson volumes piled beside me. They breathe lofty thought & calm, tho' indeed I should have that, for love & nature seem to wrap me now, so that no wound smarts. But for a recurring thought 'had I done this' or 'had we perhaps stayed here until the summer had warmed & revived him', which brings unrest, I have nothing to disturb the holy calm. Few have so much to live for.

We go again in the dark to see the little grave banked up & massed with flowers. A cloudless, serene sky, saffron & orange melting into blue, a fitting canopy.

MONDAY, JULY 11 My first moments, getting up by five, to go to the little quiet spot. Flowers withering, a fresh wind astir.

I feel it calls to me saying 'Be up, the working world has need of your life.'

THURSDAY, JULY 21 I have to take all his precious little note books, pencils, caps from his pocket. Every little thing of daily use, brims now with the tears of parting.

MONDAY, JULY 25 Have decided to have Andrews & Steadman up to put on the head & arms of the beautiful rider if this can be done, then I can show it to a few who know, & ask them to compare it with the bronze & with the wax.

WEDNESDAY, JULY 27 Andrews & Steadman came. Today, for you, I have the arms & the head set in the torso of the *Physical Energy*. I want counsel from Mr Rivière upon this point. You changed much in his back, moved the head two inches further back. There was still that work of which you said 'Oh, four days more! It was little to ask.' Is it well to cast from this as it is, just filling the joints,[1] or shall we use Parlanti's moulds? This is what I want them to decide for me.

Darling! My beloved. The outer shell of your earthly house is here today, a beautiful cast.[2]

Dear Lady Somers here for an hour talking of him till nine o'c. So sweet to me, blessing me for my love & service. How easy that was, what joy a bit of what is called menial work was to me. 'Oh what have I brought you into?' he used to say, when my heart was rejoicing.

THURSDAY, AUGUST 4 In the afternoon Alice Moore Smith comes. Choons thinks she & her brother would like to come to live here & manage the Hostel,[3] if we could get him work in London, which is possible.

---

1. This was the second bronze cast of *Physical Energy*. **2.** Watts's death mask (Watts Gallery). **3.** Part of the new Gallery was built as a hostel for the young apprentice potters. There were sometimes as many as five of them, even in the early days of the pottery, and a couple to 'manage' the organising of their day-to-day living was becoming essential.

Strange to say seeing her who never knew Signor seems to accentuate all my loss.

FRIDAY, AUGUST 5 Early to the chapel with vases. I find the birds throw out the flowers from the pots on the grave to get water so I have placed a bird's drinking bowl there, for his little brothers & sisters, the birds. What could be better for that spot!

SATURDAY, AUGUST 6 I have now taken up my old work. Nicol comes at 8.30, & at 9, dear Andrews. I went today to do some touching to the Eastbury sundial. I cried like a baby before getting to work. This is not being strong as I hoped.

Lily shepherds Edward lovingly & well. What a darling she is! She labelled the Hostel roses with the boys today, & had them here for tea. I am so grateful. They are on my mind. Poor dears. The present arrangement cannot last.

TUESDAY, AUGUST 9 All the morning in the chapel. Steadman on a ladder doing hands for me.[1] I am eyes below. I am breathing over the Seraphim, who want just that to make them better, touching up symbols with aluminium leaf, then Mr Moore Smith comes.[2] One's first impression of him is that he is too feeble, too unassertive, & too dull. Afterwards one wondered whether it was a natural & beautiful self distrust & shyness, remembering that 'The meek do inherit the earth'. I shall trust. I see both under a disadvantage, for they are overwhelmed thinking of my grief, & the emptiness here. How I trust & pray this change may be right.

WEDNESDAY, AUGUST 10 Again in the chapel.

Sir Edward Poynter came to see what the Winter Ex[3] would be. He wants 100. I think there should be more. The work is so various.

Then to see Mrs Ellice. Her sundial being set up. Then Mr Gillett & Mrs Simpson to see me. My day quite ordinary, & yet the change so great. The great silent studio.

---

1. Steadman and Mary were working on painting the hands and eyes of the angels on the walls of the chapel interior. The four seraphs, blessing the whole, near the roof, are surrounded by roundels painted with symbols. **2.** Mr Moore Smith, possibly joining his sister to manage the Hostel, the home of the pottery apprentices. **3.** The retrospective exhibition at the Royal Academy.

The little grave had fresh lilies laid by it today. I do not know by whom. Some grateful heart.

THURSDAY, AUGUST 11 A wet morning. I spend my fond hours at the Chapel. Steadman has done his best for me, & the Cherubim look far nobler & more serene.

FRIDAY, AUGUST 12 *Little Holland House* Edward & Choons leave. We travel up together.

At the little House. Saw Mr Spielmann. The book is not written he says.[1]

Both Mr Rookes are painting there.[2] I did not get to Parlanti's.

MONDAY, AUGUST 15 Up at 5.

I go first to the Portrait Gallery.

Then to Parlanti's to see about the *Physical Energy*.

TUESDAY, AUGUST 16 Mrs Lowry comes to see about the house.[3] I think what she offers might be accepted with advantage. If she gives it up in 3 years, artists might be then more prosperous & able to take it.

I wonder if my beloved is near me when I make decisions of this sort! Ah, if one knew how near or how far.

Miss Jekyll came, but I was resting & Lily kept her away. If Mrs Lowry takes our house, I shall just have a month & a half to clear out everything.

My nightly engagement is to read a little bit of 'Fatima' & live again with my beloved, & hear his simple words.

THURSDAY, AUGUST 18 Got up & did my needlework. It is strange that this soothes me more than anything. Mr Hamilton Aidé came for luncheon, & dear Annie Ritchie came later. It is comforting to have these beloved friends to talk to.

Lily read me the article on Julian Sturgis[4] in the evening.

---

1. The biography of Watts that Marion Spielmann had intended to write. **2.** Thomas Matthew Rooke (1842–1942) and his son Noel Rooke (1881–1953). Thomas Rooke painted the watercolour of Watts's studio at Little Holland House. **3.** Mary was already looking for a tenant for Little Holland House, so soon after Watts's death. Her heart was, and had been for some time, at Limnerslease. Mrs Lowry was not, eventually, a suitable tenant as she wanted to sublet the studio and gallery. **4.** Julian Sturgis (1848–1904), barrister, novelist, poet, librettist. He built himself a country house near Compton, Wancote, designed by Voysey. He died two months before Watts, and Mary designed one of her most exceptional graves for him in the chapel cemetery.

FRIDAY, AUGUST 19 To London by 9.30. to meet Parlanti. Had to arrange for much further casting of the Bronze.

With Andrew, driving across the green drive I took my darling over those last days of May, when he seemed so tired, & consented to let me drive him.

Here I am with flowers for his grave in my arms, white lilies.

THURSDAY, SEPTEMBER 1 *Little Holland House* A dim light at four o'clock, when I first awoke, thinking how on July 1st my beloved's voice sounded last in my ears. I got up & picked a leaf of his dear eucalyptus, wet & fresh from a night of rain, remembering his dear hand bringing it to me last year. My fear lest it should die in the winter. I tried to keep death away from our little home, but I could not. Thompson died,[1] & then my dear one mourned, & worked, perhaps foresaw, for indeed he was a seer.

Alone in my first home with him. Dear little Emma wonderful. So much to settle. I may not sit down & think. That is as he wished it to be.

I slept in Lily's room. All unfamiliar, I am glad to say.

An exquisite painting by Mr Rooke of the studio, the beloved studio.

FRIDAY, SEPTEMBER 2 *Little Holland House* To Coutts, & on to meet Lily at Waterloo. My sweet child[2] comes back to me & I am glad, laden with bulrushes she had been by train to get for me.

SATURDAY, SEPTEMBER 3 *Little Holland House* I wonder if I have had my last night under this roof? What does it matter? My heart seems dead to all the feeling of goodbye to it. I hope I shall soon know the lease for 3 years is signed, & I shall shut the door thankfully.

THURSDAY, SEPTEMBER 8 *Limnerslease* Busy preparing the Hostel for the Moore Smiths who come tomorrow.

FRIDAY, SEPTEMBER 9 A beautiful autumn day. What shall I say for the gift of gentle warmth, golden air, peace over nature. A selfish cry is kept back. Instead I try to think he, out of unutterable peace & light, looks

---

1. Thompson had died in the Spring of 1904. **2.** Lily had become very close to Watts and Mary. Her life was completely integrated into theirs as their ward, and she often spoke of Mary as her 'mother'. Watts's letters to her when she was at school at Roedean are very affectionate, and she kept them for the rest of her life. She lived to be 93. In 1907 she married Captain Michael Chapman of the Grenadier Guards, and they had two children, Ronald and Anthea. Chapman was killed in action in April, 1918, and Lily returned to Limnerslease, where she and Mary brought up the children together. Lily stayed there until Mary's death in 1938.

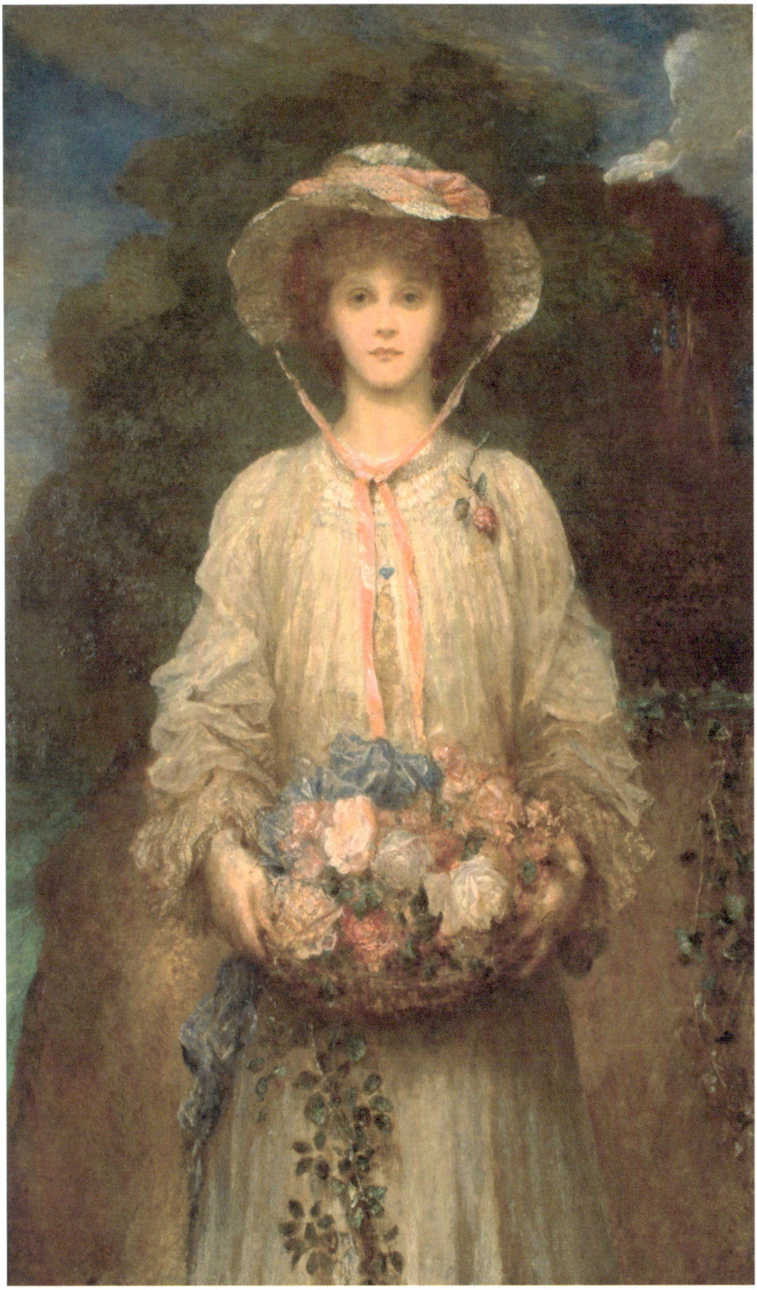

G.F. Watts, *Lilian*, 1904, oil on canvas, Watts Gallery

back & is glad that we have this golden summer, & so he does share it with me. Dear Bill here. He came in his motor. Mr & Miss Moore Smith came in the evening. Out of their van-load of luggage leapt a nice north-country woman, who has come as cook. There was something simple and delightful in the arrival. Surely I am blest in these people.

TUESDAY, SEPTEMBER 13 Andrews & Steadman go to Little H.H. about the horse, that comes back.[1] I try to design all the morning & cannot. Why? My hands can work, & work, but not my head.

Mary Head[2] leaves after all these years. A widower brother claims her.

I wish I could say as I often think of Browning's words, 'Rejoice that man is hurled from change to change, his soul's wings never furled'. Rather I feel the grief we must feel when changes & parting comes, is proof that we have a part knowledge or foreknowledge of something better, where every tear is wiped away.

WEDNESDAY, SEPTEMBER 14 Mike[3] & Lily & I go up to London.

A wet day again so that I cannot properly enjoy the great horse, now safely back, & the Rider on it. How grand it looks, & certainly greatly improved by my beloved's recent work. Oh, if he could have had this summer! I feel rebellious against myself, against many things. Surely he might have been preserved for just these months! If I could have known, & have kept him here till warm July. That is my one regret!

THURSDAY, SEPTEMBER 15 A beautiful soft sweet day, the little red monthly rose is crimson against his studio wall & window. Nicol & I rush off early to Eastbury, where the masons are making a mistake about the seat going up there now. I saw the dear old lady[4] & Miss Mary came out to me several times. All looked beautiful in sweet autumn stillness.

To the Hostel. How much I like dear Alice Moore Smith's face, & kind wide open eyes. Lily & Mike drive to Crooksbury, where he stays to see his father.[5] I write & then going to my little grave, so sadly neglected these days, I meet May.

---

1. The second bronze cast of *Physical Energy* was completed, and the plaster original was back at Little Holland House. **2.** Mary Head had been Watts's cook for many years. **3.** Michael Chapman was not yet decided on a career but after some time in Canada later joined the Grenadier Guards. **4.** Mrs Ellice, owner of Eastbury Manor in Compton. The first sundial made at Compton Pottery was for her. **5.** Michael Chapman's parents lived at Crooksbury, near Farnham.

FRIDAY, SEPTEMBER 16 *L.H.H. for the day* I am worried by a letter from Mr Lowry asking if he may let Signor's studio & the Gallery! Oh, dear, as if I could consent! I write my answer. The debacle goes on. But out of all the rains the big *Energy* once more is there intact!

Mike comes here later with a grave face, because he is for this year to forego advancement of income, & accept opportunity of work & further equipment. He has chosen this himself, deliberately on his father's advice, but it is in a sort of way delaying.[1]

SATURDAY, SEPTEMBER 17 I woke this morning after a wonderful dream. My beloved was well & alive. We were going to take up sweet life together, & undo all my mistakes! I questioned myself & asked if it could be a dream, I, bashing my head against a wall. No! I was quite awake. It was all true. I knew he had been dead but he was here again living our life. It was true, so unutterably wonderfully & sweet. But I did wake.

This is the first dream I have had of him since he went away.

WEDNESDAY, SEPTEMBER 21 The two vanloads arrive.[2] What chaos.

THURSDAY, SEPTEMBER 22 With the help of Mr Nicol & the boys we get going on unpacking 15 cases of books.

FRIDAY, SEPTEMBER 23 The little beloved Red Hall is all as it was always, till autumn when I borrowed for the drawing room. The drawing room is in order & the East studio. Strange to say, with more furniture the house looks bigger.

MONDAY, SEPTEMBER 26 The house is still most unrestful in its disorder. I am trying to get on top of it.

TUESDAY, SEPTEMBER 27 *Little Holland House* I have to go to London about moving all the sculpture & pictures.

First to the quadrangle of the Academy to see the *Physical Energy*. It looks so grand.

Then arriving at the bare little house! I ran to the sculpture studio, but could not judge of the difference. One stands too high & too near.

---

1. Michael Chapman was to go to Canada, but since he and Lily were engaged, Mary felt it might delay their wedding. 2. This was a furniture and books from Little Holland House. Mary was gradually bringing down the possessions she wanted to have round her at Limnerslease.

Agnes Poynter[1] came, & went all over the little house. It seems too good to believe, but really I am hopeful of them being his successors!

My darling Gerry came. I look at all the material & work & wonder if I can make use of it all at the great barn some day, arranging it so that all can work & do.

My darling Gerry. A real mourner in our empty house.

WEDNESDAY, SEPTEMBER 28 *Limnerslease* Home to sleep in my new room! Better bareness than emptiness, I think, & oh, I have so much. His bed, his chair, the last he sat in. The rug that he last stood upon, & I shall have my *Love Triumphant*.

THURSDAY, SEPTEMBER 29 I wake to see my little Raphael drawing (the sixpenny autotype I picked up once!), holding up her hands. Aspire, aspire.

FRIDAY, SEPTEMBER 30 *Little Holland House* Andrews & I at the final packing in the sculpture studio, my studio, the Iron House.

Desolation everywhere. The garden a sad wreck.

SATURDAY, OCTOBER 1 Came home reading a little book about the Tennysons.

'Came home'! What is it now? An empty house. To go away, is to come back to tears. But I have my blessed work, & will not be weak.

SUNDAY, OCTOBER 2 To church in Compton.

Mike here for luncheon. A storm of rain. Mike supposed to leave, but cannot.

Finally says goodbye & goes out into the rain & dark, & then comes back to say his lamp won't work, & so he stays.

MONDAY, OCTOBER 3 Mike leaves at six o'clock.

Another long day in London, sculpture packing, turning out the Iron studio to find such a mess as you never saw.

Under my big 'throw' the floor has rotted. No ventilation & damp & decay were vigorous, so in the Iron house at the back. Lily with me, but oh, to leave it all is not so bad as to come back here, to see the lamps

1. Agnes Poynter was married to Edward Poynter, President of the Royal Academy. Georgiana Burne-Jones was her sister. The Poynters were contemplating renting Little Holland House.

shining out just they always did, when my heart leapt to think my beloved was inside.

Nothing brings the hot tears more quickly.

WEDNESDAY, OCTOBER 5 When I went out to the Barn, seeing a gleaming pantechnicon van, I picked a heap of roses.

Two vans filled with cast busts & the sculpture work. When I saw the unfinished *Dawn* carried out I could not keep back my tears & had to go away. He was so full of hope when he last worked upon it, but the better Dawn came to him first.

All my beloved's things are out now in two rooms! I must disperse them as soon as possible.

THURSDAY, OCTOBER 6 Letters, to Eastbury, & to my little grave to put the autumn crocus there!

So tired.

FRIDAY, OCTOBER 7 *Little Holland House* Andrews, Steadman & I went to London. Emma met us. All swept & bare now. The pictures & furniture stacked in my studio.

The great strong man & horse alone triumphant, going forward.

THURSDAY, OCTOBER 13 I work all day, trying to get the 'Little flower from the crannied wall'[1] done for the hand of Tennyson, & also varnishing his pictures, *Earth*, *The Court of Death*, *Outcast Goodwill*, *Industry & Greed*. The pictures! The five in the studio, seemed for a moment to promise that he was coming! But only that wonderful shadow of him was there all day with me. Oh, I am tired, tired.

FRIDAY, OCTOBER 14 Still working at the little plant, trying to get it exactly right. It seems simple, but the more right I get it, the more like the ivied leaved toadflax of nature, the more wrong it seems for the statue.

SATURDAY, OCTOBER 15 I was awake in the night, & suddenly after a weary recurrence of the knowledge that my little flower was all wrong, I <u>saw</u> what it should be, much more general, far less particular. I got

1. Watts's figure of Tennyson for Lincoln Cathedral (see page 242) looks down at a flower he is holding in his hand. It represents a quotation from the laureate's poem of that title, musing on the lack of understanding we have of the intricacies of nature. The flower had not been modelled and Mary completed the sculpture by designing it in metal.

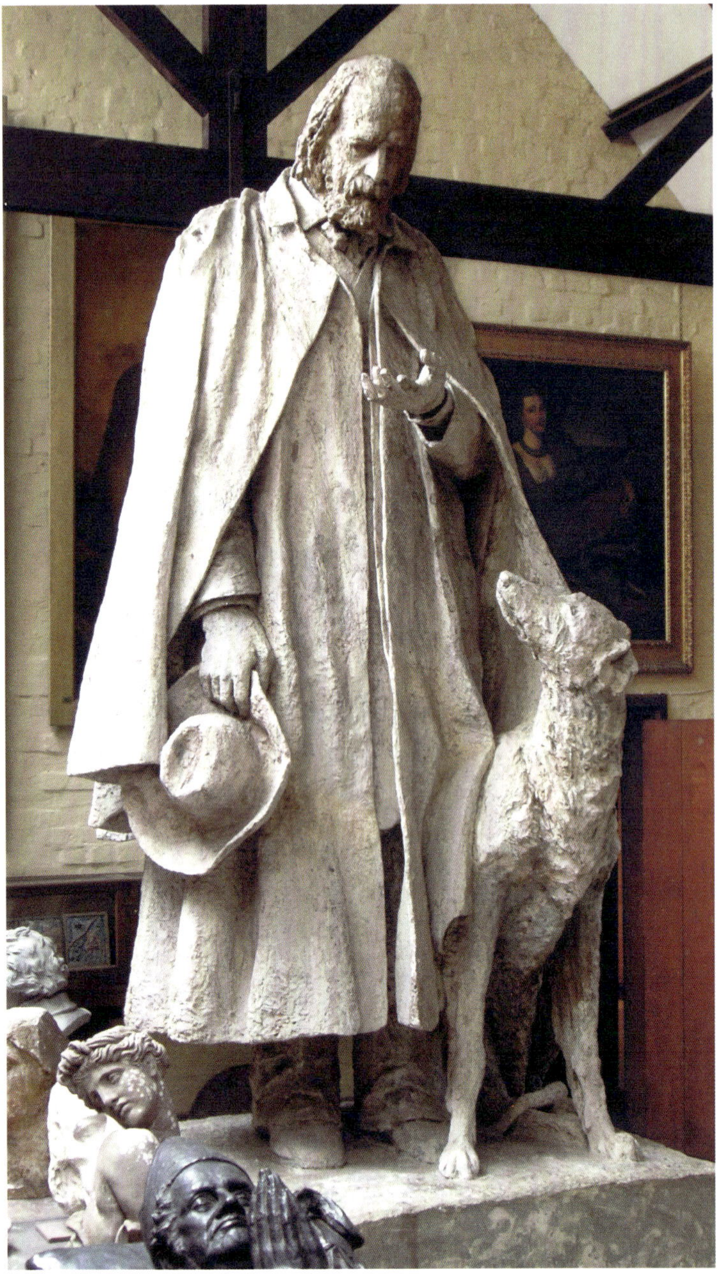

G.F. Watts, *Tennyson*, 1903, plaster of his bronze sculpture for Lincoln Cathedral, Watts Gallery

green wax today from my studio, & warming it well, at last I got the thing more right.

MONDAY, OCTOBER 17 I finish & pack the little flower from the crannied wall. It took my day.

THURSDAY, OCTOBER 20 I wonder if in any planet, an English October day at its best, can be more beautiful.

Hollyer here all day doing many photographs from the pictures.

FRIDAY, OCTOBER 21 We have had our St Luke's summer. Now it is grey, tho' so warm.

I design a little figure more carefully, for Tom.[1]

SATURDAY, OCTOBER 22 St Luke has slipped back to us again. I counted some eighty crimson roses hanging like heart's blood between our bedroom window & Signor's studio window & on the border. Below, the earth is crimson with petals shed from its abundance.

Lily went to London. Mike had arranged luncheon for her.

SATURDAY, OCTOBER 29 A telegram from Lord Grey, saying he would be here at 10.30 o'clock, & he is, soon after. Oh, he looks tired. What a happy morning I had with him. He wished he had not forgotten something Signor had said about the sun shining on a rusty plough once by our chapel, one of his exquisite little parables. He goes full of youth & energy & hope to Canada.[2]

TUESDAY, NOVEMBER 1 All Saints.

A dear little letter unsigned, came, thanking 'My Saint'.

The letter touches me profoundly. It is from Eton, & the writer is in trouble, but says she will be comforted by kneeling near the *Sir Galahad*.[3]

MONDAY, NOVEMBER 14 Alas, the breaking of the little head of Tom's first little figure, *Gathering*, happened today. Tom takes it well. Walter, the breaker, very distressed.

Miss Crabbe, who has lost her mother & is in deep sorrow, has found comfort in going to my chapel. She calls it her pilgrimage. I can fancy

---

1. Thomas Wren, apprentice potter and talented modeller. He was only 17 when he modelled the figure of Watts for the memorial in the cloister at the Watts Cemetery Chapel. **2.** Lord Grey was to take up the position of Governor-General of Canada in December 1904. **3.** The painting by Watts hangs in the chapel at Eton College.

how from the heart of Aldershot, the quiet village & this little bit out a life of thought & reverence from beauty & its holiest side, may be a contrast, & a pleasure!

TUESDAY, NOVEMBER 15 I write & then try to design. But no.

Strange after much letter writing, I cannot.

The effort made me quite unwell, & I went to bed.

WEDNESDAY, NOVEMBER 16 Start early. Travel with Andrew & May. I see Dr Knightly who will help me to be well. Then with May to St Paul's.[1] My sweetest beloved's spirit filled the place for me. They sang his hymns. They sang 'Peace come away', divinely sung. It was all for him, as far as my heart was concerned, & I hoped those who had loved Val much have seen ideals of which I knew nothing. Tonight at Farnham they sing 'Peace come away' In Memory of G. F. Watts. My Beloved!

I went to dear Bill, then on to St Botolph's[2] where I must help them to complete all, & make it an example. Had I been asked, I should have said the 'Peace come away' was too intimate for a great public offering of sorrow & thanksgiving, but it is beautiful so no more need be said.

THURSDAY, NOVEMBER 17 I have heard Signor's Service once again!

'Peace, Come away. We do him wrong' sings in my ears – & has brought a certain feeling of peace & strength. I am at work on Julian Sturgis' headstone.

The whole service yesterday was so entirely Signor's that I feel it quite a strange gift to me, for how on that Thursday in July could I realize what the service was. Now it has all been said again & is in my heart till hearing dies.

The explanation of it was that no selection was made. Florence[3] wished for a service at Westminster Abbey & they said it could not be. St Paul's was chosen. Then she sent to Jim & said he must arrange the service, so he said 'let it be as Mr Watts'. That was so lovingly chosen by Gerry & Andrew for my ethereal spiritual labourer when his task here was done. It was sung there.

---

1. Valentine Prinsep's funeral. He had died at 66. **2.** Watts's Memorial to Heroic Self-Sacrifice, part of St Botolph's churchyard, and later designated as Postman's Park. **3.** Val Prinsep's wife.

SATURDAY, NOVEMBER 19 Mary Sturgis came to see the sketches for her grave, her sister & Mark & Mr Henry Sturgis with her.

FRIDAY, NOVEMBER 25[1] *34 Clarges St.* In the strange house & with help at my side! I awoke to feel my beloved cannot be far. All he has left for me is to carry on, develop further.

I have to go to L.H.H. Emma & I meet on the doorstep of the silent empty house, & kiss & try to be brave. The men from the Academy[2] came, & then to the lifting & labelling of the pictures & the work in the dark cold for some time.

To Luncheon at Lady Somers, then I go to darling Choons. Strange to say, we spend our two birthdays together this year. Not once before since 1871 has this happened. I had her darling letter, saying she, with so many my life had helped, was glad I had been born. Thank you, darling Choons, & I thank God for my Lily's loving arms.

TUESDAY, NOVEMBER 29 Gerry here, who came to Burlington House, where we went through the lists of pictures once more.

It suddenly came to me that I must stay one more night in London, to see the removal tomorrow at Little Holland House, & so I sent Lily off. She wished to go back to her Jerry, her dog, & I stayed. Our rooms were relet so I had to climb to a bedroom at the top.

There Gerry came, & later the man servant announced Sir Edward Poynter. I said 'Is there any room downstairs that I can see him in?' 'I've got him here' said the man, & then poor Sir Edward was breathless at my bedroom door! He had to come in & then we went through Mr Spielmann's list.

Later at Paddington with Gerry we watched the wonderful sight of Her Majesty's 'Royal Mail', scarlet van upon van. Scarlet-coated men doing their wonderfully arranged work. It is a glimpse into civilisation, the meaning of the best side of it.

WEDNESDAY, NOVEMBER 30 Emma & I met & cleared out the little Iron house, my studio. Nothing now remains, save *Clytie* for Lord Wemyss, the baby portrait for Lady Airlie, & the great Rider on the great Horse.

---

1. Mary's birthday. **2.** Royal Academy staff were collecting the paintings for the exhibition of Watts's work in Winter 1904–5.

Back to the Academy with the *John Burns* portrait & the drawing of the *Recording Angel.* Then to see my beloved's beautiful drawing of Phillips.[1]

Then home. My sweet Lily, my dear kind Andrews always a welcome, but the darling empty shell, & I cry in my room at night. Ungrateful grief, I know.

Signor, help me!

THURSDAY, DECEMBER 1 *Limnerslease* See Nicol. Then to the Pottery, to the Hostel about records, then to see about all the frames Steadman has made, & the new rose bed.

I am so tired at night. I can only read *The Times* & then nap. When shall I have less various work & be able to concentrate?

Tonight Lily & I go over the list of clothes we have to give & assign them as far as possible quite justly.

FRIDAY, DECEMBER 2 Little red roses still bloom by Beloved's window. Lily is dusting & sorting photographs & drawings downstairs. The Van arrives with all the pictures from L.H.H. I do not see them, for Andrews has them simply lifted into the Gallery till next week to keep this house clearer.

Afternoon spent clearing two rooms full of dear clothes. They are nearly all assigned now. Only a few that must go through the Artists Benevolent.

One must not hoard. Moth tells us this, but I keep one coat, & his fur I shall use, & his dear Inverness.[2]

Lily busy with French in the evening.

SUNDAY, DECEMBER 4 I have a day of work. Work, not prayer. Work that is prayer. Two pictures to varnish. The frame for Mary Anderson's portrait, always so disfiguring because it closely frames the picture, has had 4 carved corners added by Steadman, & so has *Love Triumphant.* These bright new bits of gilding have to be carefully toned, & I work till dusk. Ethel & Mike here. I began Georgie Burne Jones' book.[3] I go, a tired work-woman, to bed early.

---

1. Watts's chalk drawing from the 1850s of Henry Wyndham Phillips. It was probably made when Phillips took over Watts's studio in Charles Street. They spent time together, too, at the Cosmopolitan Club, of which they were both founder-members. **2.** Watts's sealskin coat, which he had altered for Mary, and the Inverness cape they had bought in 1899 on Watts's only visit to Aldourie with Mary. **3.** *Memorials of Edward Burne-Jones* (1904) by Georgiana Burne-Jones.

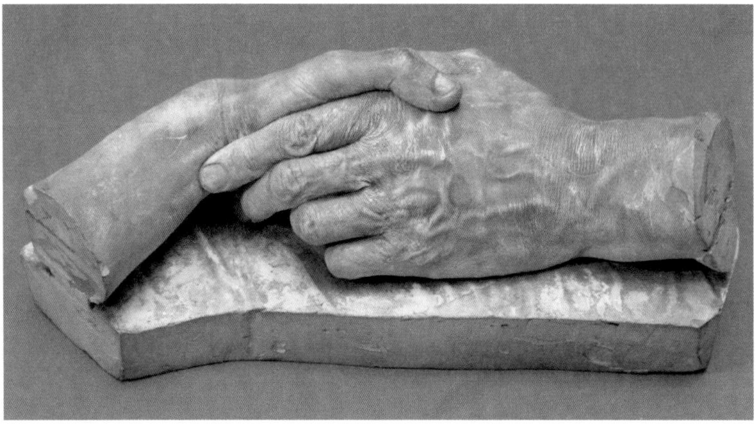

Plaster cast of the joined hands of George Frederic and Mary Watts

MONDAY, DECEMBER 5 A day of work. But how well rewarded, when I see that wonderful portrait in our drawing room, *Mary Anderson*, & the *Love Triumphant*, framed as they should be.

How I wish my beloved had seen them thus. Steadman has done wonders, & the touching of the gold now leaves no recognisable join. The 1st van is at the Gallery door. The 2nd comes tomorrow. I read 'G. B.-J.' to Lily. It is thoroughly well written, terse, descriptive, & bright.

We have just got to the Oxford days.

TUESDAY, DECEMBER 6 New days! The vans are at the door & one after another his pictures are carried out. They seemed like a part of his very life, limb after limb taken away. When I went back into the empty studio I cried, as if now for the first time I knew that he was dead, but he is not dead.

FRIDAY, DECEMBER 9 I write all day, the last dates of pictures. Later in the evening, hunting up dates of recent pictures, I turn to my journals, my 'Fatima'.

Alas, that I should have not been able to keep it better all these last years, but I am grateful for it. It is like opening drawers to find pictures of our dear life together, & of the steps on which we rise to better & better, until the 'well done' sounds for us, the door opens, & we pass beyond the grave.

Today, I say, I will go on with 'Fatima', anyhow for another year.

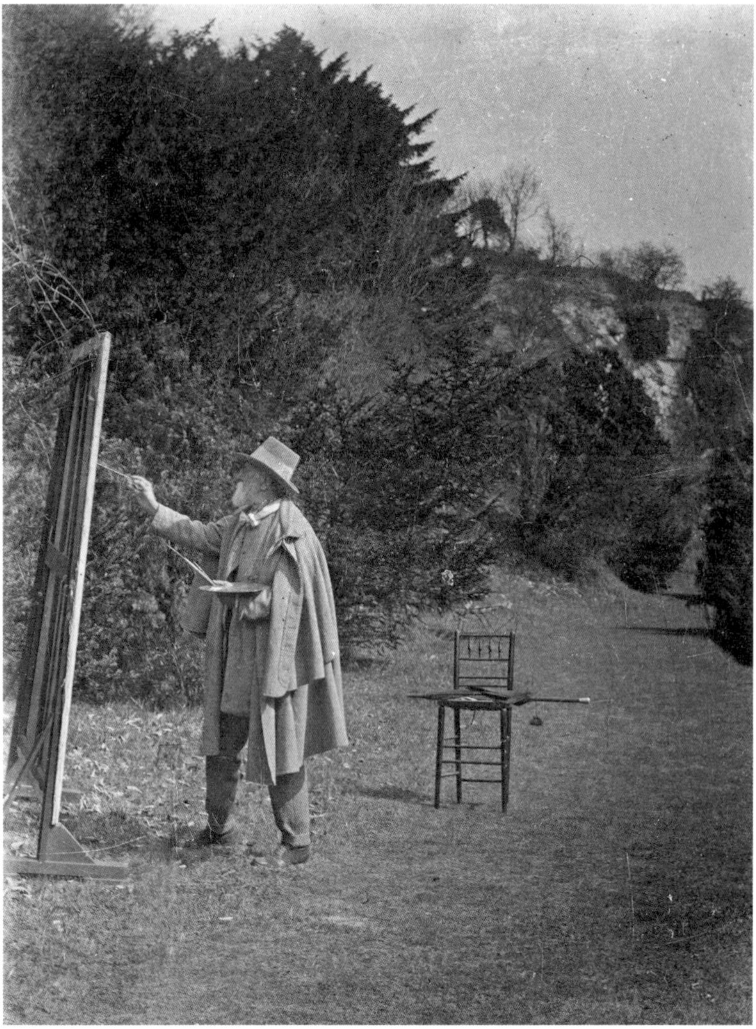

Watts painting at Monkshatch wearing the Inverness cape

SATURDAY, DECEMBER 10 My schemes for spending on others must cease, & I must only try for using what I have got as well as possible. My fear is debt, or having too little to be just to all about me at Limnerslease.

Strange. If he knows it he will be sorry, but perhaps he sees that conflict & difficulties are necessary for me. Anyhow, I pray to adapt myself to whatever is possible now for the highest, my utmost! Money is not everything. I go to see Bill.[1]

SUNDAY, DECEMBER 11 I could not sleep last night for nerves, & wonder if I shall be able to meet all expenses, all the unknown death duty sums! I do not know what they may be.

Walked with Bill, a lovely wide glorious sea of brown fern and rolling down, in the bright winter sun. I am beginning to adjust myself, but in the process feel irritable & querulous, & must be a bad companion for Bill. In the evening I said to myself the Brahmin thought, 'When ceasing to desire, every activity is good, to breathe in Atman', & I quieted myself & slept well.

WEDNESDAY, DECEMBER 14 Designed a new figure for Tom.

Dear little Mr Turnor[2] came. I gave him a message & pencil, marked *Hostel* & our initial letters on it.

THURSDAY, DECEMBER 15 Dear little Mr Turnor made time to come back again this morning. I was touched. How good it is to have someone who knew Signor, & who is young & good & clever, to see one, & encourage one.

He says the work grows, month by month. He sees that clearly, coming back to it.

FRIDAY, DECEMBER 16 To London, to see L.H.H. To Hollyer's. To the Academy about the catalogue.

Sent Emma for Mr Rooke's beautiful drawing of my beloved's studio & brought it back in my arms.

SUNDAY, DECEMBER 25 Hoping for 8.30 service at little Compton. Choons, Ethel, & I went & May & Andrew! Shut doors! Oh, Christmas cares!!

WEDNESDAY, DECEMBER 28 To the Academy where I spend most of the day, wandering amongst my beloved's work. How wonderful. There was a good deal to correct in the Catalogue & I was there till nearly eight.

---

1. Mary was beset with complications arising from Watts's will. Death duty on his body of paintings and other work, a clause that gave her responsibilities for financing the running of the Watts Gallery, and bequests to the Royal Academy and other provincial galleries combined to make her anxious as to whether she could meet her obligations. Her half-brother, Bill, was very helpful in his role as the executor. **2.** Watts Gallery, designed by Christopher Hatton Turnor, opened to the public in 1904.

I cannot say what that great room must ever be to my mind. My beloved there himself, with folded hands (so it seemed to me) awaiting! The great work round him & indeed the greatest seemed to be of 1903 & 1904. 'I am learning to paint' he used to say, & so he is. The Portrait is on Sir Joshua Reynolds' easel!

Back to dine with darling May, & that kindest of Andrews!

THURSDAY, DECEMBER 29 Luncheon at May's. Lily's birthday, bless her.

FRIDAY, DECEMBER 30 Reading Georgie Burne Jones' *Life*. I envy her all the precise & clean history she has of her beloved. Of mine I can but garner here & there facts out a mist! How well she writes. How vivid!

I think all day of my beloved, that vision of him sitting calmly awaiting the verdict of his work which is there all about him in that great gallery. The Pressmen are there today, but scribbling does not make or mar his story.

SATURDAY, DECEMBER 31 The last year, the last golden year for me, dies. Now for me it must be all looking forward, forward[1] to the day when death's gates open to the beyond. If only I may meet Signor & say 'I have followed, worked, loved as you did, beloved.'

There is a red rose now upon his wall. Its face is turned against the stone as if it kissed it. I have an hour or two working out the angels to sit above dear Mr Sturgis' grave.

I get the roses in at the cemetery.

I think of the many feet passing through the great rooms where my beloved's work, his spirit, is shining down. Of some who will be moved to see him there himself, so quiet, so serene, in the midst of it all. How I thank God for that picture.

---

1. Mary had many years of looking forward ahead of her. She ran the Compton Pottery, and designed for it well into her eighties; she helped Lily to bring up her children at Limnerslease after her husband, Michael Chapman, was killed in the First World War; she was President of the Godalming Suffrage Society; she designed the decorative scheme for the Military Chapel at Aldershot; she managed the Watts Gallery and organised numerous exhibitions of Watts's work. She wrote the almost complete catalogue of his paintings, the three-volume *Annals of an Artist's Life* and *The Word in the Pattern*, her book about the Watts Cemetery Chapel. Mary more or less abandoned diary-writing, adding only one or two entries in a journal about incidents that struck her in the years 1906–8. She was trying hard, and succeeding, from then onwards to look forward.

Select Bibliography

Abdy, Jane and Charlotte Gere, *The Souls*, Sidgwick & Jackson, London, 1984

Ady, Julia Cartwright (Mrs Henry Ady), *The Life and Works of G.F. Watts*, Art Journal Easter Annual, London, 1896

Alston, Rowland, *The Mind and Work of G.F. Watts*, Methuen, London, 1929

Barrington, Mrs Russell, *G.F. Watts: Reminiscences*, Macmillan, London, 1905

Bills, Mark, *An Artist's Village: G.F. and Mary Watts in Compton*, Philip Wilson, London, 2011

Bills, Mark, *Watts Chapel: A Guide to the Symbols of Mary Watts' Arts and Crafts Masterpiece*, Philip Wilson, London, 2010

Bills, Mark and Barbara Bryant, *G.F. Watts, Victorian Visionary*, Yale University Press, New Haven and London, 2008

Bryant, Barbara, *G.F. Watts in Kensington: Little Holland House and Gallery*, Watts Gallery, Compton, 2009

Burne-Jones, Georgiana (G.B.-J.), *Memorials of Edward Burne-Jones*, 2 vols, Macmillan, London, 1904

Chapman, Ronald, *The Education of Davey Porteous*, Collins, London, 1969

Chapman, Ronald, *The Laurel and the Thorn: A Study of G.F. Watts*, Faber and Faber, London, 1945

Gleeson-White, J., 'A mortuary chapel, designed by Mrs G.F. Watts', *The Studio*, vol.24, 1898

Gould, Veronica Franklin, *G.F. Watts: The Last Great Victorian*, Yale University Press, New Haven and London, 2004

Gould, Veronica Franklin, *Mary Seton Watts 1849–1938: Unsung Heroine of the Art Nouveau*, Watts Gallery, Compton, 1998

McMahon, Mary, *The Making of Mary Seton Watts*, Watts Gallery, Compton, 2013

Macmillan, Hugh, *The Life-Work of George Frederic Watts*, J.M. Dent, London, 1903

Ormond, Leonée and Richard, *G.F. Watts: The Hall of Fame. Portraits of His Contemporaries*, Watts Gallery, Compton, 2012

Rooke, Thomas, *Burne-Jones Talking*, John Murray, London, 1982

Tromans, Nicholas, *Hope: The Life and Times of a Victorian Icon*, Watts Gallery, Compton, 2011

Ward, Chloe, *The Drawings of G. F. Watts,* Philip Wilson, London, 2015

Watts, M.S., *George Frederic Watts: Annals of an Artist's Life*, 3 vols, Macmillan, London, 1912

Watts, M.S., 'Manuscript catalogue of G.F. Watts' portraits and subject paintings', 3 volumes, unpublished

Watts, M.S. *et al.*, *The Word in the Pattern: A Facsimile with Seven Essays*, Society for the Arts and Crafts Movement in Surrey, Lymington 2012

Acknowledgements

My heartfelt thanks to those who have helped me in editing, annotating and bringing to light the personality of this remarkable woman. Watts Gallery staff have been unfailingly supportive, both practically and in their belief in the project, in particular Dr Chloe Ward and Dr Beatrice Bertram. I am very grateful to Dr Nicholas Tromans for the time he has given in support both practical and moral. My thanks, too, to Dr Lucy Ella Rose and Gail Naughton, both of whom have helped with some of the transcribing. I am very grateful indeed to the Finnis Scott Foundation, and the Dr Lee MacCormick Edwards Foundation for the funding which has enabled the project to go ahead. Lastly, my thanks to Lucy Clark and Sarah Thorowgood at Lund Humphries who have been a delight to work with. *Desna Greenhow*

THE FINNIS SCOTT FOUNDATION

The publication of this book has been made possible through the generosity of the Finnis Scott Foundation. The Foundation was set up in 2008 to assist in artistic and horticultural projects, these being the abiding interests of a remarkable couple, Sir David Scott KCMG OBE (1887-1986) and his wife Valerie Finnis VMH (1924-2006). Sir David was a career diplomat who became one of the twentieth century's most distinguished collectors of Victorian art. With Valerie, a well-known gardener and photographer, he completed an exquisitely beautiful tree and shrub garden at Boughton House in Northamptonshire, Sir David's home for many years. In 2008 the famous collection of art was sold to create the Finnis Scott Foundation, whose first gift was to Watts Gallery, then under restoration. In supporting the publication of the diary of the wife of G.F. Watts, one creative couple has now supported both members of another, for which kindness we are enormously grateful. *Watts Gallery Trust*

Index

Note: Page numbers in italics refer to illustrations; those followed by *n* to information in a footnote. GFW = George Frederic Watts

... is a put hopeless of
... such strides, so I turn on
... he comes back at five &
... side me making coffee for me!
... thoughtful — bless him, I was
... way from him keeping my
... I went to 35 Dover Street
... Loan & Gen Ctd. &c = Chaos,
... from morning to night.
... splendid church embroideries sanctuary
... things. but before I left at 6.30
... the rooms looked well —
... afternoon. then morning hard
... Mrs. Board & her daughter's a most prosperous
... in Berkeley Square
... Mrs. Robbie Benson — bring my mar-
... what she had had his brother
... Lord Rosebery had been for
... Signor got something in
... & thoughtful — quite
... ... man
... went out today, she
... work but the squabble
... not yet work together
... & she says it is
... then she can do with
... acter training of public
... person! What g...

to suffer – it is just hopeless of
to such strides, so I turn on
like he comes back at five &
side me making coffee for me!
& thoughtful – bless him, I love him
away from him keeping my
den. I went to 35 Dover Street
ver Loan & Guild Ex = Chaos,
nd from morning to night –
splendid church embroideries sanctuary
things. but before I left at 6.30
the rooms looked well –
Afternoon. then morning had
Mrs Boord & her daughters & Maud ...
on in Berkeley Square
Mrs Robbie Benson bring my ...
ment shoes had had his broth.
Lord Rosebery had been for
signor got something in –
& thoughtful – quite
... man
... went out today, she
work but the squabbles
not yet work together
is & she says it is
then she can do with –
aracter training of public
suppose,' Wit ...